Presidential Power
and the Constitution

Presidential Power
and the
Constitution ESSAYS

by EDWARD S. CORWIN

Edited with an Introduction
by RICHARD LOSS

Cornell University Press ITHACA AND LONDON

First published 1976 by Cornell University Press.
Published in the United Kingdom by Cornell University Press Ltd.,
2-4 Brook Street, London W1Y 1AA.

International Standard Book Number 0-8014-0982-9
Library of Congress Catalog Card Number 75-38000
Printed in the United States of America
Librarians: Library of Congress cataloging information appears on the last page of the book.

For Drew Hyland

Contents

Introduction

by RICHARD LOSS

Edward S. Corwin (1878-1963) ranks among the titans of American constitutional law because of his influence on judicial views of the Constitution. "I find I have frequent occasion to draw upon your learning,"[1] Associate Justice Benjamin Cardozo once told Corwin, who over a thirty-two-year period was the only non-lawyer among the ten legal writers most often cited by the Supreme Court of the United States.

Born near Plymouth, Michigan, Corwin graduated from the University of Michigan in 1900 and received his doctorate from the University of Pennsylvania in 1905. He was soon asked by Woodrow Wilson, then President of Princeton University, to become one of the original preceptors there. He continued to teach at Princeton until his retirement in 1946. A prolific author, Corwin published over sixty articles in legal and professional journals and twenty-three in journals of opinion and periodicals. He also wrote eighteen books as sole author and two as co-author in addition to editing the 1953 annotated Constitution of the United States. In 1935 he served as constitutional adviser to the Public Works Administration, in 1936 as special assistant and in 1937 as constitutional consultant to the Attorney General. Corwin's biography, though, asserted that "in politics he is an independent."

One of his most important books, *The President: Office and Powers* (first published 1940), describes the "reciprocal interplay of human character and legal concepts" in the "development and contemporary status of presidential power and of the presidential office under the Constitution." Corwin discerned a "revolutionary reversal of constitutional values" in which "the Presidency has reached a position of unhealthy dominance in the system."[2]

1. Cardozo to Corwin, July 31, 1935, category 1, carton 1, Corwin Papers, Princeton University Library.
2. Corwin, "Our Constitutional Revolution and How to Round It Out," 19 *Pennsylvania Bar Association Quarterly* 261, 284 (April, 1948), reprinted in this volume.

That treatise, though authoritative, is austere and somewhat forbidding. By reprinting most of Corwin's essays on the Presidency, the present book not only makes Corwin's argument more accessible, but also forms a bridge to the treatise. The essays are related to, but distinct from, the treatise. Only "The President as Administrative Chief," which is included here to preserve continuity, directly overlaps.

Presidential Power and the Constitution is a selection of twelve articles on the growth, constitutional impact, and control of presidential power from Woodrow Wilson through Harry Truman. Corwin's method is to study constitutional law and political thought through examples: he examines American entry into World War I, the Depression, the New Deal, Franklin Roosevelt's effort to pack the United States Supreme Court, the impact of "total war" on individual liberties, and the surge of presidential power in the Cold War.

These essays are of contemporary importance not only because they deal with the topic of presidential power, but also because they grapple with two conflicting interpretations of the Constitution which are still being debated today. One interpretation emphasizes "constitutional theory": the idea of a higher, natural law standard, the consideration of the Framers' intention, and limitations on popular majorities, governmental power, and the Presidency.[3] The other supports the idea of an organic or "living Constitution": the substitution of the majority's felt needs of "this day and hour" for the Framers' intention of what the Constitution is or ought to be, and a dominant Presidency, perhaps one without statable limits upon its power.[4]

Neither interpretation clearly dominates Corwin's thought, though

3. See, for example, Corwin, "The Natural Law and Constitutional Law," 3 *Proceedings of the Natural Law Institute* 47–81 (1950), reprinted in this volume.

4. Alexander Bickel has called the idea of organic constitutional growth the "strongest and most searching" argument in support of the contemporary dominant Presidency: "The idea of organic constitutional growth . . . [through] usage, gradual changes by successive degrees to a point where a change in kind may be perceived – these, it is said, have been the life of the American Constitution. 'Our Constitution,' Justice Brandeis once wrote, 'is not a strait-jacket. It is a living organism. As such it is capable of growth – of expansion and of adaptation to new conditions'" ("The Constitution and the War," 54 *Commentary* 53 [July, 1972]). See also Bickel, *The Least Dangerous Branch* 106–7 (1962). For Corwin's acceptance of a living Constitution idea, see "Constitution v. Constitutional Theory," 19 *American Political Science Review* 302 (May, 1925).

he leaned toward the living Constitution idea by attacking an alternative to it, study of the Framers' intention. He sometimes denied the existence of objective, non-arbitrary criteria for preserving the Constitution, and he ruled out the use of "speculative ideas about what the framers of the Constitution or the generation which adopted it intended it should mean. . . . Such ideas . . . have *no* application to the main business of constitutional interpretation."[5] No one can verify, he said, whether judicial interpretation preserves or fails to preserve the Constitution because it is "obviously impossible in this year of grace to know what *was* intended 'by the Constitution,' or by the framers or the ratifiers thereof, with regard to matters which did not exist in 1787."[6] Such arguments led some to ask if Corwin was to be "the Moses to lead us from the land of the Constitution as our Fathers knew it."[7]

But he later criticized the implications of the idea of a living Constitution "palpitating with the purpose of the hour": "So we emerge more and more upon a scene dominated by the political process and political forces — or more concretely — by electoral majorities, however contrived, however led."[8] And Corwin emulated what he termed the "historical approach [exemplified by] Aristotle: 'If you would understand anything, observe it in its beginnings and its development.' "[9] Corwin, for example, observed of one of George Washington's writings that "the same sense of command over the resources of political wisdom appears again and again in the debates of the Convention, in the pages of *The Federalist*, and in the writings of contemporaries."[10] One of his most famous articles concludes that the doctrine of vested rights "represented the essential spirit and point of view of the founders of American constitutional law, who saw before them the same problem that had confronted the Convention of 1787, namely, the problem

5. Corwin, "Constitution v. Constitutional Theory" 303, italics added.

6. Corwin, "The Dissolving Structure of Our Constitutional Law," 20 *Washington Law Review* 193 (November, 1945), reprinted in this volume.

7. Powell, "Comment on Mr. Corwin's Paper," 19 *American Political Science Review* 308 (May, 1925).

8. Corwin, "Constitution v. Constitutional Theory" 303; Corwin, *Constitutional Revolution, Ltd.* 116 (1941).

9. Corwin's handwritten note, category 6, carton 2, Corwin Papers.

10. Corwin, "The Progress of Constitutional Theory Between the Declaration of Independence and the Meeting of the Philadelphia Convention," 30 *American Historical Review* 512 (April, 1925).

of harmonizing majority rule with minority rights."[11] The idea of the importance of "private and personal rights " (that is, property rights) also aided Corwin's assessment of presidential power in his treatise, which suggests that he sometimes found the Framers' intention and "political wisdom" highly germane to current problems.[12]

The President: Office and Powers exemplifies Corwin's method in presidential studies and begins to explore some of the themes that the essays of this volume more fully develop. The approach is "partly historical, partly analytical and critical." Executive power is described as a "term of uncertain content," an "indefinite residuum" of methods for dealing with emergencies that lack sufficient "stability or recurrency" to permit their being dealt with under a rule of law.[13] The determination of executive power under Article II of the Constitution leaves "considerable leeway for the future play of political forces." The Constitution "reflects the struggle between two conceptions of Executive power: that it ought always to be subordinate to the supreme legislative power, and that it ought to be, within generous limits, autonomous and self-directing."[14] "On the whole" the autonomous and self-directing Presidency has triumphed. The history of the Presidency is a "cyclical" or discontinuous aggrandizement interrupted by congressional preponderance from 1809 to 1829, from 1865 to 1885, and with exceptions, to McKinley's death.[15] "Not more than one in three" Presidents enlarged presidential power; under other incumbents presidential power either stabilized or receded: "What the Presidency is at any particular moment depends in important measure on who is President."[16] The architects of the "great accession to presidential power in recent decades" were Theodore Roosevelt, Woodrow Wilson, and above all, "the second Roosevelt who beyond all twentieth-century Presidents put the stamp, both of *personality* and *crisis,* on the Presidency."[17]

The essays reprinted here form a coherent whole in examining whether

11. Corwin, "The Basic Doctrine of American Constitutional Law," 12 *Michigan Law Review* 276 (February, 1914).

12. Corwin, *The President: Office and Powers* 312 (4th ed. 1957).

13. Corwin, *President: Office and Powers* 3; cf. Locke's definition of prerogative, *Second Treatise* par. 160 (Laslett ed.).

14. Corwin, *President: Office and Powers* 307.

15. *Id.* at 30, 307, 309.

16. *Id.* at 30.

17. *Id.* at 310-11.

limited constitutional government is possible, or even conceivable, under an ascendant Presidency. They begin with an explanation of the natural law doctrine that justifies limited constitutional government and curbs the Presidency and other branches of government short of plenary power. Earlier, in 1934, Corwin had written that "Locke's (Second) *Treatise on Civil Government,* chap. v, was perhaps the most important source of the ideas of 'the Founding Fathers' regarding property."[18] But the doctrines of vested rights and due process of law, which had blended Lockeanism into the American political tradition, were "irrelevant . . . to the solution of the questions of governmental power raised by the New Deal."[19] That these ideas "once represented valid hypotheses of constitutional interpretation need not be disputed — the point is that modern conditions subordinate them to an entirely different set of ideas," notably those of John Dewey, a critic of Lockean natural rights.[20] The New Deal signifies popular acceptance of the "idea that government should be active and reformist," "especially in matters affecting the material welfare of the great masses of the people."[21] It is an era "whose primary demand upon government is no longer the protection of rights but the assurance of security."[22]

Corwin, however, later reversed his 1934 opinion that Lockeanism and related individual rights were irrelevant to the New Deal.[23] The essay which leads off this volume holds that, "as the matrix of American constitutional law, the documentary Constitution is still, in important measure, natural law under the skin." "Natural law . . . [is] a challenge to the notion of unlimited human authority," and "American constitutional law is the record of an attempt to implement that challenge." The concluding essay of this volume, also written after World War II, reiterates his stand that constitutional provisions delineate the structures of the national government, define its powers, and affirm certain individual rights against the powers of the national government.[24]

This idea of individual rights guided Corwin's later investigations of

18. Corwin, *The Twilight of the Supreme Court* 197 n.7 (1934).
19. *Id.* at 97.
20. *Id.* at 98.
21. Corwin, *President: Office and Powers* 294, 311.
22. Corwin, *Total War and the Constitution* 172 (1947).
23. Corwin, *Twilight of the Supreme Court* 97.
24. Corwin, "Our Constitutional Revolution" 261.

the power of the national government, particularly of the Presidency. He deplored the "unhealthy dominance" of the Presidency because he had an explicit standard of political health — based on the notion of individual rights against the national government — with which to understand presidential power. He criticized Mr. Justice Holmes' rejection of natural rights, and though undeveloped in detail, this criticism nevertheless took an important step towards a re-examination of the theory of the New Deal Presidency.[25] Corwin's last book review was written, appropriately enough, on the *Declaration of Independence and What It Means Today*. He disputed the argument that "'the weakness of the natural law philosophy is that, in the opinion of modern "positivist" jurists, it confounds the separate realms of law and morals.' But, conversely," said Corwin, "the *separation* of these realms is precisely the weakness of modern legal positivism, and one which points mankind toward the monolithic state."[26]

The middle essays of this volume explain the thrust that Wilson, Roosevelt, and Truman gave to the constitutional revolution in presidential power. In his 1917 essay on Wilson, Corwin welcomes the "beginnings of what may well prove to be revolutionary developments in our system. . . . Thus war has overtaken us at a peculiarly favorable moment for effecting lasting constitutional changes." The 1919 essay on Wilson warns that "today the question is . . . the preservation of constitutional government in face of an almost world-wide tendency towards one-man power"; Corwin specifically warned the Senate against abdicating its participation in shaping diplomacy. He concludes that Wilson converted the Presidency into a "global institution . . . with a world-wide, non-voting constituency," made the President a leader of the legislative process, and "established the precedents for presidential dictatorship in time of war or of grave international crisis." Wilson paved the way for Roosevelt's Presidency.

In the first essay on F.D.R., Corwin confidently predicts that "the Constitution of the United States can accommodate itself to the revolution which the Nira [National Industrial Recovery Act, 1933] undoubtedly does spell," and the "gradual diminution in the years to come of the role of the Supreme Court in the determination of national

25. Corwin, "Natural Law and Constitutional Law" 80–81.
26. Corwin, Review of Edward Dumbauld, *The Declaration of Independence and What It Means Today* (1950), in 37 *Cornell Law Quarterly* 345 (Winter, 1952).

policies." Our attitudes toward the Constitution "will consequently become less legalistic and more political." The second essay on Roosevelt discusses his attempt to enlarge the Supreme Court after it had precipitated a crisis by striking down such New Deal legislation as the National Industrial Recovery Act in 1935. If, as eventually happened, the Supreme Court should restrict itself in limiting executive power, how effectively would Congress limit the President? The essay on the President as administrative chief concludes that, though the President's removal power is constitutionally subject to congressional control, Congress has declined to fetter it and has delegated discretion to the President. In 1943 Corwin draws the "chief lesson of the war to date for constitutional interpretation, . . . that the Constitution is an easily dispensable factor of our war effort — perhaps one might say an 'expendable' factor."

President Truman's seizure of the steel mills persuaded Corwin that "the chief constitutional value which overextension of presidential power threatens is, of course, the concept of a 'government of laws and not of men' — the 'rule of law' principle." He pointed out the "moral" of the steel seizure: "Escape must be sought from 'presidential autocracy' by resort not to judicial power, but . . . by resort to timely action by Congress." "The President's Power" (1951) takes vigorous issue with the "high-flying prerogative men," such as Arthur Schlesinger, Jr., who ascribed to the President "a truly royal prerogative in the field of foreign relations . . . without indicating any correlative legal or constitutional control to which he is answerable." "Indeed," these men "appear to resent the very idea that the only possible source of such control, Congress to wit, has any effective power in the premises at all." Given, however, the actual long-run retreat of Congress and the Supreme Court before presidential power, what implications did this trend hold for constitutional law?

Clearly Corwin's inquiries conclude with a warning on the unhealthy impact of presidential dominance upon American constitutional law, and with suggestions on how to "round out" the constitutional revolution in favor of democracy. The next-to-last essay, in which Corwin synthesizes a lifetime of constitutional study, contends that the judicial validation of the New Deal transformed and enfeebled "the two main structural elements of government . . . in the past," dual federalism and separation of powers. These changes in the structure of constitutional law will on the whole be permanent ones: "In Thomas Wolfe's poignant words, 'We can't go home again' — if indeed we should wish to.'' The last essay defines the constitutional revolution in presidential power and proposes to solve the "unhealthy dominance" of the President with popular understanding, a new conception of government as a job of housekeeping, and a new kind of Cabinet.

The preceding comments have anticipated to a great extent my assessment of Corwin's scholarly contribution. More than any other writer, he weaves together human character, legal concepts, and political and moral ideas in recounting the development and contemporary status of presidential power and the presidential office. He demonstrates the risks and dangers no less than the opportunities and achievements of the strong Presidency. And his inquiries are "radical" in the most literal sense because they go to the roots of the Presidency in our political and constitutional tradition.

Some limitations of Corwin's thought, however, are illuminated by Aristotle's contention that political science has four themes: the best regime in principle, the best regime under existing conditions, the origin and preservation of a given regime, and the most suitable regime generally.[27] Reflection on the best regime in principle gives one a critical distance from the salient features of existing regimes. Clearly Corwin avoided comparing American democracy to the best regime in principle; nor did he systematically discuss whether the United States was the best regime under actual conditions. Although Corwin thought more comprehensively about the Presidency than most others who came after him, his failure to pursue either of the two themes just mentioned limits the value and depth of his assessment of the American political tradition. Corwin has a tendency, which must be neither exaggerated nor ignored, to take for granted the merits of American liberal democracy as he dwells instead on its origin and development.

His presidential studies, though, exclude detailed consideration of the *origin,* for example, the Framers' intention. By underemphasizing this factor, he made it more difficult to alert Congress to its role of balancing executive power and *preserving* "some of our constitutional liberties," presumably liberties intended by the Framers.[28] Corwin adopted a perplexing course in discussing whether the New Deal was consistent with the fundamental Lockeanism of the United States or

27. Aristotle, *Politics* 155 (trans. Ernest Barker 1962).
28. Corwin, "Our Constitutional Revolution" 277.

represented a change of regime. On the one hand, he claimed that "Locke . . . was the philosopher *par excellence* of the American Revolution," and that "the general purpose of the New Deal legislation is much more fairly represented as an effort to realize the Lockean and early American conception of property . . . than as an attempt to overthrow it."[29] On the other hand, he felt "that such notions of property are for the most part irrelevant to any discussion of the political morality of the New Deal."[30] Corwin's discussion does not clarify whether the preservative element of the New Deal predominated over its novelty.

For a time Corwin hoped that congressional participation with the executive might serve as an effective brake on the excesses of presidential power. The final edition of Corwin's treatise withdraws the call for a Joint Cabinet and relies on the personality of incumbent Presidents to minimize the risks of a dominant Presidency. Corwin ignores the problem of identifying which sorts of presidential personality can lessen the risks of the Presidency, though he agrees with a recent authority in picking Eisenhower as a model President.[31] Rather than any specific solution he advanced, Corwin's legacy is his breadth, penetration, sense of the perennial themes of politics, sense of history, acuteness in dealing with doctrine, and his belief that abiding values undergird the Constitution.

Corwin's approach is undoubtedly strongest where alternative approaches are weakest. Both the advocates of presidential power, such as Clinton Rossiter and Richard Neustadt, and the authors of the "reform" literature exemplified by Schlesinger's *Imperial Presidency* lack an explicit and non-arbitrary standard of political health with which to assess presidential power.[32] Only a relatively small number of people can make the specialized judgments required to apply the standard of psychological health in James Barber's *Presidential Character*.[33] Whatever its scientific credentials, Barber's standard would, for most citizens

29. Corwin, "The New Deal in the Light of American Political and Constitutional Ideas," address to the Federation of Bar Associations, Western New York, June 27, 1936, pp. 19–21, category 6, carton 2, Corwin Papers.

30. *Id.* at 20.

31. Hargrove, *The Power of the Modern Presidency* 58 (1974).

32. See Loss, "Dissolving Concepts of the Presidency," 4 *Political Science Reviewer* 147–68 (Fall, 1974).

33. Hargrove, *Power of the Modern Presidency* 77.

who wished to screen campaign candidates, be impossible to apply. Even before President Nixon's resignation, Alexander George observed that "post-Watergate hindsight makes more noticeable the importance of old-fashioned moral character and the difficulty of incorporating this concept into character typologies such as Barber's."[34] The passage of time has persuaded many that "constitutional *desiderata"* will not necessarily take care of themselves, and that if a choice must be made, a President's moral character is more important than his ability to acquire "effective influence" over people.[35]

Post-Corwin and pre-Nixon presidential studies have with few exceptions lacked a coherent substantive doctrine of the liberal democratic regime and have implied that presidential power as such is morally good. In the 1970's some critics believe that power, especially in national security and foreign affairs, is morally tainted. If, in fact, power is morally neutral, then a standard external to the power-seeker is needed to appraise the uses and outcomes of presidential power; such a standard might perhaps be elaborated from the Constitution and the political theory it reflects. The cautious suggestion offered here is that the thought of Edward S. Corwin can assist the recovery of a standard external to Presidents and their quest for power.

At the end of his career Corwin pondered the New Deal's extension of governmental power in relationship to the Framers' intention. His occasion was the opinion of Chief Justice Stone speaking for a unanimous Court in United States v. Darby (312 U.S. 100 [1941]). Stone had cited Chief Justice Marshall's definition of congressional power over interstate commerce in Gibbons v. Ogden and Marshall's interpretation of "necessary and proper" in McCulloch v. Maryland. "Can it be supposed," wrote Corwin of the "great Chief Justice" Marshall, "that if he had been present in person he would have consented willingly to be thus conscripted in the service of the New Deal? . . . The answer to the above question must undoubtedly be 'No.' . . . At no time . . . did he contemplate the desirability, or even the feasibility, in a free state, of greatly altering by political action the existing relations of the component elements of society. Liberty, the spacious

34. George, "Assessing Presidential Character," 26 *World Politics* 249 n.21 (January, 1974).

35. See Richard Neustadt's review of Corwin, *President: Office and Powers,* in 43 *Cornell Law Quarterly* 736–37 (Summer, 1958).

liberty of an expanding nation, not social equality, was the lode-star of his political philosophy."[36] Corwin, the Moses who led us from "the land of the Constitution as our Fathers knew it," bowed to the "great Chief Justice" and the Framers' constitution of liberty.

A final note about the selection of these essays. My intention has been to reprint the essays that best delineate Corwin's argument, and I have chosen these after carefully examining his published work on the Presidency and the Corwin Papers at Princeton. Some essays concerning the Presidency were omitted because of overlap; for example, "The President, Court and Constitution," *Christian Science Monitor,* July 3, 5, 6, 1935, and "The Presidency," 25 *Princeton Alumni Weekly* 80 (October 22, 1924). The inclusion of "President and Court: A Crucial Issue" obviated the need to include the former background piece, and the latter is an introductory lecture largely taken from a previous publication. The omission of other essays, which either were remotely related to the theme of this book or added nothing to Corwin's argument, is not meant to prejudge their importance among his publications.

This book differs from the now out-of-print volume edited by Alpheus Mason and Gerald Garvey, *American Constitutional History: Essays by Edward S. Corwin* (New York: Harper & Row, 1964), whose theme was the "theory and practice of judicial review" (Editorial Note, p. vi). The present volume is the first collection of Corwin's essays on the Presidency. It stresses his idea of limited constitutional government and reprints the complete texts of essays and footnotes instead of "severely abridged" versions (Mason, p. vii). The reader is therefore able to evaluate Corwin's evidence for himself. For the student of Corwin's thought, this book also lists additions to the Mason-Garvey bibliography of Corwin's writings.

As for editorial policy, I have made some minor changes in the essays for consistency and ease of reading. Since there was considerable variation between essays, and since some of the essays had been carelessly edited, I have taken the liberty of standardizing the following items: capitalization and punctuation (according to Corwin's most frequent use), titles of books, names of cases, possessive forms, inclusive page

36. Corwin, "John Marshall, Revolutionist *Malgré Lui,*" 104 *University of Pennsylvania Law Review* 22 (October, 1955).

numbers, and the form of the footnotes, and I have modernized the most obvious old spellings. Any editorial comments of mine in the text have been placed in braces to distinguish them from Corwin's brackets.

I. The Basis of Limited Constitutional Government

1. The Natural Law and Constitutional Law

Ancient Chinese philosophers were wont to distinguish the passive and active elements of Being, called respectively *yin* and *yang*. If I may be permitted to employ this locution for a moment, the "yang" element of American constitutional law is judicial review, the power and corresponding duty of a court to pass upon the validity of legislative acts in relation to a higher law which is regarded as being binding on both the legislature and the court. By the same token the "yin" element is the aforesaid higher law. Today this role is ordinarily filled by a constitutional document, the Constitution of the United States being the supreme example; but earlier, natural law or some derivative concept took the part of "yin." Hence the purpose of this discourse — which is to demonstrate how very large a part of its content American constitutional law has always owed, and still owes, to its natural law genesis. As the matrix of American constitutional law, the documentary Constitution is still, in important measure, natural law under the skin.

Of natural law there is no end of definitions, as a casual examination of Sir Thomas Erskine Holland's *Elements of Jurisprudence* suffices to show. I venture to quote a few passages from the 13th edition:

Aristotle fully recognizes the existence of a natural as well as of a legal Justice. He mentions as an ordinary device of rhetoric the distinction which may be drawn between the written law, and "the common law" which is in accordance with Nature and immutable.

The Stoics were in the habit of identifying Nature with Law in the

From 3 *Proceedings of the Natural Law Institute* 47-81 (1950). Reprinted by permission.

higher sense, and of opposing both of these terms to Law which is such by mere human appointment. "Justice," they say, "is by Nature and not by imposition." "It proceeds from Zeus and the common Nature."

The same view finds expression in the Roman lawyers. "Law," says Cicero, "is the highest reason, implanted in Nature, which commands those things which ought to be done and prohibits the reverse." "The highest law was born in all the ages before any law was written or State was formed. . . ." "We are by Nature inclined to love mankind, which is the foundation of law. . . ."

S. Thomas Aquinas: "Participatio legis aeternae in rationali creatura lex naturalis dicitur."

Grotius: "Jus naturale est dictatum rectae rationis. . . ."[1]

For our purposes it is not essential to choose nicely among these definitions of what Cicero and St. Thomas call *lex naturalis* and Grotius terms *jus naturale.* We are concerned only with certain juristic connotations of the concept: first, that natural law is entitled by its intrinsic excellence to prevail over any law which rests solely on human authority; second, that natural law may be appealed to by human beings against injustices sanctioned by human authority.

I. Natural Law into Natural Rights

In a famous passage in the *Rhetoric,* Aristotle advised advocates that when they had "no case according to the law of the land," they should "appeal to the law of nature," and, quoting from *Antigone* of Sophocles, argue that "an unjust law is not a law."[2] While this advice scarcely reveals any deep devotion on Aristotle's part to the natural law concept, it does evidence the short step, which even at that date existed in men's minds, between the concept and the idea of a *juridical* recourse to it. Three hundred years later we find Cicero in his *De Legibus* contrasting *summa lex* and *lex scripta; summum jus* and *jus civile; universum jus* and *jus civile;* and on one occasion appealing in the Senate to *recta ratio* against the *lex scripta.*[3]

It was during the Middle Ages, however, that the conception of natural law as a code of human rights first took on real substance and

---

1. Holland, *Elements of Jurisprudence* 32-34 (13th ed. 1924).
2. *Id.* at 32 n.4.
3. *Id.* at 33 n.6; see also the present writer's book, Corwin, *Liberty Against Government* 15-17 (1948) and accompanying notes.

importance. This was so even on the Continent,[4] albeit institutions were lacking there through which such ideas could be rendered effective practically. In England, on the other hand, this lack was supplied by the royal courts, administering the common law. The impregnation of the common law with higher law concepts proceeded rapidly in the fourteenth century under Edward III. Of the thirty-two royal confirmations of the Charter noted by Sir Edward Coke, fifteen occurred in this reign; and near the end of it, in 1368, to the normal form of confirmation the declaration was added by statute that any statute passed contrary to Magna Carta "soit tenuz p'nul," words which seem clearly to have been addressed to the royal officials, including the judges.[5]

Here, to be sure, Magna Carta fills the role of natural law, but it is a Magna Carta already infused with natural law content, as is shown by Bracton's earlier designation of chapter 29 as *constitutio libertatis;* and in the fifteenth century the *lex naturae* has completely replaced Magna Carta in the juristic equation. This is notably so, for example, in the pages of Fortescue's famous *In Praise of the Law of England* (*De Laudibus Legum Angliae*), which was but one of many similar encomia. As Father Figgis has written of this period:

> The Common Law is pictured invested with a halo of dignity peculiar to the embodiment of the deepest principles and to the highest expression of human reason and of the law of nature implanted by God in the heart of man. As yet men are not clear that an Act of Parliament can do more than declare the Common Law. It is the Common Law which men set up as an object of worship. The Common Law is the perfect ideal of law; for it is natural reason developed and expounded by a collective wisdom of many generations. . . . Based on long usage and almost supernatural wisdom, its authority is above, rather than below that of Acts of Parliament or royal ordinances, which owe their fleeting existence to the caprice of the King or to the pleasure of councillors, which have a merely material sanction and may be repealed at any moment.[6]

Thus the common law becomes higher law, without at all losing its quality as positive law, the law of the King's courts and of the rising Inns of Court. Nor does Fortescue fail to stress its dual character. As-

4. See Gierke, *Political Theories of the Middle Ages* 80–81 (Maitland's trans. 1927).
5. The preceding sentence is taken from Corwin, *Liberty Against Government* 26.
6. As quoted in *id.* at 28.

serting the identity of "perfect justice" with "legal justice," and the subordination of the King to the law, i.e., the law courts, he proceeds to counsel his Prince as follows:

> ... There will be no occasion for you to search into the arcana of our laws with such tedious application and study. . . . It will not be convenient by severe study, or at the expense of the best of your time, to pry into nice points of law: such matters may be left to your judges; . . . furthermore, you will pronounce judgment in the courts by others than in person, it being not customary for the Kings of England to sit in courts or pronounce judgment themselves (*proprio ore nullus regum Angilae judicium proferre uses est*). I know very well the quickness of your apprehension and the forwardness of your parts; but for that expertness in the laws which is requisite for judges the studies of twenty years (*viginti annorum lucubrationes*) barely suffice.[7]

In short, natural law has become a craft mystery — the mystery of Bench and Bar — what it has remained, now in greater, now in lesser measure ever since.

A century and a half later we find Lord Coke, Chief Justice of the Common Pleas, describing a scene[8] which reads like a re-enactment of that imagined by Fortescue. But to his predecessor's work of edification, Coke adds official recognition that judicial custodianship of the common law signifies the power and duty of the law courts to apply its measure both to the royal prerogative and to the power of Parliament. The latter claim appears in his famous "dictum," so-called, in Dr. Bonham's case,[9] which reads:

> And it appears in our books, that in many cases, the common law will controul Acts of Parliament, and sometimes adjudge them to be utterly void: for when an Act of Parliament is against common right and reason, or repugnant, or impossible to be performed, the common law will controul it and adjudge such Act to be void. . . .[10]

And this was said, it should be noted, at the end of a century in which the thesis of Parliament's absolute power to alter and abrogate any and all laws had been asserted again and again;[11] and not only asserted but

---

7. *Id.* at 30.

8. 12 Rep. 63–65, 77 Eng. Rep. 1341–43 (1609).

9. 8 Rep. 113b, 77 Eng. Rep. 646 (1610).

10. *Id.*, 8 Rep. at 118a; see also Proclamations, 12 Rep. 74, 77 Eng. Rep. 1352 (1611).

11. See Corwin, *Liberty Against Government* 32–33 and notes.

demonstrated by its part in the Tudor ecclesiastical and religious revolution.

Eighty years after Dr. Bonham's case, "the great Mr. Locke" produced his second *Treatise on Civil Government*, in which the dissolution of natural law into the natural rights of the individual — the rights of "life, liberty and estate" — is completed through the agency of the social compact. Of judicial review, to be sure, Locke appears to have no inkling. He relied for the protection of the individual's inherent and inalienable rights on: first, Parliament; second, the right of revolution. Even so, Locke's contribution to both the doctrinal justification of judicial review and to the theory of its proper scope is first and last a very considerable one.

Coke and Locke are the two great names in the common Anglo-American higher law tradition, and the contribution of each is enhanced by that of the other. Locke's version of natural law not only rescues Coke's version of the English constitution from a localized patois, restating it in the universal tongue of the eighteenth century, it also supplements it in important respects. Coke's endeavor was to put forward the historical *procedures* of the common law as a permanent restraint on power, and especially on the power of the English crown. Locke, in the limitations which he imposes on legislative power, is looking rather to the security of the *substantive* rights of the individual — those rights which are implied in the basic arrangements of society at all times and in all places. While Coke extricated the notion of fundamental law from what must sooner or later have proved a fatal nebulosity, he did so at the expense of archaism. Locke, on the other hand, in cutting loose in great measure from the historical method of reasoning, opened the way to the larger issues with which American constitutional law has been called upon to grapple in its latest maturity.[12]

II. Natural Law and Judicial Review

The *fons et origo* of both the doctrine and the practice of judicial review in the United States is Coke's invocation in Dr. Bonham's Case of "common right and reason," which as explained by the sixteenth-century author of *Doctor and Student,* was the term used "by them that be learned in the laws of England" in place of the term "law and

12. Parts of the above paragraph are taken from *id.* at 50-51.

nature."[13] Commended by two Lord Chief Justices, Hobart and Holt, the dictum had won repeated recognition in various legal abridgments and digests before the outbreak of the American Revolution.[14] In the early 1700's, it was relied on by a British colonial law officer as affixing the stigma of invalidity to an act of the Barbadoes assembly creating paper money.[15] In 1759, we encounter a casual reference by Governor Cadwallader Colden of the Province of New York to "a judicial power of declaring them [laws] void."[16]

But just as Coke had forged his celebrated dictum as a possible weapon for the struggle which he already foresaw against the divine rights pretensions of James I, so its definitive reception in this country was motivated by the rising agitation against the mother country. The creative first step was taken by James Otis in February, 1761, in his argument for the Boston merchants against an application by a British customs official for a general warrant authorizing him to search their cellars and warehouses for smuggled goods. An act of Parliament "against natural Equity," Otis asserted, was void. "If an Act of Parliament," he continued, "should be made in the very Words of this Petition, it would be void," and it would be the duty of the executive courts to pass it "into disuse."[17] Four years later, according to Governor Hutchinson of Massachusetts, the prevailing argument against the Stamp Act was that it was "against Magna Charta and the natural rights of Englishmen, and therefore, according to Lord Coke, null and void," testimony which is borne out by a contemporaneous decision of a Virginia county court.[18] On the very eve of the Declaration of Independence, Judge William Cushing, later to become one of Washington's appointees to the original bench of the Supreme Court, charged a Massachusetts jury to ignore certain acts of Parliament as "void and inoperative" and was congratulated by John Adams for doing so.[19]

And meantime, in 1772, George Mason had developed a similar argument against an act of the Virginia assembly of 1682, under which

13. See *id.* at 35, 35 n.40.
14. *Id.* at 39 n.43.
15. See 2 Chalmers, *Opinions of Eminent Lawyers* 27-38 (1814).
16. 2 New York Historical Society Collections 204; see also Chalmers, *Political Annals,* in 1 New York Historical Society Collections 81 (1868).
17. Adams' report of Otis' argument in Paxton's case, Quincy (App. 1) 474 (Mass. 1761).
18. Quincy (App. 1) 519 n.18 (Mass. 1761).
19. 5 McMaster, *History of the People of the United States* 395 (1905).

certain Indian women had been sold into slavery. The act in question, he asserted, "was originally void of itself, because contrary to natural right."[20] And, he continued:

> If natural right, independence, defect of representation, and disavowal of protection, are not sufficient to keep them from the coercion of our laws, on what other principles can we justify our opposition to some late acts of power exercised over us by the British legislature? Yet they only pretended to impose on us a paltry tax in money; we on our free neighbors, the yoke of perpetual slavery. Now all acts of legislature apparently contrary to natural right and justice, are, in our laws, and must be in the nature of things, considered as void. The laws of nature are the laws of God; whose authority can be superseded by no power on earth. . . . All human constitutions which contradict his laws, we are in conscience bound to disobey. Such have been the adjudications of our courts of justice.[21]

Mason concluded by citing Coke and Hobart. The court adjudged the act of 1682 repealed.[22]

Nor did the establishment of the first American constitutions cause this course of reasoning to be abandoned. To the contrary, the most eminent judges of the first period of American constitutional law, which comes to an end approximately with the death of Marshall in 1835, appealed freely to natural rights and the social compact as limiting legislative power, and based decisions on this ground, and the same doctrine was urged by the greatest lawyers of the period without reproach. Typical in this connection is the case of Wilkinson v. Leland, which was decided by the Supreme Court in 1829.[23] Attorney for the defendants in error was Daniel Webster. "If," said he, "at this period there is not a general restraint on Legislatures in favor of private rights, there is an end to private property. Though there may be no prohibition in the constitution, the Legislature is restrained . . . from acts subverting the great principles of republican liberty and of the social compact. . . ."[24] To this contention his opponent William Wirt responded thus: "Who is the sovereign? . . . Is it not the Legislature of the State, and are not its acts effectual . . . unless they come in contact

20. Robin v. Hardaway, Jeff. 109 (Va. 1772).
21. *Id.* at 114.
22. *Id.* at 114, 123.
23. 2 Pet. 627, 7 L. Ed. 542 (1829).
24. *Id.,* 2 Pet. at 646.

with the great principles of the social compact?"[25] The act of the Rhode Island legislature under review was upheld, but said Justice Story speaking for the Court: "That government can scarcely be deemed to be free where the rights of property are left solely dependent upon the will of a legislative body without any restraint. The fundamental maxims of a free government seem to require that the rights of personal liberty and private property should be held sacred."[26] Indeed, fourteen years before this the same court had unanimously held void, on the basis of these same principles, an act of the Virginia legislature which purported to revoke a grant of land.[27]

In short, *judicial review initially had nothing to do with a written constitution.* In point of fact, the first appearance of the idea of judicial review in this country antedated the first written constitution by at least two decades. Judicial review continued, moreover, in a relationship of semi-independence of the written constitution on the basis of "common right and reason," natural law, natural rights, and kindred postulates throughout the first third of the nineteenth century. But meantime, a competing conception of judicial review as something anchored to the *written constitution* had been in the process of formulation in answer to Blackstone's doctrine that in every State there is a *supreme, absolute power,* and that this power is vested in the *legislature.* From this angle judicial review based on "common right and reason," or on natural law ideas, was an impertinence, as Blackstone took pains to point out in his *Commentaries.*[28] But suppose that the supreme will in the State was not embodied in the *legislature* and its *acts,* but in the *people at large* and their *constitution* – what conclusions would follow from this premise? In *The Federalist* No. 78, Hamilton suggested an answer to this question, and in 1803, in Marbury v. Madison,[29] Chief Justice Marshall elaborated the answer: it is the duty of courts when confronted with a conflict between an act (i.e., a *statute*) of "the mere agents of the people" (that is, of the ordinary legislature) and the act of the people themselves (to wit, the constitution) to prefer the latter.

The inevitable clash between the two conceptions of judicial review

25. *Id.,* 2 Pet. at 652.
26. *Id.,* 2 Pet. at 657.
27. Terrett v. Taylor, 9 Cranch 43, 3 L. Ed. 650 (1815).
28. 1 *Blackstone Commentaries* *46, 91.
29. 1 Cranch 137, 2 L. Ed. 60 (1803).

was first unfolded in the case of Calder v. Bull, decided by the Supreme Court in 1798.[30] There it was held that the "ex post facto" clause of Article I, section 10 of the Constitution applied only to penal legislation and hence did not protect rights of property and contract from interference by a state legislature; but Justice Samuel Chase endeavored to soften this blow to proprietarian interests by citing the power of the state courts to enforce extra-constitutional limitations on legislative power, such as many of them were in fact already doing. Said he:

> I cannot subscribe to the *omnipotence* of a *state Legislature,* or that it is *absolute and without controul;* although its authority should not be *expressly* restrained by the *constitution,* or *fundamental law,* of the state. . . . There are certain *vital* principles in our *free Republican governments,* which will determine and overrule an *apparent and flagrant* abuse of *legislative* power. . . . The *genius,* the *nature,* and the *spirit* of our state governments, amount to a prohibition of *such acts of legislation;* and the *general principles of law and reason* forbid them.[31]

To hold otherwise, it was stated, would be "political heresy, altogether inadmissible."[32]

Chase belonged to the older generation of American lawyers and had been brought up on Coke-Littleton, having received much of his legal education in London in the Inns of Court. Alongside him on the Supreme Bench, however, sat a very different type of lawyer, one of "that brood of young lawyers," characterized by Jefferson as "ephemeral insects of the law," who had imbibed their law from Blackstone's *Commentaries.* This was James Iredell of North Carolina, who demurred strongly to Chase's natural rights doctrine. "True," said he, "some speculative jurists" had held "that a legislative act against natural justice must, in itself, be void; but the correct view, he stated, was that:

> If . . . a government, composed of legislative, executive and judicial departments, were established, by a Constitution, which imposed no limits on the legislative power, . . . whatever the legislative power chose to enact, would be lawfully enacted, and the judicial power, could never interpose to pronounce it void. . . . Sir William Blackstone, having put the strong case of an act of parliament, which should authorize a man to try his own cause, explicitly adds, that even in that case,

---

30. 3 Dall. 386, 1 L. Ed. 648 (1798).
31. *Id.,* 3 Dall. at 387–89.
32. *Id.*

"there is no court that has power to defeat the intent of the legislature when couched in such evident . . . words. . . ."[33]

The debate thus begun was frequently renewed in other jurisdictions; and long before the Civil War, Iredell had won the fight — but as we shall see, more in *appearance* than in *reality*. In 1868, Judge Cooley, in considering the circumstances in which a legislative enactment may be declared unconstitutional, wrote:

> The rule of law upon this subject appears to be, that, except where the constitution has imposed limits upon the legislative power, it must be considered as practically absolute, whether it operate according to natural justice or not in any particular case. The courts are not the guardians of the rights of the people of the State, except as those rights are secured by some constitutional provision which comes within the judicial cognizance.[34]

Yet, six years later we find the Supreme Court of the United States pronouncing a statute of the state of Kansas void on the very grounds that had been laid down in Chase's dictum. Speaking for an all but unanimous Court, Justice Miller said:

> It must be conceded that there are . . . rights in every free government beyond the control of the State. A government which recognized no such rights, which held the lives, the liberty, and the property of its citizens subject at all times to the absolute disposition and unlimited control of even the most democratic depository of power, is after all but a despotism. It is true it is a despotism of the many, of the majority, if you choose to call it so, but it is none the less a despotism. It may well be doubted if a man is to hold all that he is accustomed to call his own, all in which he has placed his happiness, and the security of which is essential to that happiness, under the unlimited dominion of others, whether it is not wiser that this power should be exercised by one man than by many.[35]

One Justice dissented, asserting that such views tended to "convert the government into a judicial despotism."[36]

But vastly more important is the fact that in the very process of discarding the doctrine of natural rights and adherent doctrines as the

33. *Id.,* 3 Dall. at 398–99.

34. Cooley, *Constitutional Limitations* 168 (3d ed. 1874).

35. Citizens' Savings & Loan Ass'n v. Topeka, 20 Wall. 655, 662, 22 L. Ed. 455 (1874).

36. *Id.,* 20 Wall. at 669.

basis of judicial review, the courts have contrived to throw about those rights, which originally owed their protection to these doctrines, the folds of the documentary constitution. In short, things are not always what they seem to be, even when they seem so most.[37] The indebtedness of the institution of judicial review and of the rights protected by it to natural law ideas is by no means sufficiently summed up in the glib statement that nowadays judicial review is confined to the four corners of the written constitution.

III. How Natural Law Doctrines Were Used to Fill a Gap in the Written Constitution

It is a commonplace that the doctrine of natural rights was conveyed into the American written Constitution by bills of rights, the earliest example of which was the Virginia Declaration of Rights of June 12, 1776. This commonplace is, however, only a half of the truth, and indeed the lesser half. As has been indicated, the type of judicial review which stemmed from Coke's dictum supplied a second avenue for natural rights concepts into the constitutional document. In this section I shall first illustrate this proposition with the doctrine of vested rights.

Not all the early state constitutions were accompanied by bills of rights. Moreover, the availability of such bills of rights as existed as a basis for judicial inquiry into the validity of legislative measures was sharply challenged at times. Even more important was the fact that, as it came early to be appreciated, bills of rights or no bills of rights, the early state constitutions left proprietarian interests in a very exposed position vis-à-vis the new popular assemblies, for which the prerogatives of the British Parliament itself were sometimes claimed.[38]

The formidable character of legislative power in these early instruments of government as regards the property interest was exhibited in more ways than one. In the first place, in the prevailing absence of courts of equity, legislative assemblies interfered almost at will with judicial decisions, and particularly those involving disputes over property. The case of Calder v. Bull, mentioned earlier, affords an example of this sort of thing.[39] The Connecticut courts, having refused to probate

37. See e.g. Cooley, *Constitutional Limitations* 174–76, where the principle of the separation of powers is made to do duty for natural law concepts.
38. See Coxe, *An Essay on Judicial Power and Unconstitutional Legislation* 223 *et seq.* (1893); 5 *Hamilton's Works* 116 (Lodge ed. 1904); 7 *id.* at 198.
39. Note 30.

a certain will, were to all intents and purposes ordered to revise their decision, which they did, with the result that the heirs at law to an estate were ousted, after a year and a half of possession, by the beneficiaries of the will. A second and highly impressive proof of early state legislative power is afforded by the ferocious catalogue of legislation directed against the Tories, embracing acts of confiscation, bills of pains and penalties, even acts of attainder. One sample of such legislation came under the scrutiny of the United States Supreme Court in 1800, in the case of Cooper v. Telfair.[40] Said Justice Washington: "The presumption, indeed, must always be in favor of the validity of laws, if the contrary is not clearly demonstrated."[41] On this ground and one or two others, the Georgia act was sustained, although Justice Chase opined that with the federal Constitution now in effect such an act would be clearly void; but this act was passed during the Revolution. Thirdly, with the general collapse of values early in 1780, every state legislature became a scene of vehement agitation on the part of the widespread farmer-debtor class in favor of paper money laws and other measures of like intent. For the first time, the property interest was confronted with "the power of numbers," and, in the majority of cases, the power of numbers triumphed.

Could the state bills of rights withstand the flood? It soon transpired that they were an utterly ineffective bulwark of private rights against state legislative power. And so the movement was launched which led to the Philadelphia Convention of 1787. That abuse by the state legislatures of their powers had been the most important single cause leading to the Convention was asserted by Madison early in the course of its deliberations, and others agreed.[42] So far as we are concerned, the most important expression of the Convention's anxiety to clip the wings of the high-flying local sovereignties is to be found in the opening paragraph of section 10 of Article I, which reads:

No State shall enter into any Treaty, Alliance, or Confederation; grant Letters of Marque and Reprisal; coin Money, emit Bills of Credit; make any Thing but gold and silver Coin a Tender in Payment of Debts; pass any Bill of Attainder, ex post facto Law or Law impairing the Obligation of Contracts, or grant any Title of Nobility.

40. 4 Dall. 14, 1 L. Ed. 721 (1800).
41. *Id.,* 4 Dall. at 18.
42. See 1 Farrand, *The Records of the Federal Convention* 48, 133–34, 255, 424, 525, 533; 2 *id.* at 285 (1937).

The provision which here claims attention is the prohibition of *ex post facto* laws. What did those who urged their insertion in the Constitution think these words meant? Some of them, we know, thought the clause would rule out *all* "retrospective" legislation, meaning thereby legislation which operated detrimentally upon existing property rights.[43] But as we have seen in Calder v. Bull, the clause was confined to penal legislation, to statutes making criminal an act which was innocent when done. That the Court was thoroughly aware of the breach it was thus creating in the Constitution, the opinions of all the Justices, except that of the Blackstonian Iredell, make amply apparent; and going beyond apology, Chase sought to show how the gap could be stopped by the local judiciaries by recourse to extra-constitutional limitations, "the spirit of our free republican governments," "the social compact," considerations of "natural justice," and the like. The local judiciaries responded to the suggestion with varying degrees of alacrity, and the sum total of their efforts was one of the most fertile doctrines of American constitutional law, the doctrine of vested rights, the practical purport of which was that the effect of legislation on existing property rights was a *primary* test of its validity, and that by this test legislation must stop short of curtailing existing rights of ownership, at least unduly or unreasonably.[44]

But in fact, Chase's dictum only stimulated a movement already begun. Three years prior to Calder v. Bull, we find Justice Paterson charging a federal jury in a case involving vested rights in these words:

. . . The right of acquiring and possessing property and having it protected, is one of the natural, inherent and unalienable rights of man. Men have a sense of property: Property is necessary to their subsistence, and correspondent to their natural wants and desires; its security was one of the objects, that induced them to unite in society. . . . The preservation of property . . . is a primary object of the social compact, and, by the late constitution of Pennsylvania, was made a fundamental law.[45]

Indeed, a majority of the cases of judicial review after the Cokian model, referred to in Section II of this paper, involved property rights. Nor should the great name of Chancellor Kent be overlooked in this connection. First as judge, then as Chancellor in his home state, and finally

---

43. On this point see Corwin, *Liberty Against Government* 60–61 n.4.
44. *Id.* at 72 *et seq.*
45. Van Horne's Lessee v. Dorrance, 2 Dall. 304, 310, 1 L. Ed. 391 (1795).

as author of the famed *Commentaries,* Kent developed the doctrine's fullest possibilities and spread its influence fastest and farthest.

Yet even as Kent was vaunting private property as an instrument of God for realizing his plans for the advancement of the race, it was becoming less and less practicable to urge such considerations on American judges. The old-type Cokian judge had about disappeared — Blackstone was in the saddle in the law offices and in the court houses. What is more, with the accession of Jackson to the Presidency there took place an immense resurgence of the doctrine of popular sovereignty. Of the numerous corollaries into which the doctrine proliferated, two are relevant to our interest: first, the Constitution was an ordinance of the people, and its supremacy sprang from the fact that it embodied their will; second, of the three departments of state government, the legislature stood nearest the people. It followed that the courts had better go slow in holding state legislative acts invalid; and that on no account must they do so except for a plain violation of the Constitution, i.e., of the people's will as there expressed.

Bench and Bar were confronted with a dilemma: either they must cast the doctrine of vested rights to the wolves or they must bring it within the sheepfold of the written Constitution. The second alternative was adopted in due course. Ultimately the doctrine found a home within the "due process" clause, "no person shall be deprived of life, liberty, or property without due process of law." The original significance of the clause was purely procedural — nobody should be punished without a trial by jury or "writ original of the Common Law." In the revamped clause the term "due process of law" simply fades out and the clause comes to read, in effect, "no person shall be deprived of property, period." Thus was the narrow interpretation which was planted on the ex post facto clause in Calder v. Bull revenged in kind.[46]

This achievement was consummated in the famous case of Wynehamer v. People, in which, in 1856, the New York Court of Appeals set aside a state-wide prohibition law as comprising, with regard to liquors in existence at the time of its going into effect, an act of destruction of property not within the power of government to perform "even by the forms of due process of law."[47] An interesting feature of Judge Comstock's opinion in the case is his repudiation of all arguments

46. See Corwin, *Liberty Against Government* 84–115.
47. 13 N.Y. (3 Kern) 378 (1856).

against the statute sounding in natural law concepts, like "fundamental principles of liberty," "common reason and natural rights," and so forth. Such theories said he — squinting, one suspects, at the anti-slavery agitation — were subversive of the necessary powers of government. Furthermore, there was "no process of reasoning by which it could be demonstrated that the 'Act for the Prevention of Intemperance, Pauperism and Crime' is void, upon principles and theories outside the Constitution, which will not also, and by an easier induction, bring it in direct conflict with the Constitution itself."[48]

The expansion of the "obligation of contracts" clause of Article I, section 10, by resort to natural law concepts follows a similar, though briefer course. The master craftsman was Chief Justice Marshall, and this time the infusion of the constitutional clause with natural law concepts was direct. The great leading case was Fletcher v. Peck,[49] in which, in 1810, Marshall, speaking for the Court, held that a state legislature was forbidden "either by general principles, which are common to our free institutions, or by the particular provisions of the constitution of the United States"[50] to rescind a previous land grant; while Justice Johnson based his concurring opinion altogether "on the reason and nature of things; a principle which will impose laws even on the Deity."[51] It is true that when, in 1819, the doctrine of Fletcher v. Peck was extended to the charters of eleemosynary corporations, the Court contented itself with invoking only the obligations clause.[52] The dependence, however, of the holding on natural law premises still remains. The constitutional clause presupposes a *pre-existent* obligation to be protected. Whence, if not from natural law, can such an obligation descend upon a public grant?

Of the four great doctrines of American constitutional law which the American judiciary developed prior to the Civil War, three (the doctrine of judicial review, the substantive doctrine of due process of law, and the doctrine that the obligation of contracts clause protects public contracts) are products of the infusion of the documentary Constitution with natural law, natural rights concepts. The fourth doctrine, that of dual federalism, was the creation of the Supreme

48. *Id.* at 392.
49. 6 Cranch 87, 3 L. Ed. 162 (1810).
50. *Id.*, 6 Cranch at 139.
51. *Id.*, 6 Cranch at 143.
52. Dartmouth College v. Woodward, 4 Wheat. 518, 4 L. Ed. 629 (1819).

Court at Washington under the presidency and guidance of Chief Justice Taney. It, of course, rests on different, highly political considerations. Yet even in this case, natural law may claim some credit if, as Thomas Hill Green argues in his *Principles of Political Obligation,* the notion of sovereignty is also, in final analysis, rooted in the doctrine of natural law.[53] Green, of course, was thinking of "sovereignty" as it is known to Western political thought, not the kind of sovereignty that is the offspring of Byzantine absolutism married to Marxian materialism.

IV. The Bench and Bar Present Us with an Up-to-Date Doctrine of Natural Law

In 1868, the Fourteenth Amendment was added to the Constitution. The first section of it reads as follows:

All persons born or naturalized in the United States, and subject to the jurisdiction thereof, are citizens of the United States and of the State wherein they reside. No State shall make or enforce any law which shall abridge the privileges or immunities of citizens of the United States; nor shall any State deprive any person of life, liberty or property, without due process of law; nor deny to any person within its jurisdiction the equal protection of the laws.

The fifth and final section gave Congress the power "to enforce, by appropriate legislation, the provisions of this Article."

In the understanding of most people at the time, the intended beneficiaries of the amendment were the recently emancipated freedmen, but in the very first cases to reach the Supreme Court under it, the famous Slaughter House cases of 1873,[54] this assumption was sharply challenged by counsel, John Archibald Campbell of New Orleans, a former Justice of the Court. No doubt, Campbell argued, the freedmen would and should derive benefit from the amendment, but their doing so would only be incidental to the realization of its much broader purpose, that of giving legal embodiment to the principle of "laissez-faire individualism which had been held by the colonists ever since they came to this soil."[55] "What," he asked, "did the colonists and their posterity seek for and obtain by their settlement of this conti-

53. Green, *Principles of Political Obligation* (1901).
54. 16 Wall. 36, 21 L. Ed. 394 (1873).
55. These words are from Twiss, *Lawyers and the Constitution* 53 (1942).

nent? . . . *Freedom, free action, free enterprise — free competition.*
It was in freedom they expected to find the best auspices for every
kind of human success."[56]

Campbell lost his suit, by the narrow margin of five Justices to four;
but he had sown an idea which, in the course of the next thirty years,
imparted to judicial review a new and revolutionary extension. In 1878,
the American Bar Association was founded from the elite of the American bar. Organized as it was in the wake of the "barbarous" decision —
as one member termed it — in Munn v. Illinois, [57] in which the Supreme
Court had held that states were entitled by virtue of their police power
to prescribe the charges of "businesses affected with a public interest,"
the association, through its more eminent members, became the mouth-
piece of a new constitutional philosophy which was compounded in
about equal parts from the teachings of the British Manchester School
of Political Economy and Herbert Spencer's highly sentimentalized version of the doctrine of evolution, just then becoming the intellectual
vogue; plus a "booster" — in the chemical sense — from Sir Henry
Maine's *Ancient Law,* first published in 1861. I refer to Maine's famous
dictum that "the movement of the progressive societies has hitherto
been a movement *from Status to Contract.*"[58] If hitherto, why not
henceforth?

In short, the American people were presented *a new doctrine of
natural law,* the content and purport of which appear — to take a specific example — in Professor William Graham Sumner's *What Social
Classes Owe to Each Other,* which was published in 1883. I quote a
passage or two:

> A society based on contract is a society of free and independent men,
> who form ties without favor or obligation, and cooperate without
> cringing or intrigues. A society based on contract, gives the utmost
> room and chance for individual development, and for all the self-reli-
> ance and dignity of a free man. . . . It follows that one man, in a free
> state, cannot claim help from, and cannot be charged to give help to,
> another.

And again:

> All institutions are to be tested by the degree to which they guaran-

56. *Id.* at 54, quoting Campbell's brief, pp. 42–44. Emphasis supplied.
57. 94 U.S. 113, 24 L. Ed. 77 (1876).
58. Maine, *Ancient Law* 165 (3d Amer. ed. 1873).

tee liberty. It is not to be admitted for a moment that liberty is a means to social ends, and that it may be impaired for major considerations. Any one who so argues has lost the bearing and relations of all the facts and factors in a free state. He is a centre of powers to work, and of capacities to suffer. What his powers may be — whether they can carry him far or not; what his fortune may be, whether to suffer much or little — are questions of his personal destiny which he must work out and endure as he can; but for all that concerns the bearing of the society and its institutions upon that man, and upon the sum of happiness to which he can attain during his life on earth, the product of all history and all philosophy up to this time is summed up in the doctrine, that he should be left free to do the most for himself that he can, and should be guaranteed the exclusive enjoyment of all that he does. . . . Social improvement is not to be won by direct effort. It is secondary and results from physical or economic improvement. . . . An improvement in surgical instruments or in anesthetics really does more for those who are not well off than all the declamations of the orators and pious wishes of the reformers. . . . The yearning after equality is the offspring of envy and covetousness, and there is no possible plan for satisfying that yearning which can do aught else than rob A to give to B; consequently all such plans nourish some of the meanest vices of human nature, waste capital, and overthrow civilization. . . .[59]

It is interesting to compare this new type of natural law, and its tremendous exaltation of individual effort, with the ancient type, which was set forth in the texts quoted in Section I of this paper. There are two differences, the first of which approximates that between a *moral* code, addressed to the reason, and natural law in the sense in which that term is employed by the natural sciences. The former operates *through* men; the latter *upon* men, and altogether independently of their attitude toward it, or even of their awareness of its existence. The results of its operation would therefore be of no moral significance, except for one circumstance, the assumption, to wit, that *compliance with it — whether conscious or unconscious — forwarded Progress.* Thus, according to Maine, it was *the progressive societies* which had heretofore moved from *status* to *contract;* while with Spencer *progressive societies* were destined to "evolve" from the *military state* into the *industrial society* — a process not yet completed, however, or the State would have vanished. In short, the laissez-faire version of natural law contrived, in the end, to combine the *moral* prestige of the older concept with the *scientific* prestige of the newer.[60]

59. Extracted from Mason, *Free Government in the Making* 607-8 (1949).
60. Parts of this paragraph are taken from Corwin, *Liberty Against Government* 198.

The second difference can be put more briefly, although it is perhaps the more important one. The natural law of Cicero, of St. Thomas, Grotius — even of Locke — always conceives of man as *in* society. The natural law of Spencer, Sumner, et al., sets man, the supreme product of a highly competitive struggle for existence, *above* society — an impossible station in both logic and fact.

The chief constitutional law precipitate from the new natural law, the doctrine of freedom of contract, confirms and illustrates this fatal characteristic of it. By this doctrine, persons *sui juris* engaged in the ordinary employments were entitled to contract regarding their services without interference from government; as reciprocally were those who sought their services. Endorsed by such writers as Cooley, Tiedemann, James Coolidge Carter, J. F. Dillon, and by a growing procession of state high courts headed by those of New York, Pennsylvania, Massachusetts, and Illinois, the doctrine attained culminating expression in 1905 in the famous Bakeshop case.[61] There a New York statute which limited the hours of labor in bakeries to ten hours a day and sixty hours a week was set aside five Justices to four as not "a fair, reasonable and appropriate exercise of the police power of the state" but "an unreasonable, unnecessary and arbitrary interference with the right of the individual to his personal liberty. . . ."[62]

How was this result reached? Very simply: it was the automatic result of the conception of an area of individual action *any* interference with which by the state put upon it a burden of justification not required in other cases. On this basis the Court came to operate a kind of "automatic" judicial review, the product of which was labelled by its critics "mechanical jurisprudence." Nor is this type of jurisprudence extinct today, as I shall now point out. Its application has merely been transferred to a different set of values and interests.

V. Natural Law and Constitutional Law Today

In 1925, in the now famous Gitlow case,[63] which involved a conviction under the New York Anti-Syndicalist Act, the Supreme Court adopted tentatively the thesis, which it had rejected earlier, that the word "liberty" in the Fourteenth Amendment adopts and makes effective against state legislatures the limitations which the First Amend-

---

61. Lochner v. New York, 198 U.S. 45, 25 S. Ct. 539, 49 L. Ed. 937 (1905).
62. *Id.,* 198 U.S. 56.
63. Gitlow v. New York, 268 U.S. 652, 45 S. Ct. 625, 69 L. Ed. 1138 (1925).

ment imposes upon Congress in favor of "freedom of speech and press." Then in 1940 in the Cantwell case,[64] the Court upset a conviction under Connecticut law of two Jehovah's Witnesses for breach of the peace on the ground that the proselyting activities of the said Witnesses did not under the circumstances constitute a "clear and present danger" to public order; and since then a majority of the Court has gone to the verge, at least, of making the "clear and present danger" formula a direct test of legislation, although in the Gitlow case it had rejected the rule as spurious.

And what has all this to do with natural law? The answer is discovered when we note the rule by which the Court professes to be guided when interpreting the word "liberty" in the Fourteenth Amendment in the light of the Bill of Rights. Not all the provisions of the latter are regarded as having been converted by the Fourteenth Amendment into restrictions on the states, but only those that are protective of the "immutable principles of justice which inhere in the very idea of free government"; of the "fundamental principles of liberty and justice which lie at the base of all our civil and political institutions"; of the "immunities . . . implicit in the concept of ordered liberty"; of principles of justice "rooted in the traditions and conscience of our people"; principles, the violation of which would be "repugnant to the conscience of mankind."[65]

This is entirely in line with the natural law tradition. But does it suffice to elevate the rights it deals with into a *super-constitution,* so that any law touching them is *ipso facto* "infected with presumptive invalidity"? As we have seen, this is precisely what happened in the case of "liberty of contract"; and today, "liberty of contract" thus distended "is all," as they say in Pennsylvania; and may not a like fate overtake freedom of speech, press, and religion in time if the same slide-rule methods are applied to legislation touching them? I am thinking especially of such decisions as those in Saia v. New York,[66] McCollum v.

64. Cantwell v. Connecticut, 310 U.S. 296, 60 S. Ct. 900, 84 L. Ed. 1213 (1940).

65. Louisiana v. Resweber, 329 U.S. 459, 470-72, 67 S. Ct. 374, 91 L. Ed. 422 (1947), quoting from Holden v. Hardy, 169 U.S. 366, 389, 18 S. Ct. 383, 42 L. Ed. 780 (1898); Hebert v. Louisiana, 272 U.S. 312, 316, 47 S. Ct. 103, 71 L. Ed. 270 (1926); Palko v. Connecticut, 302 U.S. 319, 325, 58 S. Ct. 149, 82 L. Ed. 288 (1937); Snyder v. Massachusetts, 291 U.S. 97, 105, 54 S. Ct. 330, 78 L. Ed. 674 (1934).

66. 334 U.S. 558, 68 S. Ct. 1148, 92 L. Ed. 1574 (1948).

Board of Education,[67] and Terminiello v. City of Chicago.[68] These were very ill-considered decisions to my way of thinking, and in fact the first of these has already been repudiated by the Court,[69] at least four of the five Justices who were responsible for it lugubriously so assert. I contend, in short, that any patent formula or device which relieves the Justices from considering relevant, however recalcitrant facts, or which exonerates them of the characteristic judicial duty of adjusting the universal and eternal to the local and contingent, the here and the now, is to be deplored. I contend further that the "clear and present danger" rule is just such a patent formula.

How are we to assess the importance of the natural law concept in the development of American constitutional law? What it all simmers down to is essentially this: while that distinctive American institution, judicial review, is regarded today as stemming from the principle of popular sovereignty, it sprang in the first instance from "common right and reason," the equivalent with men of law in the sixteenth-century England of natural law. What is more, popular sovereignty in the last analysis is itself a derivative from the natural law postulate, being neither more nor less than a sort of ad hoc consolidation of the natural right of human beings to choose their own governing institutions.

And the indebtedness of American constitutional law to natural law, natural rights concepts for its content in the field of private rights is vital and well-nigh all-comprehensive. It is, of course, true that not all of the corollaries that the courts have endeavored to attach to their premises have survived; and few have survived without modification. Yet it is a striking fact that while hundreds of constitutional provisions have been adopted since judicial review was established, not one has ever proposed its abolition and only very few **its** modification. And meantime the American states have continued to incorporate in their successive constitutions, virtually without comment, the constitutional clauses – the due process clause, for example – that today incorporate the principal judicial doctrines which I have traced to natural law bases. It is true, as I just remarked, that some of these doctrines have become extinct and others have been qualified; but invariably these results have been achieved by judicial massage, as it were – sometimes a rather rugged massage – and not by legislative or constitutional surgery.

67. 333 U.S. 203, 68 S. Ct. 461, 92 L. Ed. 649 (1948).
68. {337} U.S. {1}, 69 S. Ct. 894 (1949).
69. The reference is to Kovacs v. Cooper, 336 U.S. 17, 69 S. Ct. 448 (1949).

Not that the doctrine of natural law itself has escaped disturbing comment at times, even from American jurists. Frequently cited in this connection is the late Justice Holmes' discourse on "Natural Law." "It is not enough," said Justice Holmes in a characteristic passage, "for the knight of romance that you agree that his lady is a very nice girl, — if you do not admit that she is the best that God ever made, you must fight"; and the same demand, he opines, "is at the bottom of the jurist's search for criteria of absolute validity."[70]

We can readily concede that such criteria may never be established in this far from perfect, and always changing world. Yet that admission does not necessarily discredit the search; perhaps, indeed, it makes it more necessary, as an alternative to despair. Holmes, in fact, exposes himself when he goes on to advance as an argument against natural law that the right to life "is sacrificed without a scruple whenever the interest of society, that is, of the predominant power of the community, is thought to demand it."[71] But the answer is plain: the right to life is more than the right to live — it is also the right to spend life for worthwhile ends; and so long as one is guaranteed a free man's part in determining what these ends are, natural law has *pro tanto* received institutional recognition and embodiment. But, of course, it is essential to this argument that the free man's part be kept a really vital one.

Our present interest, however, has been in natural law as a challenge to the notion of unlimited human authority. American constitutional law is the record of an attempt to implement that challenge. The record is a somewhat mixed one, but it is clear that in the judgment of the American people it has been on the whole a record of successes. May it continue to be!

70. Holmes, *Collected Legal Papers* 310 (Laski ed. 1920).
71. *Id.* at 314.

II. Wilson and "Precedents for Presidential Dictatorship"

2. War, the Constitution Moulder

The concentration of power and responsibility demanded by war is apt to give a system grounded on the rigid maxims of republicanism a somewhat violent wrench. Fortunately the framers of the Constitution were not wholly unaware of the difficulty, which they proceeded to meet by conferring on the President as Commander-in-Chief of the army and navy all the prerogatives of monarchy in connection with war-making except only the power to declare war and the power to create armed forces. The clause of the Constitution which makes the President Commander-in-Chief may accordingly be described as the elastic block in the closed circle of constitutionalism; in the heat of war the powers it confers are capable of expanding tremendously, but upon the restoration of normal conditions they shrink with equal rapidity. The true nature of the presidential prerogative in war time was comprehended by Lincoln perfectly, who, when he was confronted with the argument that some of his measures were likely to constitute precedents injurious to liberty, answered the objection in his character-istic strain: "Nor," said he, "am I able to appreciate the danger appre-hended that the American people will, by means of military arrests during the rebellion lose the right of public discussion, the liberty of speech and the press, the laws of evidence, trial by jury, and habeas corpus, throughout the indefinite peaceful future which I trust lies before them, any more than I am able to believe that a man could con-tract so strong an appetite for emetics during a temporary illness as to persist in feeding upon them during the remainder of his healthful

From *The New Republic*, June 9, 1917, pp. 153–55.

life." History has amply vindicated Lincoln's judgment in this matter, for the direct effect of the Civil War in the way of enlarging national power or of altering the relations of the different branches of the national government to one another was comparatively slight.

Will those of us who survive be able to say the same of the present war fifty years hence? Probably not, at any rate if the war is prolonged. For it requires no inordinate insight to recognize already the beginnings of what may well prove to be revolutionary developments in our system.

Despite much that has been said implying the contrary, it is extremely unlikely that our participation in the present war will exact of us sacrifices at all approaching those with which our forefathers met the war for the Union. But our participation will be for the most part, it seems probable, of a different order and so will produce different results. The Civil War was *war* in the most elementary sense of the term; our assistance to the Allies, even though we eventually send a considerable army abroad, must still be primarily financial and industrial. And this means the regimentation of industry and commerce on a national scale. It means, if Congress follows the President in this matter, lodging in the hands of the national executive the power to direct transportation, to control exports, to prevent − in the President's own words − "all unwarranted hoarding of every kind and the control of food stuffs by persons who are not in any legitimate sense producers, dealers, or traders," the power to requisition food supplies to meet public need, and the equipment necessary to handle them, the power to prohibit unnecessary and wasteful use of foods, and finally the power to fix maximum and minimum prices. No doubt, many of the measures suggested in the President's statement of Saturday, May 19, which I have just paraphrased, will be of a purely emergency character, and so will pass out of existence with the war. Yet it is clear that for some of them, and for others of a similar nature, the way had already been paved both by industrial development and political agitation long before our entrance into the war had been thought of. Measures of this description look toward the permanent reshaping of both our governmental and our industrial systems, and the power upon which they rest will be relaxed only in part, if at all, with the return of peace.

  This, however, is but the beginning of the changes which the war promises to engraft upon our constitutional arrangements. For the new faculties with which the national government will find itself endowed new channels must be provided or else existing channels must be enlarged. The latter is the more economical course, and already it is being resorted to. Moreover, we again perceive the stress of the immediate exigency striking hands with developments which were originally launched much earlier. In this connection it is interesting to refer to a paragraph in Mr. Wilson's own work, *The State,* in which he comments upon the administrative powers of the French executive in the following manner: "The Executive is expected to shape the laws to the cases that arise, and to supplement them where they lack completeness. The laws are, accordingly, for the most part themselves without detailed provisions. They give the officers of state, who are to execute them a principle by which to go rather than a body of minute instructions." He also makes it clear that this way of legislating presents a distinct contrast to the English-American method.

But these words were written nearly thirty years ago. Since then Congress, influenced partly by a growing appreciation of its own inability to provide wisely for the multiple phases of the complex matters that today frequently fall within its regulating power, and partly by the rising reputation of the "scientific expert," has fallen more and more into the French way of proceeding. Thus it has authorized the Commerce Commission to fix "reasonable" maximum rates for interstate transportation; it has authorized the Secretary of the Treasury to say what varieties of tea are fit for importation; it has authorized the Secretary of Agriculture to prescribe regulations for governing the use of the public grazing lands; it has invested the Federal Reserve Board, the Federal Trade Commission, and the Shipping Board with the broadest kind of discretion within their several fields; and illustrations of the same character might be multiplied almost indefinitely. Such legislation plainly derogates from the principle of the separation of powers and the corollary doctrine that the legislature cannot delegate its powers. It had therefore, at first, a rather difficult gauntlet to run with the courts. But today the federal Supreme Court at least has definitely yielded its scruples on these points, and will sustain such legislation simply on the score of necessity. (See Buttfield v. Stranahan, 192 U.S., and Grimaud v. U.S., 220 U.S.) Necessity, however, is at best a vague concept, and it is especially so in wartime. One of the most conspicuous features, accordingly, of the legislation at present pending in Congress is the extent to which it relies upon executive discretion to supplement its provisions.

An even more striking possibility in the way of constitutional development than those just referred to is foreshadowed by section 6 of the Conscription Act. This section authorizes the President "to utilize the services" not only of all officers and agents of the United States and territories, but of the several states as well, and it further provides that any person "who in any manner shall fail or neglect fully to perform any duty required of him in the execution of this act, shall, if not subject to military law, be guilty of a misdemeanor and, upon conviction in the District Court of the United States having jurisdiction thereof, be punished by imprisonment for not more than one year." Students of constitutional law will at once appreciate how radically these provisions transgress the principle of dual sovereignty which has hitherto underlain our federal system, a corollary of which is that the national government can impose legal duties upon state officers only with the consent of and upon the terms imposed by the states themselves. It was upon this principle that the first Fugitive Slave Act was pronounced partially void in 1842 in the famous case of Prigg v. Pennsylvania, 16 Pet., while a few years afterward the Court held, on the same ground, that the "duty" with which the governor of a state is charged by the act of 1793 in connection with the rendition of fugitives from justice is not a legally enforcible one (Ky. v. Dennison, 24 How.). The Conscription Act is, however, vindicated to some degree by certain later utterances of the Court (see especially *Ex parte* Siebold, 100 U.S.), and at any rate it is clearly harmonious with the original intention of the Constitution. The younger Pinckney, speaking in this reference on the floor of the Philadelphia Convention, said: "They [the states] are the instruments upon which the Union must frequently depend for the support and execution of its powers." Then the Constitution itself requires an oath of fidelity from all state officers, commenting upon which fact, Hamilton wrote in *The Federalist* as follows: "Thus the legislatures, courts, and magistrates of the respective members will be incorporated into the operations of the national government as far as its just and constitutional authority extends, and will be rendered auxiliary to the enforcement of its laws." An interesting possibility is thus suggested: that, as the states diminish in importance in the legislative field, through the extension of congressional power, they may be afforded an opportunity to justify their continued existence in the capacity of administrative agents of the national government, and so our dual system would be gradually replaced by a federal system approximating to the German and Swiss type.

The general bearing of some other developments of the moment is not so easily perceived. What, for instance, will be the ultimate fate of such unofficial bodies as the Council of National Defense — are they merely "sports" which the body politic has put forth under an extraordinary stimulus and destined therefore to wither away when this stimulus is removed, or are they true species, the beginnings of valuable institutions? Again, what will be the permanent outcome of the President's notable efforts these days at "common counsel" with the congressional leaders — will they be likely to pave the way for the gradual displacement of the Cabinet in the American sense with a Cabinet in the British sense? Yet again, there is the ever-present question of budgetary reform. Must not the government's increasing resort to those forms of taxation which are most directly burdensome to the taxpayer bring this problem evermore to the front? And will not the recent reform of the Senate's rules, forced from the White House, have a similar tendency? To be sure, the practice of doing business by unanimous consent sometimes thwarted the congressional logrollers, as where an individual Senator or two held up a rivers and harbors bill at the end of the session; but ordinarily it promoted it, by giving disgruntled seekers after "pork" in the House a second chance to force their demands through friends in the upper chamber. Now, however, this opportunity for blackmail is at an end, together with the special defense that has hitherto existed against the worst scandals of logrolling. In both ways the case for executive budget-making will be considerably strengthened with Congress itself.

Thus war has overtaken us at a peculiarly favorable moment for effecting lasting constitutional changes. For several years forces have been accumulating behind the barriers of the old Constitution, straining and weakening them at many points, yet without finding adequate enlargement. Where the stress of war falls coincident with such forces we may expect it to thrust aside accepted principles, not for the time only, but permanently. Certainly if the war is considerably prolonged, we may expect our system to emerge from it substantially altered in numerous ways, with the result, however, it may be, of postponing more radical alterations many years.

3. Wilson and the Senate

The issue between the President and the Senate over the ratification of the {League of Nations} Covenant is developing a struggle for power between parties and between two branches of the national government that is of really historic dimensions. It is true that thus far both sides to the controversy have deprecated the charge of "partisanism" as explanatory of their respective attitudes, but there is no good reason why they should do so; and still less is there reason for the senatorial opponents of the league to fight shy of the other charge which has been leveled against them, that they are waging war upon the President's program in order to vindicate "the dignity and prerogatives of the Senate." The maintenance of the constitutional prerogatives and dignity of an important branch of the government is itself a matter of moment; and that must be an exigent issue indeed which is capable of relegating it to a secondary or incidental role.

In a striking passage of his *Promise of American Life,* Mr. Herbert Croly passes estimate upon the outcome of the protracted struggle which took place in Jackson's time between the President and the Senate. It resulted, he says — I quote from recollection — in a victory for the President "because the people decided for him," "as they must always do" when the occupant of the presidential chair is a man "no worse than Andrew Jackson" and his antagonist a man "no better than Henry Clay." Is this interesting verdict applicable to the contest which today impends? That is to say, Woodrow Wilson being no worse than he is and Henry Cabot Lodge being no better than *he* is, which way ought popular sympathy to incline in a struggle for power between the institutions represented by these two men?

There is no quarreling with Mr. Croly's complacency over Jackson's triumph, for had not the presidency been aggrandized at the moment when John Marshall was sinking into his grave and the powers of Congress were being brought more and more under the surveillance of a jealous particularism, of which the Senate itself was the very citadel, the cause of the Union would have had in 1861 no rallying-point. But the situation has altered since then, and today the question is not the preservation of the Union, it is the preservation of constitutional gov-

From *The Weekly Review,* July 26, 1919, pp. 228–29.

ernment in face of an almost world-wide tendency towards one-man power. Confronted with such a situation, the Senate may be very well warranted in feeling that it ought to insist somewhat upon "its dignity and prerogatives."

In his lectures on "Constitutional Government in the United States," which were published in the spring of 1908, Mr. Wilson discovers three seats of authority in the national government, to wit, the Presidency, the Senate, and the Speakership of the House of Representatives. Since then the Speakership has been put in commission in great part, so that today, if the President is to be effectively checked, it is the Senate which must do the business. Nor has any writer presented the claims of the Senate to popular confidence more appealingly than Mr. Wilson himself, in the volume just cited. The Senate, he declares, "represents the country, as distinct from the accumulated populations of the country, much more fully and much more truly than the House of Representatives does." It is a place too "of individual voices," and "the suppression of a single voice would radically change its constitutional character." (There is no thought here, it will be noted, of stigmatizing the "willfulness" of "little groups.") Again, the men who make up the Senate are "men much above the average in ability and in personal force," and if they are not always wise counselors, still their "experience of affairs is much mellower than the President's can be," for "the continuity of the Government lies in the keeping of the Senate more than in the keeping of the executive, even in respect of matters which are of the especial prerogative of the presidential office."

Turning then to the subject of the relations of the President and the Senate in the control of appointments to office and treaty-making, Mr. Wilson writes:

> There can be little doubt in the mind of any one who has carefully studied the plans and opinions of the Constitutional Convention of 1787 that the relations of the President and Senate were intended to be very much more intimate and confidential than they have been; that it was expected that the Senate would give the President its advice and consent in respect of appointments and treaties in the spirit of an Executive Council associated with him upon terms of confidential cooperation rather than in the spirit of an independent branch of the Government, jealous lest he should in the least particular attempt to govern its judgment or infringe upon its prerogatives.

Unfortunately this idea has not in general prevailed, and the relations

between the two branches have fallen too often under the control of
a spirit of distrust, mitigated to some extent by a sort of "customary
modus vivendi, as of rival powers. The Senate is expected in most
instances to accept the President's appointments to office, and the President is expected to be very tolerant of the Senate's rejection of treaties,
proposing but by no means disposing even in this chief field of his
power." However, there have been "one or two Presidents of unusual
sagacity" who have recurred to something like the earlier practice, as
any President is free to do:

He may himself be less stiff and offish, may himself act in the true
spirit of the Constitution and establish intimate relations with the
Senate on his own initiative, not carrying his plans to completion and
then laying them in final form before the Senate to be accepted or
rejected, but keeping himself in confidential communication with the
leaders of the Senate while his plans are in course — in order that
there may be veritable counsel and a real accommodation of views
instead of a final challenge and contrast. The policy which has made
rivals of the President and Senate has shown itself in the President as
often as in the Senate, and if the Constitution did indeed intend that
the Senate should in such matters be an Executive Council it is not only
the privilege of the President to treat it as such, it is also his best
policy and his plain duty.

Could a more telling indictment be penned of President Wilson's
entire course in connection with the League of Nations Covenant?
Here is a proposal of vital interest to every section of the country, a
proposal not needing to be elaborated in secret, certainly not after
the first draft of it was published some months ago, a proposal furthermore for the final perfection of which the utmost allowance of
time is even yet available, since it is now the announced intention
of the Allies to act for some months to come in carrying out the peace
treaty through the Council of Five. Yet not only has the President
never consulted with the Senate as a body about this proposal, nor
with any of its leaders except in the most cursory fashion, but he has
expended the greatest ingenuity in an endeavor to deprive the Senate
of all freedom of action with reference to the proposal when this shall
finally come before it. Writers on our political system with a bias in
favor of executive authority are prone to criticize the legislative "rid-
er," a device whereby a measure of minor importance is put safely
past the danger of veto on the back of a more important or more urgent

measure. It is safe to say, however, that concocters of "riders" now have a new record in audacity set them. And in this connection it is pertinent to recall the announcement which was first given out from Paris regarding the proposed guaranty treaty with France. The President, we were told, had not positively committed himself to the arrangement but had promised to refer it to the Senate, presumably for advice. Yet, as compared with the covenant, the guaranty treaty would mark a relatively slight departure from our national traditions. Little wonder that the President has subsequently abandoned his scruples about the lesser compact — the discrepancy in procedure would have been too glaring. Yet even as matters stand, the Senate is to be allowed a free hand with the guaranty treaty.

There are certain other facts which cast additional light upon the constitutional significance of the impending struggle over the covenant that may be set down more or less at random. On the debit side of the ledger for the President appear such facts as the Ishii agreement, which was never referred to the Senate; also the understanding between the United States and Great Britain, which was testified to by General March the other day before the Senate Military Committee, that both these powers shall maintain a military establishment four times larger than before the war (we know now, perhaps, why President Wilson appealed to the country last autumn for a Democratic Congress); again, such facts as the numerous instances during the present Administration of wars waged without congressional sanction, indeed, without congressional knowledge; and the still more numerous instances of diplomatic appointments without reference to the Senate. Meantime, the demand for "open diplomacy," at least for democratic control of diplomacy, has been rising higher and higher throughout the world, while by the Seventeenth Amendment the Senate has been rendered a democratic body as never before.

Finally, it requires no extraordinary insight to perceive that if the League of Nations Covenant is ratified, the opportunity — indeed, the necessity — for independent presidential action in the diplomatic field will be much augmented. This is not of itself a conclusive argument against ratifying the covenant were it otherwise satisfactory, but it is a very powerful argument against the Senate's consenting to any unnecessary abdication of its participation in the shaping of our diplomatic policies.

4. Woodrow Wilson and the Presidency

When Thomas W. Wilson, Princeton '79, found it essential to select a theme for his senior essay — the institution goes back that far, apparently — he chose "Cabinet Government in the United States." The choice was dictated by two circumstances: first, by the fact that he had been reading, especially in Bagehot's misnamed *English Constitution,*[1] about the British cabinet system and had come to admire it; secondly, by the scars which as a Southerner he bore vicariously from the enormities of Congressional Reconstruction.

It can hardly be claimed that young Wilson's essay was a literary masterpiece. The style is turgid, spasmodic, and the work abounds in repetition. For all that, it was, for so young a man, a notable production, in that it marked an effort to assess government under the Constitution *functionally,* in contrast to the customary legalistic approach. How good a government are we really getting under the Constitution was the question presented.

What Wilson found was, in effect, that Congress was a tyrant, indeed, a faceless, voiceless tyrant, all of its powers being at the disposal of a proliferation of committees, whose proceedings and decisions, when they reached the American public at all, did so haphazardly, sporadically. Above all, Congress lacked a central guiding leadership.

What then was the remedy? In *Cabinet Government* young Wilson goes back a half century to Story's *Commentaries* and takes from it the suggestion that heads of departments be allowed, like territorial delegates, seats in the House of Representatives, "where they might freely debate without a title to vote."[2] But then he broaches a much bolder suggestion. "The highest order of responsible government," he writes, "could . . . be established in the United States only by laying upon the President the necessity of selecting his Cabinet from among

From 42 *Virginia Law Review* 761–83 (October, 1956). Reprinted by permission.

1. Bagehot, *The English Constitution* (1901).
2. Wilson, *Cabinet Government in the United States* 8 (1947).

the number of representatives already chosen by the people, or by the legislatures of the States"[3] — in other words, from the House of Representatives and the Senate — in brief, by setting up a cabinet after the British model. Only thus, he argued, could governmental policy attain coherency; only thus could talent be drawn into the government. He continued:

Responsible ministers must secure from the House and Senate an intelligent, thorough, and practical treatment of their affairs; must vindicate their principles in open battle on the floor of Congress. The public is thus enabled to exercise a direct scrutiny over the workings of the Executive departments, to keep all their operations under a constant stream of daylight. Ministers could do nothing under the shadow of darkness; committees do all in the dark.[4]

Apparently Wilson's instructor was well pleased with the young man's performance. *Cabinet Government in the United States* was published in the August, 1879, issue of *International Review,* the editor of which was one Henry Cabot Lodge!

In *Congressional Government,*[5] which was his Hopkins doctoral thesis, and which issued from the press in 1885, Wilson renewed and extended the argument of *Cabinet Government.* I quote some characteristic passages:

The noble charter of fundamental law given us by the Convention of 1787 is still our Constitution; but it is now our *form of government* rather in name than in reality, the form of the Constitution being one of nicely adjusted, ideal balances, whilst the actual form of our present government is simply a scheme of congressional supremacy.[6]

It is said that there is no single or central force in our federal scheme . . . but only a balance of powers and a nice adjustment of interactive checks, as all the books say. How is it, however, in the practical conduct of the federal government? In that, unquestionably, the predominant and controlling force, the center and source of all motive and of all regulative power, is Congress. . . .[7]

Congress [is] the dominant, nay, the irresistible, power of the federal

3. *Id.* at 11.
4. *Id.* at 23.
5. Wilson, *Congressional Government: A Study in American Politics* (1900).
6. *Id.* at 6.
7. *Id.* at 11.

system, relegating some of the chief balances of the Constitution to an insignificant role in the "literary theory" of our institutions.[8]

And again:

Congress is fast becoming the governing body of the nation, and yet the only power which it possesses in perfection is the power which is but a part of government, the power of legislation.[9]

With this, contrast the position which Wilson assigns the President of that period:

Except in so far as his power of veto constitutes him a part of the legislature, the President might, not inconveniently, be a permanent officer; the first official of a carefully-graded and impartially regulated civil service system, through whose sure series of merit-promotions the youngest clerk might rise even to the chief magistracy. He is a part of the official rather than of the political machinery of the government, and his duties call rather for training than for constructive genius. If there can be found in the official systems of the States a lower grade of service in which men may be advantageously drilled for Presidential functions, so much the better. The States will have better governors, the Union better presidents, and there will have been supplied one of the most serious needs left unsupplied by the Constitution, – the need for a proper school in which to rear federal administrators.[10]

And the consequence of the low estate of the President was that "no office [was] set apart for the great party leadership in our government. ... [T]he presidency is ... too little like a premiership and too much like a superintendency."[11]

In short, the Presidency was written off as a bad job. But a decade later, in consequence of the Spanish-American War, Wilson indicates a disposition to revise his estimate of the potentialities of the office, at least in some measure. Thus in his preface to the 15th impression of *Congressional Government* written August 15, 1900, he says:

Much the most important change to be noticed [i.e., since 1885] is the result of the war with Spain upon the lodgment and exercise of power within our federal system: the greatly increased power and opportunity for constructive statesmanship given the President, by the

8. *Id.* at 23.
9. *Id.* at 301.
10. *Id.* at 254.
11. *Id.* at 203-4.

plunge into international politics and into the administration of distant dependencies, which has been that war's most striking and momentous consequence. When foreign affairs play a prominent part in the politics and policy of a nation, its Executive must of necessity be its guide: must utter every initial judgment, take every first step of action, supply the information upon which it is to act, suggest and in large measure control its conduct. The President of the United States is now, as of course, at the front of affairs, as no president, except Lincoln, has been since the first quarter of the nineteenth century, when the foreign relations of the new nation had first to be adjusted. There is no trouble now about getting the President's speeches printed and read, every word. Upon his choice, his character, his experience hang some of the most weighty issues of the future. The government of dependencies must be largely in his hands. Interesting things may come out of the singular change.[12]

The real herald of the twentieth-century Presidency, however, its John the Baptist, was not Woodrow Wilson: it was a Pittsburgh editor named Henry Jones Ford, whose brilliant volume *The Rise and Growth of American Politics* spotlights the Presidency in the tradition of its successes, not of its failures.[13] In these discerning pages we read:

The agency of the presidential office has been such a master force in shaping public policy that to give a detailed account of it would be equivalent to writing the political history of the United States. From Jackson's time to the present day it may be said that political issues have been decided by executive policy.[14]

The rise of presidential authority cannot be accounted for by the intention of presidents: it is the product of political conditions which dominate all the departments of government, so that Congress itself shows an unconscious disposition to aggrandize the presidential office.[15]

The truth is that in the presidential office, as it has been constituted since Jackson's time, American democracy has revived the oldest political institution of the race, the elective kingship. It is all there: the precognition of the notables and the tumultuous choice of the freemen, only conformed to modern conditions. That the people have been able to accomplish this with such defective apparatus, and have been

12. *Id.* at xi–xii.
13. Ford, *The Rise and Growth of American Politics* (1914).
14. *Id.* at 279.
15. *Id.* at 284.

able to make good a principle which no other people have been able to reconcile with the safety of the state, indicates the highest degree of constitutional morality yet attained by any race.[16]

There is, to be sure, considerable exaggeration here. It is quite untrue that after Jackson's day political issues had been settled by executive policy. The issue of slavery in the territories first arose in Congress and was settled — temporarily to be sure — by the Supreme Court, eventually by war; and the issue of Reconstruction, as well as that of the tariff, was settled in Congress. But Ford's notable volume was really oriented toward the future, and the future came to its rescue.

The first exponent of the new Presidency was Theodore Roosevelt. Assessing his performance in the illumination sparked by Ford's volume and the Spanish-American War, Woodrow Wilson wrote in his Blumenthal Lectures given at Columbia University in 1907:[17]

He cannot escape being the leader of his party except by incapacity and lack of personal force, because he is at once the choice of the party and of the nation. . . . He can dominate his party by being spokesman for the real sentiment and purpose of the country, by giving direction to opinion, by giving the country at once the information and the statements of policy which will enable it to form its judgments alike of parties and of men. . . . His is the only national voice in affairs. Let him once win the admiration and confidence of the country, and no other single force can withstand him, no combination of forces will easily overpower him. His position takes the imagination of the country. He is the representative of no constituency, but the whole people. . . . He may be both the leader of his party and the leader of the nation, or he may be one or the other. If he lead the nation, his party can hardly resist him. His office is anything he has the sagacity and force to make it.

Some of our Presidents have deliberately held themselves off from using the full power they might legitimately have used, because of conscientious scruples, because they were more theorists than statesmen. . . . The President is at liberty, both in law and conscience, to be as big a man as he can.[18]

The following year the lectures were published under the title *Constitutional Government in the United States.* The same year Wilson,

16. *Id.* at 293.
17. Wilson, *Constitutional Government in the United States* (1927).
18. *Id.* at 67–70.

as president of Princeton University, offered its author {Wilson} a professorship in politics, which the latter in due course accepted. His indebtedness to Roosevelt Mr. Wilson was less prompt to acknowledge. In the index to *Constitutional Government* T.R.'s name appears just once, and the reference is of no significance. Indeed, without mentioning Roosevelt, who had just emerged victorious from a hard fought battle with the Senate over certain pending legislation — the famed Hepburn Act — Wilson contrives to read him a lecture on how Presidents ought to treat that august body. "If," he writes, "he [the President, has] character, modesty, devotion and insight as well as force, he can bring the contending elements into a great and efficient body of common counsel."[19] Little did he foresee that ten years later he would be describing the Senate as "the only legislative body in the world which cannot act when its majority is ready for action. A little group of willful men, representing no opinion but their own, have rendered the great Government of the United States helpless and contemptible"![20]

Woodrow Wilson abandoned academic and entered public life in 1910. Was it *contingency* or *predestination* that determined this, the most momentous choice in his career? The question is the more intriguing for the reason that, as a sound Calvinist, Mr. Wilson undoubtedly believed in predestination, and identified with it his own destiny. Still that there was at the outset an element of contingency in his decision cannot be gainsaid, inasmuch as it was in the first place the consequence of his defeat in his controversy with Dean West over the location of the Graduate College. Was the college to be located on the Princeton campus or on the Princeton golf course? President Wilson wanted the former; Dean West the latter.

Early in 1910 William Cooper Procter, of Ivory Soap fame, offered Princeton $500,000 to be expended in furtherance of Dean West's plan, but when Mr. Wilson demanded that the condition be rescinded, Mr. Procter withdrew the gift. So far the President enjoyed the support of his Trustees, albeit by a precarious margin. In June, however, the news broke upon the world that a person named Wyman, of Marblehead, Massachusetts, had died leaving Princeton substantially his entire

19. *Id.* at 141.
20. II *The Public Papers of Woodrow Wilson,* vol. 2, 435 (Baker and Dodd ed. 1927).

estate, which was variously estimated as falling "somewhere between three and thirty millions of dollars." The condition on which the bequest hinged was that it should be used to forward Dean West's design. Confronted with this turn of affairs, Mr. Wilson remarked with adequate decision, "The size of the gift alters the perspective," and the following October resigned as president of the university, whereupon he was quickly snatched up by expectant politicans and run for Governor of New Jersey.

For all that, I am quite convinced that Mr. Wilson would have resigned his academic post sooner or later to run for public office — and sooner rather than later — Wyman or no Wyman. Not only was there that hovering brood of politicians, which was headed in New Jersey by "Jim Smith Junior," there was also the redoubtable George Harvey, editor of the *North American Review* and *Harper's Weekly,* who had been for some years carrying Mr. Wilson's name at the mastheads of his publications as just the man needed to spike T.R.'s Square Deal. I also place reliance on the testimony of Mr. Talcott Williams, distinguished Philadelphia editor, who came to Princeton in 1906 or thereabouts to give a lecture. Following the talk, he and Mr. Wilson repaired to "Prospect," where they had a long conversation in the course of which Mr. Wilson told about certain reading he had been recently doing, including, mayhap, Mr. Ford's book. Mr. Williams listened with increasing intentness, and at the conclusion of Mr. Wilson's remarks charged the latter with harboring political ambitions, and Mr. Wilson admitted the soft imperchment {impeachment?}.

The real reason why Woodrow Wilson finally decided to enter public life was a two-fold one. On the one hand, he had learned that in the potentialities of the Presidency public life in the United States did, after all, afford ample field for talent. On the other hand, his defeat in his battle against the club system and his impending defeat — which he no doubt clearly foresaw— in the battle over the location of the Graduate College, had revealed a mission to him. What this mission was he clearly expressed in his famous Pittsburgh Speech of April 16, 1910. Referring to the question of the location of the Graduate College, Mr. Wilson asked:

What does the country expect of Princeton? It expects of Princeton what it expects of every other college, the accommodation of its life to the life of the country.

The colleges of this country are in exactly the same danger that the churches are in. I believe that the churches of this country, at any rate the Protestant churches, have dissociated themselves from the people of this country. They are serving the classes and they are not serving the masses. They serve certain strata, certain uplifted strata, but they are not serving the men whose need is dire. The churches have more regard to their pew-rents than to the souls of men, and in proportion as they look to the respectability of their congregations to lift them in esteem they are depressing the whole level of Christian endeavor.

Where does the strength of the nation come from? From the conspicuous classes? Not at all. It comes from the great mass of the unknown, of the unrecognized men, whose powers are being developed by struggle, who will form their opinions as they progress in that struggle, and who will emerge with opinions which will rule.

What we cry out against is that a handful of conspicuous men have thrust cruel hands among the heartstrings of the masses of men upon whose blood and energy they are subsisting.

The universities would make men forget their common origins, forget their universal sympathies, and join a class — and no class ever can serve America.

The great voice of America does not come from seats of learning. It comes in a murmur from the hills and woods and the farms and factories and the mills, rolling on and gaining volume until it comes to us from the homes of common men. Do these murmurs echo in the corridors of universities? I have not heard them.[21]

Thus was "the New Freedom" born which first spread its healing wings over New Jersey, then over the nation, then, bereft, to be sure, of some of its plumage, over "abroad."

In 1911 Mr. Wilson informed Editor Harvey that he wished the latter to discontinue his attentions, that they had become "embarrassing." In short, Mr. Wilson was not questing for Lotus Club votes. When Harvey next adopted a candidate for the Presidency, the beneficiary was one Warren G. Harding!

I turn now to evaluate Mr. Wilson's exercise of the office of President of the United States. What was his impact on the office; and first of all, by what procedures did he convert the Presidency into an instrument of social reform? The answer is, by making the President an active partici-

21. Speech by Woodrow Wilson, Princeton alumni meeting at Pittsburgh, April 16, 1910. Copy on file at the University of Virginia Law Library.

pant in the national legislative process far beyond any of his predecessors, even T.R.; by converting it, in other words, into a species of prime ministership. Mr. Wilson had dismissed his early idea of superseding the Presidency with a cabinet government after the British model. He now substituted for that idea an amalgamation, as it were, of the British prime ministership and the Presidency.

A document of first importance in this connection is the letter which Mr. Wilson wrote a short time before his inauguration to his future Attorney General, A. Mitchell Palmer. The letter was in answer to one from Palmer urging the President-elect to endorse a plank in the Democratic platform favoring a single term Presidency. Mr. Wilson sharply demurred:

[The President] is expected by the nation to be the leader of his party as well as the chief executive officer of the Government and the country will take no excuses from him. He must play the part and play it successfully or lose the country's confidence. He must be Prime Minister, as much concerned with the guidance of legislation as with just and orderly execution of law; and he is the spokesman of the nation in everything, even the most momentous and most delicate dealings of the Government in foreign affairs.[22]

To deny the President the possibility of re-election was out of the question. To be sure:

Sooner or later it would seem he must be made answerable to opinion in a somewhat more informal and intimate fashion, answerable, it may be, to the Houses whom he seeks to lead, either personally or through a cabinet, as well as to the people for whom they speak. But that is a matter to be worked out — as it will inevitably be in some natural American way which we cannot yet even predict.[23]

In fact, Mr. Wilson himself worked "the matter out" for one contingency. He planned that if Mr. Hughes was elected in 1916, he would ask Marshall to resign from the Vice-Presidency and then appoint Mr. Hughes Secretary of State so that, under the Succession Act of 1886, the latter could assume the office of President at once, as the logic of the prime minister concept undoubtedly required.

Mr. Wilson took office on March 4, 1913. His first official act after taking the oath was to summon Congress to meet in special session on

22. Binkley, *President and Congress* 206 ((1947).
23. *Id.*

April 7. The following day he electrified the country by going up to Capitol Hill to present his first message in person, thereby returning to a practice which his great predecessor Jefferson had discarded 112 years earlier. "Gentlemen of the Congress" were his opening words, a locution which toppled an equally venerable precedent. For while the original Constitution does say "The Congress," the first amendment says "Congress," and I find no instance in which Washington, Jefferson, Lincoln, or John Marshall, not to mention sundry others, used the older form save when they were quoting directly from the Constitution.

But Wilson's greatest innovation is to be seen in the form and content of his message. The old State of the Union message which had become established custom on similar occasions, had grown to inordinate length. Some of T.R.'s ran to thirty thousand words and over. Sent up to Capitol Hill by a messenger, they were handed over to a sleepy clerk who droned along for two or three hours, while the members drowsed.

Naturally, no President would care to submit himself in person to such an ordeal. Wilson's message was brief and was devoted to a single topic, tariff reduction; and his later messages followed this same model. They dealt crisply with banking and currency reform, with antitrust legislation, and so on. They asserted for the President his legislative leadership in the achievement of specific reforms. As Professor Small remarks:

Whereas Roosevelt confused both Congress and the public by attempting to enlist its attention immediately to his entire legislative program, as expounded in a vague message or two, Wilson, by proceeding in this more methodical fashion, enabled his legislative associates to direct their undivided attention to single items of his platform, and accordingly escaped many of the delays produced by congested calendars. Wilson's method also helped him in crystalizing and mobilizing public opinion in support of his proposals.[24]

One can readily imagine the chagrin of T.R. when he read in the morning papers of April 9, 1913, what Woodrow Wilson had been up to the day before. Why had he never thought that one up!

I also cite Dr. Small for his estimate of Wilson's achievement in the

24. Small, *Some Presidential Interpretations of the Presidency* 175 (1932).

legislative field. He accords it an easy primacy, with the possible exception of that of Jefferson, whose methods were, however, vastly different, being conditioned by Jefferson's professed deference to the principle of the separation of powers. In these circumstances, while Jefferson's guidance of Congress was constant and unremitting, it was often secret and always disavowed.

Another facet of Wilson's legislative activities emerged in 1916. World War I had now broken; a presidential campaign was looming; and the Republican Party was split. To be sure, the Democrats had what many of them reckoned was a winning shibboleth, "He kept us out of war" — a slogan which Mr. Wilson himself endorsed in his Shadow Lawn speech early in September, when he warned the country, "If you elect my opponent [Mr. Hughes], you elect a war." But was this enough? Many Democrats doubted it. What the doubting Thomases demanded was that a definite effort be made to capture "Progressive" (Roosevelt) votes — but how? Looking to this end, Democratic leaders urged the passage of an anti-child labor bill. But could Mr. Wilson endorse it? Hardly, if he still adhered to the views he had expressed in his Blumenthal Lectures anent an earlier proposal of the same sort. There he wrote:

The proposed federal legislation with regard to the regulation of child labor affords a striking example [of the devitalization of the federal principle.] If the power to regulate commerce between the States can be stretched to include the regulation of labor in mills and factories, it can be made to embrace every particular of the industrial organization and action of the country. The only limitations Congress would observe, should the Supreme Court assent to such obviously absurd extravagancies of interpretation, would be the limitations of opinions and of circumstances.[25]

A bill after the pattern of the measure which Mr. Wilson had stigmatized as "absurd" passed the House of Representatives early in February, 1916, but got stalled in the Senate. On July 17 the President was warned by certain of his followers in that body that passage of the measure was "necessary," and the following day the President went to the Capitol to plead with the Democratic command of that body to permit the measure to come to a vote. The bill was finally passed

---

25. Wilson, *Constitutional Government* 179.

on August 8 and was signed by the President on September 1, "with real emotion," he said. In point of fact, the bill had already become law several days earlier owing to the President's failure to disapprove it within the required "ten Days (Sundays excepted)." His belated signing of it was nevertheless valuable politically; it may even have turned the trick in closely-contested California.

Twenty-two months later the act was held void in a five-to-four decision of the Supreme Court,[26] which rested substantially on the grounds urged by Mr. Wilson in *Constitutional Government,* to wit, its damaging effect on the federal system. Fortunately, the decision was not retroactive as to the election of 1916. Mr. Wilson continued to be President till the end of his term on March 4, 1921. Not till 1941 did the Supreme Court accept − in a unanimous judgment − the principle underlying the measure, the simple principle, to wit, of national supremacy within the realm of national powers.[27]

I now turn to Mr. Wilson's exercise of the Presidency in the field of foreign relations. Here, too, at the outset his past caught up with him. Japan was demanding a treaty from Washington which would give its subjects the right to own land in the United States. Confronted with the choice of fighting Japan or "The Sons of the Golden West," the Administration elected to pursue a middle course. By what in effect was a *modus vivendi,* Japan abandoned her attempt to get the treaty and the Administration admitted her special rights in China. Thus early was Yalta foreshadowed.

For the rest, history was on Mr. Wilson's side, history that stemmed from the time of Washington. "The transaction of business with foreign nations," Jefferson proclaimed, was "Executive altogether,"[28] doctrine which was reiterated by Jefferson's little-loved cousin, John Marshall, on the floor of Congress: "The President is the sole organ of the nation in its external relations and its sole representative with foreign nations";[29] and four years later, Marshall expounded even broader doctrine from the bench: "By the Constitution, the President is invested with certain important political powers, in the exercise of which he is to use his own discretion, and is accountable only to his country in

---

26. Hammer v. Dagenhart, 247 U.S. 251 (1918).
27. United States v. Darby, 312 U.S. 100 (1941).
28. Padover, *The Complete Jefferson* 138 (1943).
29. 2 Beveridge, *The Life of John Marshall* 470–71 (1919).

his political character, and to his conscience" — is, in brief, autonomous.[30]

This autonomy Wilson labored constantly and successfully to maintain, bringing at times his prime minister conception of the office into operation in its support. Thus he repeatedly asked Congress during the war for what was in effect a "vote of confidence." Two items from the *New York Times* illustrate the point:

Washington, July 23, 1917. — A virtual threat to veto the Administration Food Bill if the conferees retain the Senate amendment creating a joint committee to supervise war expenditures is contained in a letter sent tonight by President Wilson to Chairman Lever of the House Committee on Agriculture. The letter says the President would interpret "the final adoption of Section 23 as arising from a lack of confidence in myself."[31]

Washington, May 15, 1918. — Three moves of prime importance were made today in connection with the aircraft controversy:

President Wilson in a letter to Senator Martin, the Democratic floor leader, vehemently opposed the Chamberlain resolution for an investigation of the conduct of the war by the Committee on Military Affairs of the Senate. He said passage of the resolution would be "a direct vote of want of confidence in the Administration," and would constitute "nothing less than an attempt to take over the conduct of the war." The President called upon supporters of the Administration in the Senate to rally in his support.[32]

Mr. Wilson also contemplated resignation had he been defeated on the Panama tolls issue and in his opposition to the McLemore Resolution of March, 1916, warning American citizens to refrain from traveling in armed belligerent vessels. He got his way in all four instances.

Mr. Wilson's famous appeal to the country of October 24, 1918, in behalf of the Treaty of Versailles and the League smacks also of the same general idea of prime ministership. It read, in part, as follows:

My fellow-Countrymen, the Congressional elections are at hand. They occur in the most critical period our country has ever faced or is likely to face in our time. If you have approved of my leadership and wish me to continue to be your unembarrassed spokesman in affairs at home

30. Marbury v. Madison, 5 U.S. (1 Cranch) 137, 164 (1803).
31. *New York Times,* July 24, 1917, p. 1, col. 1.
32. *New York Times,* May 16, 1918, p. 1, col. 3.

and abroad, I earnestly beg that you will express yourselves unmistak-
ably to that effect by returning a Democratic majority to both the
Senate and the House of Representatives.

I have no thought of suggesting that any political party is paramount
in matters of patriotism. I feel too deeply the sacrifices which have
been made in this war by all our citizens, irrespective of party affiliations, to harbor such an idea. I mean only that the difficulties and
delicacies of our present task are of a sort that makes it imperatively
necessary that the nation should give its undivided support to the
Government under a unified leadership, and that a Republican Congress would divide the leadership.[33]

Although this time he failed, he neglected to resign — an omission
which some of his critics condemned as at least illogical.

The truth of the matter is that Mr. Wilson had always two strings
to his official bow — the prime minister concept and the historic traditions of the American Presidency — and he retained to the end complete liberty of choice between them. Thus, when that "little group of
willful men" in the Senate foiled him in his effort early in 1917 to
obtain congressional authorization to arm American merchantmen
plying in the war zone, backed by high legal authority, he went ahead
and did it anyway; and one of his last acts as President, following his
partial recovery from his collapse in October, 1919, was to refuse to
carry out a provision of the Jones Shipping Act of 1920, which ordered
him to denounce certain treaties which other provisions of the measure
overrode. The requirement, he asserted, invaded his prerogative in the
field of foreign relations. His partisan enemies assailed his action as
"unconstitutional" and "presumptuous." One of these same critics
was Mr. W. G. Harding, one of whose first official acts on becoming
President was to adopt his predecessor's position.

In asserting his monopoly of the right to determine the foreign relations of the United States, Mr. Wilson was fighting, as it were, a defensive action, the constitutional basis of which was the "executive power"
clause as it had been interpreted by presidential spokesmen from the
time of Washington. His direction of the domestic phases of our war
with Germany was based, in important part, on that clause of Article II
which makes the President "Commander-in-Chief of the Army and
Navy of the United States, and of the Militia of the several States when

33. 56 Cong. Rec. 11494 (1918); Farmer, *The Wilson Reader* 191 (1956).

called into the actual service of the United States. . . ." But in this case the historical record was somewhat more complicated.

Expounding the "Commander-in-Chief" clause in *The Federalist* No. 69, Hamilton had asserted that it would be altogether erroneous to compare this power with the superficially similar prerogative of the British monarch. The President was top admiral and top general, and nobody could issue him a military command; but that was all. And in 1850, in a case growing out of the Mexican War, the Supreme Court, speaking by Chief Justice Taney, substantially repeated Hamilton's language.[34] The "Commander-in-Chief" clause remained the forgotten clause of the Constitution until the day when Sumter fell, April 14, 1861. Then came the great breakthrough.

First calling Congress to assemble on July 4, then more than ten weeks away, Lincoln proceeded forthwith to take certain measures of his own, based on the idea that in the circumstances "the war power" was his; and on this premise proclaimed a blockade of the Southern ports, summoned an army of three hundred thousand volunteers, increased the regular army and navy, took over the rail and telegraph lines between Washington and Baltimore, and eventually as far as Boston, and suspended the writ of habeas corpus along these lines. Congress and/or the Supreme Court sustained all these measures as within the President's powers as Commander-in-Chief in a rebellion which had attained the dimensions of public war. Secretary Seward summed up the business more compactly in conversation with Russell, Washington correspondent of the London *Times:* "We elect a king for four years, and give him absolute power within certain limits, which after all he can interpret for himself."

Between the Civil War and World War I two profound contrasts appear in retrospect. In the first place, most of the fighting in World War I took place three thousand miles from our shores. There was, consequently, no question at any time of treating the country at large as a "theatre of military operations" in the conventional sense of that term. In the second place, however, the vast development between the two wars of the technological aspects of warfare had created in this greatest of industrial nations an industrial theatre of war of immense proportions. Great industry in the United States had, in brief,

34. Fleming v. Page, 50 U.S. (9 How.) 603 (1850).

become part and parcel of the fighting forces not only of the United States but of its allies as well, and as such it had to be subjected to detailed regimentation by the government of the United States. To meet this requirement Congress was compelled to develop a new technique in legislative practice, one capable of meeting the fluctuating demands of a fluid war situation. This it did by delegating the President at his insistence vast unchannelled powers to be exercised by him through men of his own choosing. John Locke's ban upon delegated legislation simply went by the board, nor has it since been revived so far as concerns powers which are shared by the two departments. As to these "cognate" powers, as it terms them, the Court will not attempt nowadays to plot nicely, or at all, the delimiting line. More than that, however, President Wilson took upon himself, without consulting Congress, both the government of labor relations and the screening of information regarding the war, the former function being performed by the War Industries Board, under Mr. Baruch; the latter by the Committee of Public Information, headed by Mr. Creel. Both agencies were created out of hand by the President, as was also the later War Labor Board under the joint chairmanship of ex-President Taft and Frank P. Walsh.

But his hand-made solution of the problem of "agencies" soon gave rise to another, inasmuch as the powers and duties entrusted to these bodies were frequently unknown to any statute, with the result that if their orders — or rather, "advice," as the Court termed it — was ignored by those to whom it was addressed, the latter could not be brought to book for having committed an "offense against the United States." How were such recalcitrants to be dealt with?

Another Wilsonian contrivance speedily supplied the answer. I refer to what came to be variously known as "sanctions," "administrative sanctions," or "indirect sanctions." An illustration of the way in which "sanctions" were applied is afforded by an episode involving the Remington Arms Company of Bridgeport, Connecticut, in the autumn of 1918. I am following the narrative of a member of Mr. Wilson's War Labor Board. After a protracted strike and the rendering of a decision by the board, the strikers still refused to return to work, whereupon Mr. Wilson took his pen in hand in the board's behalf. He pointed out that an appeal from that body should be made through the regular channels and not by strike, and informed the strikers that if they did not return to work at once, they would be barred from any work in Bridgeport for a year; that the United States Employment Service would not obtain jobs for them elsewhere; and that the government would no longer consider their exemptions from the draft to be justified on the theory that they were useful in war production. The narrative concludes: "That ended the strike."[35]

Mr. Wilson's performance was important for its immediate effect; it was even more so for laying the groundwork for F.D.R.'s course in World War II. World War II is World War I writ large; and F.D.R.'s conduct of it is Mr. Wilson's conduct of World War I writ large; besides which F.D.R. did not wait for war to break; he went to meet it — "looked the brink in the face," as it were.

In 1942, I wrote the Executive Office of the President and asked it to give me a list of all the war agencies and to specify to me the supposed legal warrant by which they had been brought into existence. I got back a detailed answer which listed forty-three executive agencies, of which thirty-five were admitted to be of purely executive provenience. F.D.R. also governed labor relations, at times indeed with a high hand, albeit without statutory authorization prior to the enactment of the War Labor Disputes Act of June 25, 1943. His principal technique was to seize plants in which strikes were going on, and some plants he seized for other reasons. For example, he ordered Montgomery Ward to adopt a maintenance of membership rule. Ward's at first agreed, but after Mr. Sewell Avery got to thinking the matter over he decided that the President entirely lacked authority to issue such an order, and so reneged. A morning or two later, when he got down to his office, he found that the seventy persons whom the Chicago post office was accustomed to send Ward's each day to look after their parcel post orders had not shown up. He thereupon capitulated, but not until after the touching episode in which, looking "the knight of the rueful countenance," he was carried out of his office on the joined hands of Sergeant Lepak and Private Dies. Eventually a case dealing with the episode reached the Supreme Court, which declined jurisdiction, saying that the matter had become "moot."[36]

I come now to my final topic: How did Mr. Wilson's quest for international peace affect the Presidency; and how did it affect his own

35. See Corwin, *The President: Office and Powers* 490 (3rd ed., 1948).
36. Montgomery Ward & Company v. United States, 326 U.S. 690 (1945).

standing in history? I answer as follows: it added a vast new dimension to the Presidency; and despite its tragic failure, due to Mr. Wilson's own tragic errors, it adds immeasurably to the stature of the Woodrow Wilson of history.

Mr. Wilson came early to believe that the United States must take a hand in the making of the peace that would end the war, and in the possibility of doing so beneficially. In an address to The League to Enforce Peace on May 27, 1916, he said:

We are participants, whether we would or not, in the life of the world. The interests of all nations are our own also. We are partners with the rest. What affects mankind is inevitably our affair as well as the affair of Europe and of Asia.[37]

And again on May 30, 1916, he spoke of uniting "the people of the world to preserve the peace of the world upon a basis of common right and justice";[38] and on January 22, 1917, ten weeks before he asked for a declaration of war on the Teutonic powers, he urged before the Senate that no lasting peace could ensue from a "peace forced upon the loser." The peace must be one of which "the very principle is equality and a common participation in a common benefit." "[It must be a] peace without victory."[39]

Two immense difficulties confronted Mr. Wilson from the outset of his quest for "peace without victory." The first was the commitment of our "associates" to certain secret treaties comprising mutual promises of spoliation of the common enemy when and if they defeated him. Of these Mr. Wilson had been fully apprised when we entered the war, although he later made an ineffectual effort to obscure the fact. In the second place, the President had to win the support of an isolationist Senate.

The President announced his Fourteen Points in an address to Congress on January 18, 1918. Then taking a leaf from McKinley's book, who in 1898 had incorporated in the protocol leading to the Peace of Paris all the material provisions of that peace, the President set to work to get the Fourteen Points incorporated in an armistice bringing the war with Germany to an end. On October 24, as we have seen, he appealed

37. *Public Papers of Wilson* 185.
38. *Id.* at 195.
39. 54 Cong. Rec. 1742 (1917); Farmer, *Wilson Reader* 157.

to the people of the United States to give him a majority in the approaching November election "for the sake of the Nation itself, in order that its inward duty of purpose may be evident to the world itself."[40]

A fortnight later, on November 5, to be exact, two events took place, both of ominous significance for Mr. Wilson's program of "peace without victory." First, the Allies consented to embody the Fourteen Points in the Armistice which was offered the Teutonic Allies six days later, but with "reservations" touching "Freedom of the Seas" and with the stipulation that Germany must pay reparations for the damage she had wrought in the course of the war she had herself begun. In the second place, on this same day, November 5, the American people returned the Republican opposition to power in Congress. In the Senate, to be sure, the Republican majority was a very narrow one, but counting Mr. Truman Newberry of Michigan, who was under indictment for violating the Federal Corrupt Practices Act, it was sufficient to enable the opposition to reorganize the all-important Foreign Relations Committee under the chairmanship of Senator Lodge. As Mr. Wilson caustically remarked, "the Republican majority is out on bail." In fairness, however, it should be added, that when Newberry came to trial, the measure he was convicted under was pronounced void by the Supreme Court in a six to three decision which is no longer good law.[41]

On December 4, 1918, Mr. Wilson sailed for Europe to attend the Peace Conference. The rest is familiar history. The conference opened in Paris January 18, 1919. The treaty was signed at Versailles June 26. Mr. Wilson submitted it to the Senate July 10, and straightway began a speaking tour in its behalf. Unfortunately his own following was divided, the malcontents alleging that, while he had got his League of Nations, he had got it at the expense of "peace without victory." On September 26, the President was stricken in Colorado en route to Kansas, and brought back to Washington, where on October 3 he suffered a second stroke which paralyzed his left side, and insulated him from the world for several weeks, in the course of which twenty-eight bills became laws without his signature. Later he partially recovered and was urged by his supporters in the Senate to accept a modified version

40. III *Public Papers of Wilson,* vol. 1, 287.
41. Cf. Newberry v. United States, 256 U.S. 232 (1921); Burroughs v. United States, 290 U.S. 534 (1934).

of the Lodge Reservations. He repelled the suggestion, and on March 19, 1920, the treaty was finally rejected by a vote of forty-nine for the treaty with reservations and thirty-five against it. The League of Nations was established; the United States was not a member of it.

Ought Wilson have accepted the league even with the Lodge Reservations added? It is certainly arguable in the light of subsequent events that great advantage might have ensued from his doing so. Had the United States been a member of the league, even with the Lodge Reservations to hamper its performance thereunder, Japan might well have hesitated to invade China in 1931; Mussolini might well have hesitated to invade Abyssinia in overt defiance of the League in 1935; and Hitler might well have hesitated to invade the Rhineland, to remilitarize Germany, and to seize Austria in the years 1934 to 1938, all in arrant defiance of the Treaty of Versailles. In a word, the league would have been in position to offset the imbecilities of British foreign policy which culminated in the Munich Pact and which, instead of giving us "peace in our time," led directly to World War II.

"Wisdom after the event," you may say. Yes; but not after events that could by no chance be foreseen or the league would never have been proposed in the first instance. For the rest, I find very persuasive the following passage from a recent defense by Henry Cabot Lodge, Jr., of his grandfather's course in 1920:

The Senate majority, in 1919 and 1920, wanted to change the covenant in three major ways: (a) So that United States military actions to preserve the territorial integrity of a nation under Article X would first be approved by Congress; (b) so that the United States would be the sole judge of whether a matter involving its interests was or was not a domestic question; and (c) so that the United States would not have merely equal power with the small nations. These are all implicit in the United Nations Charter today. No one even debates them any more.[42]

In short, President Wilson demanded of the American people things they still would not concede even a quarter of a century later; or indeed, even today.

What was the motivation of Wilson's fight for the league; and how did the fight affect the Presidency? In his brilliant volume, *Woodrow Wilson and the People,* Professor Bell stresses the religious quality of

42. *New York Times Magazine,* January 22, 1956, p. 72, col. 3.

Wilson's crusade.[43] From the first, and even before our own entrance into the war, Wilson, as I have noted, advanced the idea that it must eventuate in a peace embracing all men; and, as Professor Bell shows, his language is tinged not infrequently with an apocalyptic quality. Even so, I regard Mr. Wilson's quest for peace to be of essentially the same stamp as his quest for social justice; to have been governed by the same compassionate concern for the common lot. He was fighting the battle, as he thought, of the common man, always the helpless, hopeless victim of war and its outrages.

On the other hand, while Mr. Wilson was indeed a deeply religious man, I am constrained to add there were times when his Calvinistic faith hindered rather than assisted his last great fight, by stiffening his own stubborn nature. It compelled him to reject any accommodation with the infidel — with those, to wit, who disagreed with him.

"The office of President," Mr. Wilson remarked on one occasion, "is so much greater than any man could honestly imagine himself to be that the most he can do is to look grave enough and self-possessed enough to seem to fill it."[44] And that is just what he himself was able to do. In this connection, I quote, with a few emendations, some words which I penned at the request of a friend at the time of Mr. Wilson's death:

The event of main interest this week has been Wilson's death. Though the University administration is largely in the hands of those who were in the opposition in his closing days here, everything in recognition of the occasion is being done which the demise of Princeton's most illustrious son properly calls for. Thus while individuals pass on, institutions remain, and recruit strength from the fame even of those whom in their lifetime they did not always support or even repudiated. My own opinion is that the elements of greatness were so intermingled in Wilson with cramping limitations that his fame, like that of Jefferson before the New Deal came to his rescue, will be slow to emerge from the folds of controversy. Wilson was a finished speaker, and this with his personal dignity made him a splendid figure on great occasions. But it also exposed him to the danger of self-deception, and to the temptation to substitute words for facts. A pure amateur when he entered politics, he soon displayed a finesse, an imperturbability, and a strategic skill that have been rarely equalled in American political annals. But, owing to his long residence in the shades of Academia, he was accessible much

43. Bell, *Woodrow Wilson and the People* (1945).
44. Rossiter, *The American Presidency* 137 (1956).

more readily to intellectual currents — or to intellectualized currents — than to the spontaneous reactions of the people, wherein he contrasted with his robustious rival Roosevelt. For problems that demanded an intellectual approach he was masterly, but his emotional appeals did not always ring true, as in his unfortunate "too proud to fight" speech. When indeed was he ever too proud to fight?

Wilson's critics were wont to charge that he was more concerned with the appearance of achievement than in the solid reality, since the former most affected his fortune and fame at the moment, but certainly he did not sin more grievously in this respect than most public men do, and are constrained to do, in a democracy. It is perhaps as a judge of men that Mr. Wilson shone least in his day-to-day conduct of affairs, being prone to evaluate them for their attitude toward himself, rather than their ability or their competence for the assigned task. Partly this was egotism, but partly again it was political expediency. Woodrow Wilson was no snob, he was devoid of social ambitions, and unquestionably sympathized with the common lot. But the core of his being was a flaming ambition, which his religion fanned rather than quenched, by presenting it with successive programs of reform. And along with ambition went an impatient craving for immediate domination which was kept reasonably in curb by his own good sense until health deserted him. His career ended in defeat when he refused to accept much of the substance of what he was fighting for because the offer was not accompanied by tokens from his opponents of their discomfiture and surrender.[45]

Then, as to his impact on the Presidency — he not only filled it; he added dimensions to it, in three respects. In the first place, he made the President the leader of the legislative process. He made of the office what, in the words of Walter Lippmann, it ought always to be, "the active . . . the asking and the proposing power [of the State]."[46] Secondly, he established the precedents for presidential dictatorship in time of war or of grave international crisis — a condition of affairs that is likely to remain a factor of our daily lives for many years to come. Finally, he converted the Presidency into an international, a global institution — into an office with a world-wide, non-voting constituency. To be sure, in this respect his performance was outstripped by that of the second Roosevelt. He, nevertheless, set the pattern; he created the precedents, he took that indispensable first step.

45. See Myers, *Some Princeton Memories* 34–35 (1946).
46. Lippmann, *The Public Philosophy* 30 (1955).

III. Roosevelt and Constitutional Revolution

5. Some Probable Repercussions of "Nira" on Our Constitutional System

The notable feature of the President's message addressed to Congress the other day was undoubtedly his announcement that he considered the National Industrial Recovery Act a permanent part of the American arrangement of things. This announcement seems to have shocked some people. As Will Rogers said in the *Times* the other day, "Mr. Roosevelt proposed in his speech that the NRA and a lot of these other Government-regulated business ethics should be made permanent. Well, that was a terrible blow to some business men. They figured that they would only be required by the Government to be honest until the emergency was over."

I think, however, that those who have reflected on this subject must have come to the conclusion, prior to the President's announcement, that the "Nira," if not itself permanent, would undoubtedly lead to something permanent. The Nira was originally enacted as an emergency measure, to be sure, but the emergency was of a particular character. It was an emergency in the sense of a distressful condition that needed remedying, but it was not an emergency in the sense of being the extraordinary result of extraordinary causes. It was the normal result of normal causes operating in an environment to which those causes had become ill-adapted, and causes which could be counted on to

Reprinted from "Some Probable Repercussions of 'Nira' on Our Constitutional System" by Edward S. Corwin in volume no. 172 of *The Annals* of The American Academy of Political and Social Science, © 1934 by The American Academy of Political and Social Science. All rights reserved.

resume their operation if the control represented by Nira, or by something equivalent, were once withdrawn.

It may be doubted, in fact, whether the Nira has been a great success as an emergency measure — whether it has accelerated rather than retarded recovery. I do not think that is the test to be applied. The real test is rather whether the Nira can so *guide* recovery as to prevent the kind of recovery that would lead again to collapse. In short, the Nira is regarded as a *reform* measure more accurately than as a *recovery* measure. And so regarding it, we see that it was good statesmanship to impose it while business was still down; because if business had been up, it would have been impossible to impose such a reform. "Don't interfere with business" would have become altogether too powerful a shibboleth to be resisted successfully.

Now, the permanency of Nira or something equivalent being taken for granted, it becomes interesting to inquire into the possible effects of this measure upon our constitutional system, and that is the subject on which I am going to address you briefly.

Constitutional Basis of Nira

The Nira may be regarded as a sort of declaratory statute; as declaratory, that is, of certain legal principles which it is hoped will prove to be adapted to the present economic situation of the United States. What, then, are the constitutional principles which this declaratory statute imports? If you turned to the Constitution of the United States, you would of course be able to obtain very little enlightenment on the question of the power of the government to enact such a statute. There probably are about twenty words out of the thirty-five hundred words in the Constitution, that have any bearing whatsoever upon the subject. The problem is one rather of constitutional law and theory.

In the first place we encounter the theory that the national government has only such powers as are quite clearly delegated to it. What clause, therefore, of the Constitution of the United States furnishes the generative source of the Nira? There is only one possible clause, that which gives Congress the power to regulate "commerce among the states." But commerce among the states is not the sum total of business, while Nira attempts to regulate the whole business structure. So at the very outset we encounter the theory upon which the National Industrial Recovery Act rests, and that is the *solidarity of American business.* Congress has the power to regulate commerce among the states, and hence has the power to protect that commerce. The theory of the Nira is that the health of commerce among the states depends upon the health of business in general, and that if commerce among the states cannot be restored except by measures which are conducive to the restoration of business in general, Congress has the power to take such measures.

Extent of Congressional Powers

The power of Congress over interstate commerce is not and never has been confined to the regulation of acts of commerce among the states. Thus, from whatever source a detriment to interstate commerce proceeds, it falls under the controlling power of Congress by virtue of Congress' power to protect interstate commerce. For example, Congress has the power to require that cars which are hauling goods from one point to another within a state shall be equipped with certain safety appliances, because such cars may link up with cars which are carrying goods from one state to another and so may become a source of danger to the latter. To repeat, Congress' power extends to matters which are not commerce among the states at all, simply by virtue of the fact that its power to *regulate* commerce includes the power to *safeguard* commerce.

A few years ago the United States Supreme Court was confronted with a case in which a man named Ferger was charged under a federal law with having issued a fraudulent bill of lading. He challenged the right of Congress to penalize such an act. He said that the issuance of a fraudulent bill of lading was not interstate commerce, in fact was not commerce of any kind, but was merely a violation of the law against fraud of the state where the act occurred. The Supreme Court nevertheless sustained Ferger's conviction under the act of Congress, Chief Justice White speaking as follows:

This argument mistakenly assumes that the power of Congress is to be necessarily tested by the intrinsic existence of commerce in the particular subject dealt with instead of by relation of that subject to commerce and its effect upon it. We say mistakenly assumes, because we think it clear if the proposition were sustained it would destroy the power of Congress to regulate, as obviously that power, if it is to exist, must include the authority to deal with obstructions to interstate commerce and with a host of other acts which because of their relation to and influence upon interstate commerce come within the power of Congress to regulate, although they are not interstate commerce in and of themselves.

But it may be objected (and it is a natural objection to make) that production, which is a great part of industry, is *local.* The Supreme Court has said that many times. It has even been said that production is "inherently" local. But the fact is that production is not local in any sense that is relevant to our present problem, and this for the reason that *the vast proportion of production is for the interstate or the national market.* For example, what proportion of the fruit of California does California consume? What proportion of the automobiles that it manufactures does the state of Michigan purchase and use? Where does the raw material out of which automobiles are made in the state of Michigan come from?

Production, in short, is a function, as is interstate commerce a function, *of the interstate or national market,* and expands and contracts as the interstate market expands and contracts. So it is upon this proposition of the solidarity of business, on the idea that business involves interstate commerce and vice versa, and that the health of interstate commerce depends upon the health of the entity of which it is a part — it is upon this proposition that the constitutionality of Nira rests.

Obsolescent State Power

At this point, however, we encounter a most formidable objection, namely, that this line of reasoning tends to destroy the federal system, inasmuch as it expels the states very largely from the field of business relations, while even such power as it leaves them it necessarily subordinates to the supreme power of Congress. Well, that has to be admitted; but I think the answer is that in the field of business relations state power has long been moribund, so that the Nira simply recognizes and gives effect to a constitutional theory which is the counterpart of a condition already long established in the facts of our everyday economic life.

In this connection I wish to quote from an address made by Professor Gulick at the Chicago Fair last summer.

The American state is finished. I do not predict that the states will go, but affirm that they have gone. And why have they gone? Because they were unable to deal even inefficiently with the imperative, the life and death tasks of the new national economy. Where were the states when the banks went under? . . . Where were the states when all the railroads were on the verge of passing into the hands of the bondholders and suspending operations? Where were the states in the regulation of power and control of utilities? Where are the states now in regulating insurance companies with their fake balance sheets and high salaries? Where were the states in controlling blue sky securities? Where were the states in preventing destructive business competition and protecting labor and the public? Where were the states in the development of security through social insurance? In none of these fields affecting economic life was it possible for any state to do anything decisive without driving business out of its jurisdiction into areas where there was no regulation and no control.

So Professor Gulick draws this conclusion: *"Nothing effective can be done in the stabilization of economic affairs unless the area of planning and control has the same boundaries as the economic structure."*

Some of that may appear to be couched in the language of exaggeration. But as a matter of fact Professor Gulick understates his case, because he confines his arraignment of the states to their regulation of business relations; while the inefficiency of the states even in the field of the criminal law is being displayed to us daily, as well as their growing dependence upon federal assistance in this, the most primitive field of state power. So, granting the premise of the solidarity of business, the Nira becomes a measure well within the power of Congress to foster and protect interstate commerce, and the federal system, the federal balance, will have to take its chances in the resulting situation, which was one of fact long before it became one of law.

Effect on Judicial Review

That brings me to another point, the probable effect of the Nira on the most distinctive feature of our constitutional system, judicial review. One of the great purposes of judicial review, which is to say, of the power of the courts to pass on the constitutionality of laws, has been of course to maintain the federal balance; but if the federal balance is at an end, then naturally judicial review loses much of its reason for being.

I am not predicting, of course, that the Supreme Court will be deprived outright of its power of judicial review, nor even that the power of judicial review will *overtly* come to an end in the near future. What I do say is that we are to look forward to the gradual diminution in the years to come of the role of the Supreme Court in the determination of national policies. It will be something like the demise of the veto power of the English King. That took place very unobtrusively, so much so that when Blackstone wrote his *Commentaries* in 1765 he still regarded the royal veto as a factor of the British Constitution, and when De Lolme wrote his book on the British Constitution ten years later, he still reckoned the veto power of the King as an essential part of that Constitution. But in fact the veto had not been exercised since the year 1707.

The Supreme Court will still have, of course, a great role in our system, as exemplified in the recent Scottsboro case. That is the sort of thing it seems to me that the Court ought to be doing — intervening in behalf of the helpless and the oppressed against local injustice and prejudice, rather than intervening in the assertion of out-of-date economic theories, as it has done too often since 1890.

Delegation of Power

Another feature of the Nira is, obviously, the tremendous role which it recognizes the President as occupying in our system. The Nira was not drawn in Congress; it was drawn in the executive offices of the United States, and it delegates vast powers to the executive. We have a maxim of constitutional law that the legislature may not delegate its powers. Although there is nothing in the Constitution to this effect, this maxim, which was stated by John Locke as far back as 1690, has received more or less lip service from our courts and from our political scientists for many generations.

Actually, however, the Supreme Court of the United States has never pronounced any act of Congress void on the ground that it unconstitutionally delegated legislative power. And in recent years the Court has developed this very interesting formula, that Congress may not delegate its power unless it becomes necessary to delegate it in order to exercise it effectively and conveniently. In other words, the maxim amounts simply to this, that Congress may not abdicate its power and so may not bind its successors. Of course, if all governmental power had to be exercised in the first instance in the form of detailed legislation, it really could not be exercised at all in a complex and rapidly changing society.

It is only to a period of simple and slowly changing conditions that the maxim can be successfully applied with literal force.

So the Nira simply underscores this result of our constitutional law to date. What will be the effect of its doing so upon legislative processes under the Constitution? I rather think it will be beneficial. It seems to me that debate in Congress may become much more vital when it is confined to questions of large, general principle and policy rather than to statutory details. And if this general idea of delegating legislative power is extended into the field of tariff making, as President Hoover was anxious that it should be, and as President Roosevelt apparently is also, then at last our Congress may be rescued from the stigma which Burke visited upon the House of Commons of his day when he called it "a bustle of local agencies." The Congress of the United States has lost power by trying to exercise too much power. It has lost its due influence in our national system by trying to act as a legislature for local interests.

Problems Created by Nira

The Nira is bound to make such a change in our constitutional system that it will have to be followed up, no doubt, by that sort of operation which in the war was called "mopping up." It is going to make such a vast change, particularly in the relationship of the national government to the states, that the question of what role the states are henceforth to occupy in our system is going to become a vital problem in the next few years, without doubt.

The question also arises, of course, as to the institutionalization of those procedures by which, for example, General Johnson and his associates have been enacting their codes. Subordinate legislation, delegated legislation, it is obvious, is going to become a very important feature of government. Are the methods that have been applied in the drawing up of these codes entirely satisfactory, however? This is a question which will have to be met sooner or later.

Then the further question comes up, whether or not the President's Cabinet is exactly the most satisfactory type of advisory board for the President in the new situation. The President, of course, has absolute freedom in the choice of his Cabinet, which is a body not known to the Constitution of the United States; it is an "extra-constitutional" body. The President is free, for example, to choose his Cabinet from the chairmen of the committees of Congress, in which case we might gradually approximate the cabinet system of government. The President is also free to choose as his advisers, as President Roosevelt certainly has chosen some of his most important advisers, not from the heads of his administrative departments but from men who are subordinate officials in those departments. Very possibly, therefore, there will be gradually built up a rather different type of Cabinet.

The question may even come up whether the taboo on the third term is a desirable thing in a new system in which so much depends on continuity of policy, and where governmental policy and business policy are so interlocked and interwoven with each other.

Generally speaking, I should say that the leitmotif of the new constitutional system that the Nira adumbrates is the idea of fusion of powers and cooperation, in contrast to those ideas of separation, of tension, of competition, on which our system was originally based. Mr. Roosevelt has frequently and justifiably spoken of the success of the efforts of the Administration as depending upon the cooperation of business and government. It depends also on the cooperation of the national government and the state governments, and on the cooperation within the national government, of the executive and the legislative — in the words of Mr. Roosevelt, on "the firm and permanent union" of these bodies.

Flexibility of the Constitution

So to sum the whole thing up, I say that the Nira to some indefinite extent imports a constitutional revolution, but that this revolution corresponds to one of which we have not been sufficiently aware but which had already taken place in our economic life, in the facts of our everyday living. In this connection permit me to quote the words of James Madison in *The Federalist* No. 41. Discussing there the objection of certain opponents of the Constitution, that the relative importance of manufacturing and of agriculture was bound greatly to change in the years to come, to the disadvantage of the states, Madison concluded an argument of reassuring tenor with these words: "A system of government meant for duration ought to contemplate these revolutions and be able to accommodate itself to them."

I think the Constitution of the United States can accommodate itself to the revolution which the Nira undoubtedly does spell. I think further that this means a change in the character of the Constitution itself. The Constitution will accommodate itself to the revolution, will be absorbed into it more or less, and our attitude toward it will consequently become less legalistic and more political. We shall value it for the aid it lends to considered social purpose, not as a lawyers' document.

A historical parallel is suggested by the position of Magna Carta in the English Constitution. In the year 1400, Magna Carta *was* the English Constitution in great part; in the year 1700, Magna Carta had been absorbed into a vast complexus of environing institutions. And so it may be with the Constitution of the United States. It does not seem to me that there is anything very terrifying about this; it is one of the results of living politically in an age which lives adventurously in other respects.

6. President and Court: A Crucial Issue

Although the President's recommendation that the Supreme Court be enlarged to fifteen members is part and parcel of a general plan for the reform of the federal judiciary, and is cogently supported by his message as a measure for dealing with superannuation on the bench, it has already drawn fire as an "adroit" way of 'packing the Court" with a membership favorable to the New Deal.

Indeed, the President himself says, at the close of his message, that if the measures which he recommends "achieve their aim, we may be relieved of the necessity of considering any fundamental changes in the powers of the courts or the Constitution of our government," words that are fairly interpretable as admitting the purpose which the critics of the proposal assert to be its controlling one.

Furthermore, the recommended enlargement of the Court appears as a logical – though not inevitable – outcome of the President's message of January 6, where, reporting on the state of the Union, he said:

From *The New York Times*, February 14, 1937, sec. 8, pp. 1, 2, 30, © 1937 by the New York Times Company. Reprinted by permission.

Means must be found to adapt our legal forms and our judicial interpretation to the actual present national needs of the largest progressive
democracy in the modern world. . . . The judicial branch also is asked
by the people to do its part in making democracy successful. We do
not ask the courts to call nonexistent powers into being, but we have
a right to expect that conceded powers or those legitimately implied
shall be made effective instruments for the common good. The processes of our democracy must not be imperiled by the denial of essential
powers of free government.

But why should not the President's supporters frankly defend the
proposal that the Court be enlarged, a measure necessary in the present
situation to readjust the balance between the departments and to
effect an application of the Constitution which is demanded by conditions and which has been sanctioned by the people?

One thing can be said at the outset, that this would not be the first
time the Court has been "packed." There is still, for instance a tenth
federal circuit for which there once existed, but no longer exists, a
corresponding member of the Court. This anomaly is a memento of
President Lincoln's well-warranted fear that the Court over which
Roger Taney presided might upset important war measures. Nor did
Lincoln act without precedent, for twenty-five years earlier the Court
had been enlarged from seven to nine justices in order — among other
things, perhaps — to water down the remnant of the old Marshall
bench.

Also, we now know that when President Grant sent to the Senate the
names of two new appointees to the Court, Messrs. Bradley and Strong,
the same day that the decision in Hepburn v. Griswold was handed
down, he did so in the fullest confidence that these gentlemen would
do just what in fact they did do some time later, turn to and bring
about a reversal of Hepburn v. Griswold. [On February 7, 1870, the
Supreme Court held in the Hepburn-Griswold case that the legal tender
act of February 25, 1862, making "greenbacks" legal tender, was unconstitutional.]

In the words of Secretary Fish's diary, the President explained —
this was some years later —

that at the time he felt it important that the constitutionality of the
law should be sustained, and while he would do nothing to exact
anything like a pledge or expression of opinion from the parties he

might appoint to the bench, he had desired that the constitutionality should be sustained by the Supreme Court; that he believed such had been the opinion of all his Cabinet at the time.

The principal justification, however, for the President's recommendation must be found, if at all, not in the past but in the here and now. The question which it raises is really that of the soundness of the assumption which underlies the passages above quoted from his message of January 6. It is there assumed that the Court today enjoys great freedom of choice in interpreting the Constitution, that it can often give the Constitution a liberal or strict application as it elects, and that it is able therefore frequently to forward its own preferences without violating correct judicial decorum.

In other words, it is the President's evident belief that the Court has become a political body, not in the narrow partisan sense of the term, but in the immensely more important sense, of a determinator of public policies – a super-legislature, in brief.

This assumption, one may be sure, will be boldly contested. The evidence in support of it, nevertheless, is impressive. Thus, the President will be able to cite the present Chief Justice's statement, made many years ago and so before the Court's censorship of acts of Congress had taken on its present scope, that "the Constitution is what the judges say it is"; also the late Mr. Root's admonition to the states in 1906 that if they did not exercise the powers theoretically belonging to them, interpretations would "be found" to enable the national government to take over those powers; likewise Justice Stone's statement in the AAA case that "while unconstitutional exercise of power by the executive and legislative branches of the government is subject to judicial restraint, the only check upon our own exercise of power is our own sense of self-restraint."

Turning, moreover, from opinion to fact, what do we find? One thing is that the number of acts, whether state or national, which the Court has disallowed has increased enormously in recent years. Between 1789 and 1865 the Court pronounced void just two provisions of acts of Congress. Between 1920 and 1932, inclusive, it overturned twenty-two such provisions, while between 1934 and 1936, inclusive, it overturned thirteen such provisions.

These statistics standing by themselves are, to be sure, open to diverse interpretations. It is only when we look for the reason back of them that they take on their proper significance; but this too becomes evident on a little consideration.

The acts of Congress which the Court has set aside for transgressing clear, unmistakable words of the constitutional document are few indeed. Rather the basis of its decision has usually been some doctrine or theory which it has itself, not without popular approval necessarily, imported into the Constitution from the outside. Indeed, the New Deal legislation which has perished at the Court's hands has almost all fallen before just such doctrines or theories.

Thus the decision in the "Hot Oil" cases was based on the maxim which finds no mention in the Constitution, that "the Legislature may not delegate its powers"; and the Railway Retirement Act was set aside on the ground that it deprived the carriers of their property without "due process of law," although the conception of "due process" thus invoked was unknown to the Supreme Court prior to the Dred Scott case.

And when we turn to the decisions setting aside the NIRA and the Coal Conservation Act we encounter yet another significant feature of the Court's present power. Both of these acts were passed on the theory that conditions surrounding production often affect interstate commerce detrimentally. This theory the Court answered by saying that such effects, however extensive or inevitable, were "indirect" and hence beyond the power of Congress to govern.

But the Constitution itself says nothing about "indirect effects," and still less — if that were possible — does it say that Congress may not safeguard interstate commerce from them. Indeed, no further back than 1923, we find the Court saying through Chief Justice Taft:

This court will certainly not substitute its judgment for that of Congress in such a matter unless the relation of the subject to interstate commerce and its effect upon it are clearly nonexistent.

Thus, not only do the Court's most important decisions frequently rest on extremely vague grounds, on grounds which are open to a variety of interpretations, but they also rest on grounds the Court's own interpretation of which has varied from time to time. Especially is this true of its decisions in recent years concerning the crucial issue of state versus national power.

In the Shreveport case, which was decided in 1914, the Court, speaking by the present Chief Justice, held that Congress was entitled to regulate the local charges of interstate carriers when they discriminated against interstate commerce. Defending at the time this holding against the argument that it authorized Congress to intrude on the reserved powers of the States, Mr. Hughes said:

Within its sphere as recognized by the Constitution, the nation is supreme. The question is simply of the Federal power as granted; where there is authorized exercise of that power, there is no reserved power to nullify it — a principle obviously essential to our national integrity, yet continually calling for new applications.

In the face of which, we find the Court, in the NIRA, the AAA, and the Coal Act cases, treating the reserved powers of the states as if they comprised an independent limitation on national power.

But, it may be asked, does not the principle of *stare decisis* [the doctrine of following rules or principles laid down in previous judicial decisions] contradict the President's assumption that the Court has become a political body? Not, it would seem, to any serious extent. In the words of Justice Brandeis, spoken a few years ago:

Stare decisis is not, like the rule of *res judicata* [a thing or matter finally decided on its merits], a universal, inexorable command. "The rule of *stare decisis*, though one tending to consistency and uniformity of decision, is not inflexible. Whether it shall be followed or departed from is a question entirely within the discretion of the court, which is again called upon to consider a question once decided."

It is true that these words occur in a dissenting opinion, but the opinions cited in support of them are not dissenting opinions. Furthermore, Justice Brandeis was able to fortify his statement with an impressive list of cases — between thirty and forty — which the court had, even at that date, overruled in whole or in part in the field of constitutional law.

Writing in 1932, Professor Thomas Reed Powell of Harvard summed up the position of the Court in relation to the Constitution in these words:

Nine men in Washington have a pretty arbitrary power to annul any statute or ordinance or administrative order that is properly brought before them. The power is an arbitrary power, even though it may not be arbitrarily exercised. It is arbitrary in the sense that in the last analysis it is exercised as five or more of the nine men think best.

The Supreme Court can hardly be said to be controlled by the Constitution because so seldom does the Constitution clearly dictate a decision. It is not controlled by its own precedents, for it feels free to overrule them. It feels even more free to make distinctions that no sensible person would think of making except to avoid confession that a precedent is being disregarded. All this remains true even though in most of the cases it is also true that applicable precedents are either followed or are not there to be invoked. The Supreme Court does what it prefers to do when it prefers to do as nearly as possible what it has done before.

Certainly nothing has happened since 1932 to cast doubt on the soundness of this verdict.

The origin of the Court's power of censorship over acts of Congress has been the subject of investigation again and again. It is a story not without support for the Cleopatra's nose view of history. One of the foremost problems confronting the Philadelphia Convention was that of providing a curb on the state legislatures, in the interest both of national power and of private rights.

The Virginia Plan, upon which the Constitution was largely elaborated, ignoring the idea of judicial review which had already appeared sporadically in three or four of the states, proposed a congressional veto. No sooner, however, did this proposal come up for discussion than the point was made that, on account of the bad condition of the roads, it must often be months before a state legislative act could be laid before Congress for its consideration. Must, it was asked, such acts be kept in suspension until passed upon, or must they be permitted to operate during the interval – either alternative being undesirable? And must Congress remain in continuous session in order to discharge its veto function?

Madison, principal author of the Virginia Plan, conceded the force of these objections, and as we know, the proposed congressional veto was ultimately tabled in favor of the idea, which is incorporated in the "supremacy" clause of the Constitution [Article VI, section 2], of making the state courts – local bodies, in other words – a first line of defense of the constitutional powers of the new government. From this concession to the badness of transportation in 1787 sprang all the rest.

There is, to be sure, no necessary relation between the power which the state courts, and on appeal the Supreme Court, exercise when they censor state legislation in relation to the national Constitution. In such instances both judiciaries may logically be regarded as wielding the prerogative of a supreme government — a prerogative, moreover, for which a clear precedent existed from colonial days. When, on the other hand, the Supreme Court sets aside an act of Congress, it asserts the right, by virtue of judicial power alone, to censor the action of a constitutionally coordinate body — indeed, in the light both of British and colonial practice and theory, that of a superior body.

Nevertheless, the principle which today furnishes both branches of judicial review a common basis in constitutional theory was brought forward in the convention fairly early in the proceedings. Thus, in addition to the bad-roads argument, Sherman of Connecticut proffered the argument against the congressional veto that it involved "a wrong principle," to wit, that "acts contrary to the Articles of Union would be valid."

In other words, the Articles of Union would be law in the strict sense of being cognizable and applicable by courts in the decision of cases. The supremacy clause, to be sure, defines "the supreme law of the land" as comprising "this Constitution, the laws of the United States made in pursuance thereof and the treaties made under the authority of the United States." But at any rate, the Constitution is treated as law in the same sense as acts of Congress are; and who would question that of "the supreme law" it is the supreme part?

And yet, did the members of the convention draw this conclusion which, obviously, is not inescapable? The answer seems to be that some did and some did not. Most of the discussion bearing on the question was evoked by another feature of the Virginia Plan, a proposal that a Council of Revision, to consist of the heads of the executive departments and "a convenient number of the national judiciary," should be vested with a veto power over national legislation.

The fact that the convention ultimately rejected this proposal also has given rise to the contention that it thereby indicated its disapproval of judicial review of acts of Congress. The conclusion is unwarranted. An argument against the Council of Revision was that, since the judges would have occasion to pass upon the constitutionality of the acts of Congress in the exercise of their judicial functions, it would be improper to associate them with the legislative process.

But, on the other hand, it would also be going too far to say that the defeat of the council proves that the convention accepted the thesis of judicial review. What the available records show is that judicial review was at the outset of the convention a still novel idea to those who had heard of it at all, that even its advocates had at first but the slightest prevision of its possible uses as a check on legislative power; that as this began to appear somewhat more clearly, the discovery was not altogether favorable to judicial review — some, Dickinson for instance, and later Madison, beginning now to recoil from the idea of so great a power in judges; and finally, that after all very few members did directly express themselves on the merits of the question during the convention.

For all these reasons the statistics which various writers have compiled to show a wide acceptance of the idea among the membership of the convention should be taken with a grain of salt. Not only do they depend far too much upon the argument from silence, but they also overlook the obvious fluctuation of opinion on the subject.

Nor is the verdict, which must be passed upon discussion of the subject while adoption of the Constitution was pending, substantially different. The great argument against the Constitution was, of course, that the new government would be dangerous to the rights of the states and the liberties of the people, and to this argument advocates of the Constitution occasionally found the idea of judicial review as a check on the national legislative power a very convenient answer. By far the most positive statement on the subject was that of Hamilton in one of the closing numbers of *The Federalist,* although he had overlooked the ideas in an earlier issue where it would have been pertinent to mention it. Without invoking any clause of the Constitution, Hamilton here asserts "the doctrine," as he terms it, that "the courts were designed to be an intermediate body between the people and the Legislature, in order to keep the latter within the limits assigned their authority."

Although the essay probably made converts, Madison was not among them. For a few months later we find him declaring with equal positiveness that judicial review made "the judiciary department paramount in fact to the legislative, which was never intended and can never be proper."

Though the question of the power of the Court to disallow acts of Congress on constitutional grounds was in form settled by Marshall's famous decision in Marbury v. Madison, it has taken many decades to unfold the full significance of this holding. Thus, as was pointed out earlier in this article, the grounds on which the Court can today overturn an act of Congress are often vague and indefinite in the extreme, while frequently they appear in pairs of alternatives which vest the Court with uncontrolled freedom of choice.

Nor is this all, for the general trend of professional opinion has come to endow the Court's interpretation of the Constitution with the authority of the latter, until they have been changed by constitutional amendment or have been overturned by the Court itself as having been erroneous. As someone has put it, "the Constitution is the Supreme Court's last guess."

With the dogma of the "finality" of the Court's interpretations of the Constitution — their finality, that is to say, as respects everybody but the Court itself — we are brought back to the President's message of January 6 and his more recent recommendation that the Court be enlarged. What he is saying, in effect, is that, as between an attempt to amend the Constitution and trusting to the Court to correct its own errors, he prefers the latter method of bringing the Constitution, as it is applied through the judiciary, into harmony with the needs of the times.

As a matter of fact, the latter is the method on which we have generally relied in the past, so why not now?

Without a sympathetic Court to interpret them, even constitutional amendments must prove disappointing. Furthermore, the adoption of a needed amendment can be prevented by thirteen states which contain less than a twentieth of the population of the country.

But there are those who say that the only "square and honest way" of bringing about constitutional change is by amendment. Such an attitude is specious. Certainly it is so unless its exponents are able to answer satisfactorily two questions: first, what course have they in mind in case an amendment which is desired by an unmistakable majority of the people is defeated? Second, would they support an amendment to make the amending process really democratic?

Besides, do they mean that the changes which the Court has in the past wrought in the Constitution were not "square and honest"? If not, what do they mean?

7. The President as Administrative Chief

I

The President's primary duty, logically if not chronologically, is to create an administration and maintain one for the faithful execution of the laws. In this capacity he enjoys in relation to his official subordinates certain powers of appointment, supervision, and removal; and it is my purpose in the present essay to treat of these in some detail. The appointment power is, of course, shared by the Senate; but for the rest the principal limitations upon presidential authority in this field — as, in fact, in most others — arise from the impinging powers of Congress.

It was formerly, and within limits is still, an element of the royal prerogative in England to create offices as well as to appoint to them.[1] At the outset indeed the two things were indistinguishable. Etymologically, an "office" is an *officium*, a duty; and an "officer" was simply one whom the King had charged with a duty. In the course of time certain frequently recurrent and naturally coherent duties came to be assigned more or less permanently, and so emerged the concept of "office" as an *institution* distinct from the person holding it and capable of persisting beyond his incumbency.

The Constitution, however, by the "necessary and proper" clause, assigns the power to *create* offices to Congress, while it deals with the *appointing power* in the following words of Article II, section 2, paragraph 2:

And he [the President] shall nominate, and by and with the advice and consent of the Senate, shall appoint ambassadors, other public

From 1 *Journal of Politics* 17-61 (February, 1939). Reprinted by permission of the *Journal of Politics*, published by the Southern Political Science Association in cooperation with the University of Florida, © 1939 by the Southern Political Science Association.

1. In the words of Hamilton in *The Federalist* No. 69 at 451 (Earle ed.): "He [the King of Great Britain] not only appoints to all offices, but can create offices." See further Todd, *Parliamentary Government in England* 609 (2d ed. 1887), 22 *Encyclopaedia Britannica* 280 (11th ed. 1913), 2 Anson, *Law and Custom of the Constitution* 405-6, 449-50 (1892).

ministers and consuls, judges of the Supreme Court, and all other officers of the United States, whose appointments are not herein otherwise
provided for, and which shall be established by law; but the Congress
may by law vest the appointment of such inferior officers, as they think
proper, in the President alone, in the courts of law, or in the heads of
departments.

Appointment must, therefore, be to an existing office.[2] Furthermore,
the choice of the appointing power to such an office may be severely
limited. Thus the Constitution itself stipulates in paragraph 2 of section
6 of Article I:

No Senator or Representative shall, during the time for which he was
elected, be appointed to any civil office under the authority of the
United States, which shall have been created, or the emoluments whereof shall have been increased, during such time; and no person holding
any office under the United States shall be a member of either House
during his continuance in office.

Neither of these clauses has turned out in practice to be quite as
potent a restraint on presidential power as it was, perhaps, originally
intended to be. Thus members of Congress have been repeatedly
designated by the President, at times with the consent of the Senate,
to represent the United States on international commissions or at
diplomatic conferences. Today, in fact, the practice has attained the
dignity of usage, one which is reconcilable with the letter of the Constitution only on the theory that such assignments, being to fairly
specific tasks and carrying with them no extra emolument, lack the
essential tests of "office."[3]

2. United States v. Maurice, 2 Brock. 96; 26 Fed. Cas. No. 15,747 (1823);
5 *Opinions of the Attorney General* 88 (1849); 10 *id.* at 11 (1861); 18 *id.* at 171
(1890). "Established by law" has not at all times meant established by act of
Congress. Until 1855 no legislation was enacted respecting diplomatic posts,
which were filled as the President, with the approval of the Senate, found necessary. This was based on the theory, as stated by Attorney General Cushing, that
the designations of such officers were "derived from the law of nations, and the
authority to appoint from the Constitution" (7 *id.* at 193–94 [1855]). Likewise
the notion that the Supreme Court is established by the Constitution itself would
appear to infer that its size is for the appointive power to determine. In point
of fact, however, its size has from the first been fixed by legislation.
3. "An office is a public station, or employment conferred by the appointment
of government. The term embraces the idea of tenure, duration, emolument and
duties" (United States v. Hartwell, 6 Wall. 385, 393 [1868]). The term is often
used, however, to comprehend any public employment even of the most transi-

And a like explanation may vindicate the course of many Presidents since the time of Washington in sending abroad "personal" and "secret" agents on diplomatic or semi-diplomatic missions;[4] as well as of a practice resorted to by the first Roosevelt, of constituting "volunteer unpaid commissions" for the purpose of investigating certain factual situations and reporting their findings to the President.[5] Indeed, Mr. Roosevelt's enthusiasm for this method of informing himself concerning "the state of the nation" came eventually to be denounced in Congress as "unconstitutional," and an amendment to the Sundry Civil Act of 1909 undertook to forbid the practice.[6] Mr. Roosevelt signed the measure even while asserting his intention of ignoring the restriction. "Congress," he argued, "cannot prevent the President from seeking advice," nor disinterested men from giving their service to the people;[7] and that this eminently sensible view has won out would seem clear from the fact that Mr. Hoover, when President, appointed literally dozens of fact-finding commissions, most of which were without statutory basis.[8] President Wilson's creation of the War Industries Board and the Committee on Public Information during the war with Germany, must on the other hand be set down, in view of the great powers which were exercised by those bodies in the President's name, as illustrating the enlargement which presidential authority is apt to undergo in all directions in wartime.[9]

tory nature, as in the following dictum of a state court: "The essence of it is the duty of performing an agency, that is, of doing some act or acts, or series of acts for the State." See generally Mechem, *The Law of Public Offices and Officers* 1–3 (1890).

Also, it should be noted that the weight of congressional opinion seems to condemn acceptance by a Senator or Representative of any post which has been created by act of Congress, however lacking in other respects such post is in the tests of office as set forth in the above quotation from the Hartwell case. See 1 Willoughby, *Constitutional Law of the United States* 606 (2nd ed. 1929); Senate Rep. No. 563, 67th Cong., 2nd sess., March, 1922.

4. Below.

5. Roosevelt, *An Autobiography* 365–69 (1913). The original inventor of this practice, however, seems to have been President Tyler, who in 1841 appointed a non-statutory commission to conduct an investigation of the New York Customs House. His action led to a demand by the House of Representatives that he inform it under what authority the commission "was raised." Tyler answered by citing his duty to "take care that the laws be faithfully executed" (4 Richardson, *Messages and Papers of the Presidents* 99–100 [1903]).

6. 27 *Opinions of the Attorney General* 309, 310 (1910).

7. Roosevelt, *An Autobiography* 416–17.

8. 34 *Current History* 491 (1931).

9. As to the vast powers actually exercised by these agencies in the name of

The opening clause of Article I, section 7, paragraph 2, recently came under public scrutiny in connection with the appointment of Justice Hugo L. Black to the Supreme Court. This was because Congress had recently improved the financial position of Justices retiring at seventy, and the term for which Mr. Black had been elected to the Senate from Alabama in 1932 had still some time to run. The appointment was defended by the argument that inasmuch as Mr. Black was only fifty-one years old at the time and so would be ineligible for the "increased emolument" for nineteen years, it was not *as to him* an increased emolument.[10] Similarly, when in 1909 Senator Knox of Pennsylvania wished to become Secretary of State in President Taft's Cabinet, the salary of which office had been recently increased, Congress accommodatingly repealed the increase for the period which still remained of Mr. Knox's senatorial term.[11] In other words, a Senator or Representative — but especially a Senator — may, "during the time for which he was elected, be appointed to any civil office under the authority of the United States, . . . the emoluments whereof shall have been increased during such time," *provided only* that the increase in emolument is not available to the appointee "during such time."

But the most serious limitations on the appointing power result from the fact that in creating an office, Congress may also stipulate the qualifications of appointees thereto. First and last, legislation of this character has laid down a great variety of qualifications, depending on citizenship, residence, professional attainments, occupational experience, age, race, property, sound habits, political, industrial or regional affiliations, and so on. It has even confined the President's selection to a small number of persons to be named by others.[12] Indeed, it has con-

the President, see Berdahl, *War Powers of the Executive of the United States* 197-200, 211-12 (1921).

10. On this and other constitutional questions raised by Justice Black's appointment, see McGovney, "Is Hugo L. Black a Supreme Court Justice De Jure?" 26 *California Law Review* 1-32 (1937).

11. 1 Willoughby, *Constitutional Law* 607.

12. On this point, examine the vast mass of data brought together in Justice Brandeis' dissenting opinion in Myers v. United States and accompanying notes. 272 U.S. 52, 264-74. Hundreds of statutory provisions are cited. "Thus," the opinion summarizes, " Congress has, from time to time, restricted the president's selection by the requirement of citizenship [some thirty distinct acts of Congress]. It has limited the power of nomination by providing that the office may be held only by a resident of the United States [act of March 1, 1855, c. 133,

trived at times, by particularity of description, to designate a definite eligible, thereby virtually usurping the appointing power.[13]

For the proposition is generally conceded that some choice, however

dealing with ministers and their subordinates] ; of a state [one act] ; of a particular state [five acts] ; of a particular district [two acts] ; of a particular territory [three acts] ; of the District of Columbia [act of May 3, 1802, and four other acts] ; of a particular foreign country [one act]. It has limited the power of nomination further by prescribing professional attainments [some fifty-six acts and joint resolutions], or occupational experience [eighteen acts and joint resolutions]. It has, in other cases, prescribed the test of examinations [seven acts, including the Civil Service Act of January 16, 1883, c. 27, sec. 2, and the Foreign Service Act of May 24, 1924, c. 182, sec. 5]. It has imposed the requirement of age [three acts] ; of sex [two acts] ; of race [one act] ; of property [act of March 26, 1804, c. 38, sec. 4, legislative council of Louisiana, to be selected from holders of realty] ; and of habitual temperance in the use of intoxicating liquors [one act — obsolete, no doubt, under the Eighteenth Amendment]. Congress has imposed like restrictions on the power of nomination by requiring political representation [eighteen acts, including those organizing the interstate commerce and federal trade commissions] ; or that the selection be made on a nonpartisan basis [twenty-three acts]. It has required, in some cases, that the representation be industrial [six acts] ; in others that it be geographic [seventeen acts and joint resolutions]. It has at times required that the President's nominees be taken from, or include representatives from, particular branches or departments of the government [twenty-six acts and joint resolutions]. By still other statutes, Congress has confined the president's selection to a small number of persons to be named by others [five acts, including act of February 23, 1920, c. 91, sec. 304, requiring that the railroad labor board consist of three to be appointed from six nominees by employees, and three to be appointed from six nominees by carriers]."

Cf. an opinion by Attorney General Sargent advising against a similar feature of the McNary-Haugen Bill, *New York Times*, February 26, 1927; also a protest by President Harding against a proposal to require that one member of the Federal Reserve Board be "a farmer" (*id.,* February 6, 1922).

13. The following item from the *New York Times* of May 20, 1916, affords an illustration:

"Another joker in the Army Reorganization bill is very interesting to those who know of the circumstances connected with it. This joker, slipped into the bill behind the closed doors of the Conference Committee, as jokers frequently are, is contained in a paragraph providing for the appointment of Judge Advocates in the reorganized regular army. Probably there never was more peculiar language employed to frame a joker than that which reads this way: 'Provided further, That of the vacancies created in the Judge Advocate's Department by this act, one such vacancy, not below the rank of Major, shall be filled by the appointment of a person from civil life, not less than forty-five nor more than fifty years of age, who shall have been for ten years a Judge of the Supreme Court of the Philippine Islands, shall have served for two years as a Captain in the regular or volunteer army, and shall be proficient in the Spanish language and laws.'

"The one man in the world that this description seems to fit is Judge Adam C. Carson of the Supreme Court of the Philippine Islands. Judge Carson is now in

small, must be left the appointing authority.[14] Thus the Civil Service Act of 1883 leaves the appointing officer the right to select from "*among* those graded highest as the result of" the competitive examinations for which the act provides,[15] and supplementary executive orders have customarily further restricted choice to the *three highest.* The Foreign Service Act of 1924 is notable in that it extended for the first time the principle of competitive examinations to certain offices

---

the United States on leave of absence. His home is at Riverton, Va., in the Congressional district of Representative James Hay, Chairman of the House Committee on Military Affairs, and Chairman of the House conferees on the Army Organization bill. Judge Carson went to Cuba after the Spanish war as an officer of one of the immune regiments. Afterwards he was an officer in the Philippine army which supplemented the work of the regular troops in suppressing the Aguinaldo insurrection. President Taft, while Governor General of the Philippines, appointed him a judge of the Court of First Instance and later he was appointed a judge of the Philippine Supreme Court."

The reader will be gratified to know that Judge Carson got the job.

With this episode should be compared President Arthur's veto, July 2, 1884, of "an act for the relief of Fitz John Porter," the enacting clause of which reads as follows:

"That the President be, and he is hereby, authorized to nominate and, by and with the advice and consent of the Senate, to appoint Fitz John Porter, late a major-general of the United States Volunteers and a brevet brigadier-general and colonel of the Army, to the position of colonel in the Army of the United States, of the same grade and rank held by him at the time of his dismissal from the Army by sentence of court-martial promulgated January 27, 1863 . . ." (8 Richardson, *Messages of the Presidents* 221).

To this the President objected:

"It is apparent that should this bill become a law it will create a new office which can be filled by the appointment of the particular individual whom it specifies, and cannot be filled otherwise; or it may be said with perhaps greater precision of statement that it will create a new office upon condition that the particular person designated shall be chosen to fill it. Such an act, as it seems to me, is either unnecessary and ineffective or it involves an encroachment by the legislative branch of the Government upon the authority of the Executive. As the Congress has no power under the Constitution to nominate or appoint an officer and cannot lawfully impose upon the President the duty of nominating or appointing to office any particular individual of its own selection, this bill, if it can fairly be construed as requiring the President to make the nomination and, by and with the advice and consent of the Senate, the appointment which it authorizes, is in manifest violation of the Constitution. If such be not its just interpretation, it must be regarded as a mere enactment of advice and counsel, which lacks in the very nature of things the force of a positive law and can serve no useful purpose upon the statute books" (*ibid.*).

The veto prevailed.

14. The above note; also 13 *Opinions of the Attorney General* 516 (1871).

15. U.S. Code, Tit. 5, sec. 633 (2).

appointment to which was formerly made with the advice and consent of the Senate.[16] But obviously there is no logical reason why this should not be done generally, there being no difference in the *nature* of the appointive power whether it is exercised by the President with the Senate, or by the President alone, or by a head of department.

Another power of Congress which must be distinguished from the appointing power is that of determining the powers and duties of officers of the United States. In the case of an existing office Congress may increase these to an indefinite extent without necessitating a reappointment to the office;[17] but it seems to be the Court's opinion and is certainly a very logical one, that new duties should be "germane" to the existing office, and especially that their assignment should not transgress the principle of the separation of powers.[18]

Another characteristic which usage has affixed to the President's power of appointment is that while the power connotes a choice among eligibles, it involves ordinarily no choice whether there shall be an appointment. Just as it is expected that a legally authorized appropriation will be spent, so it is expected that a legally authorized office will be filled. But what usage has created usage can also destroy, a fact which makes Mr. Roosevelt's success in keeping the office of Comptroller General unfilled for many months following Mr. McCarl's retirement of more than passing interest.

Except the President and Vice-President all members of the civil service of the national government are appointive and fall into one of three categories, those who are appointed by the President "by and with the advice and consent of the Senate"; "inferior" officers whose appointment Congress has vested by law "in the President alone, in the courts of law or in the heads of departments"; and "employees."

As it is here used the term "employee" bears a very special meaning. Ordinarily the term denotes one who stands in a contractual relationship to his "employer," but here it signifies all subordinate officials of the national government receiving appointment at the hands of officials who are not specifically recognized by the Constitution as capable of

16. *Id.*, Tit. 22, secs. 4, 5.
17. Shoemaker v. United States, 147 U.S. 283, 301 (1893).
18. *Id.;* United States v. Ferreira, 13 How. 40 (1851); *Ex parte* Siebold, 100 U.S. 371 (1879).

being vested by Congress with the appointing power.[19] The concept thus affords a way of circumventing the apparent purpose of the Constitution to continue the power to appoint "inferior" officers, by the authorization of Congress, to the President alone, the courts of law, and the heads of departments. As used in the statutes the term "officers" is frequently construed to cover "employees" in the above sense.

What are "inferior" officers in the sense of the Constitution has never been judicially determined, since, thanks to the jealous vigilance of the Senate, Congress has exercised its power in the vesting of appointments very sparingly. The term seems to suggest in this particular context officers intended to be subordinate to those in whom their appointment is vested, and at the same time to exclude the courts of law and heads of departments. If this is so, then it is at least doubtful whether the power may be lodged in a head of department to appoint members of an administrative commission which is intended to be independent of departmental direction; and even more questionable is such a proposal as one made in 1920 to vest in the Supreme Court the appointment of the Comptroller General, an officer whose functions lie entirely outside the judicial field.

The Constitution distinguishes three stages in appointments by the President with the advice and consent of the Senate. The first is the "nomination" of the candidate by the President alone; the second is the assent of the Senate to his "appointment"; and the third is the final appointment and commissioning of the appointee by the President. The first two stages are controlled to greater or less extent by a set of usages which go by the name of "senatorial courtesy." If the President, in nominating to an office within a state, fails to consult the preferences of the Senator or Senators of his own party from that state, he is very likely to see the appointment defeated upon an appeal to the Senate by the slighted member or members. Reciprocally, the Senate will ordinarily interpose no objection to the President's nominees for Cabinet posts. Any attempt to find a basis in the written Constitution for this interesting institution would be disappointing;

19. United States v. Germaine, 99 U.S. 508 (1878); United States v. Mouat, 124 U.S. 303 (1888).

it is the Senate, not individual Senators, whose advice and consent the Constitution requires.[20]

The only case in which the Supreme Court has had occasion to pass directly upon the participation of the Senate in the appointing power is the fairly recent one of Smith v. United States[21] which grew out of an attempt by the Senate early in 1931 to recall its consent to certain nominations by President Hoover to the Federal Power Commission. In support of its course, the Senate invoked a longstanding rule which permits a motion to reconsider a resolution of confirmation and to recall the notification thereof within "the next two days of actual executive session of the Senate." Inasmuch as the nominees involved

---

The Court will, nevertheless, be astute to ascribe to a head of department an appointment made by an inferior of such head. Ekiu v. United States, 142 U.S. 651, 663 (1892). For the view that there is an intrinsic difference between a "public office" and a "public employment," see Mechem, *Law of Public Offices* 3-5.

20. In Marbury v. Madison Marshall concedes that in the case of officers appointed by the President with the consent of the Senate, appointment and commissioning are practically indistinguishable, and the same is true of course as to officers appointed by the President alone (1 Cranch 137, 156-57). In the case, on the other hand, of officers whose appointment is vested by act of Congress in the heads of departments, appointment and commissioning are distinct, since the latter has, by the requirement of the Constitution, to be by the President. Yet even such officers are covered by the legislative provision that their commissions shall not have the seal of the department affixed to them "before the same shall have been signed by the President of the United States" (U.S. Code, Tit. 5, sec. 11), which seems to be designed to leave with the President the final say whether the appointment shall be consummated.

Senatorial courtesy is not quite automatic in the case of nominees to Cabinet posts. Taney was rejected for Secretary of the Treasury in 1834; three Tyler nominees were rejected in 1843 and 1844; and one Johnson nominee in 1868. The latest victim of senatorial wrath was Charles B. Warren, whose nomination by President Coolidge to the attorney generalship was rejected in March, 1925.

A passing word should be paid the recent controversy between President Roosevelt and Senators Glass and Byrd of Virginia, growing out of the Senate's rejection of the President's nominee, Judge Floyd H. Roberts, for a federal judgeship in that state. The President charged the Senators, who invoked senatorial courtesy against Roberts, of "usurping" the presidential power of nominating to office. And finally it would seem that what happened – as in all such cases – was a temporary abdication by the *Senate* to one or two of its members of its participation in the appointing power. On the other hand, Senator Glass, in his answer to the President, was able to adduce facts which went some way to show that the President, in an effort to "purge" the Virginia Senators, had for the time being abdicated his nominating power to Governor Price and other political foes of Senators Glass and Byrd (*New York Times,* February 8 and 9, 1939).

21. 286 U.S. 6 (1932); Cf. United States v. LeBaron, 19 How. 73 (1856).

had meantime taken the oath of office and entered upon the discharge of their duties, the President denied the request, which he stigmatized as an attempt "to encroach upon the executive function by removal of a duly appointed executive officer under the guise of reconsideration of his nomination."[22] The Senate thereupon voted to reconsider the nominations in question, again approving two of the nominees but rejecting the third, against whom by the Senate's order the district attorney of the District of Columbia forthwith instituted *quo warranto* proceedings on the ground that the Senate's rule as heretofore applied did not reach the case of an appointee who had already been installed in office on the faith of the Senate's initial consent and notification to the President.

Just how the Court became entitled to construe the Senate's rules, which it conceded were subject to change by the Senate without notice, does not appear from Justice Brandeis' opinion; but at any rate the expedient enabled the Court to evade the question whether the rule governing the reconsideration of nominations is valid once notification has gone forward to the President. Jefferson in his *Manual* asserts unqualifiedly that, "If, after the vote, the paper on which it [the Senate] passed has been parted with, there can be no reconsideration." Practice, however, has been far from supporting this sweeping assertion. Nor is its logic inescapable, for it may with equal logic be contended that the senatorial consent is only "a warrant of attorney, valid until revoked," or that it is akin to a proffer and hence may be withdrawn at any time before acceptance. In Smith's case the revocation or withdrawal — depending on the analogy adopted — clearly came too late.

Neither does the decision deal with the question whether the Senate may attach conditions to its approval of an appointment, as it frequently does to its approval of a treaty. The entire record of practice under the Constitution, nevertheless, negatives the suggestion, as also does early opinion. Madison, Hamilton, Jefferson, and Story all expressed themselves to the effect that the Senate's role in relation to appointments is only that of rejecting or confirming nominations without condition.[23] Moreover, the conditions which the Senate would attempt

22. *New York Times,* January 11, 1931.
23. 9 *Writings of James Madison* 112–13 (Hunt ed. 1900–1910); *The Federalist* No. 76 at 493–94 (Earle ed.); 3 Adams, *Life and Works of John Adams,* 575–76

to attach would be apt either to invade the powers of the office, which come from the law, or to limit the officer's tenure, which also comes from the law or is subject to determination by the removal power. And in principle at least the Senate's pretensions would extend to judicial no less than to executive appointees.

Although the Constitution says that the President "*shall* commission all officers," etc., this, as applied in practice, does not appear to mean that he is under constitutional or legal obligation to commission those whose appointments have reached that stage, but merely that it is he and no one else who has the power to commission them.[24] The sealing and delivery of the commission is, on the other hand, in the case both of appointees by the President and Senate and by the President alone, a purely ministerial act which has been lodged by statute with the Secretary of State, and the performance of which may be compelled by mandamus unless the appointee has been in the meantime validly removed.[25]

A further element of the appointing power is contained in the following provision of Article II, section 2, paragraph 3:

> The President shall have power to fill up all vacancies that may happen during the recess of the Senate, by granting commissions which shall expire at the end of their next session.

The significant word is "happen." Setting out from the proposition that the very nature of the executive power requires that it shall always be "in capacity for action," Attorneys General came early to interpret this to mean "happen to exist," and long continued practice securely establishes this construction.[26] It follows that whenever a vacancy may

---

(1850-1856). "The Senate cannot originate an appointment. Its constitutional action is confined to the simple affirmation or rejection of the President's nominations, and such nominations fail when it rejects them. The Senate may suggest conditions and limitations to the President, but it cannot vary those submitted by him, for no appointment can be made except on his nomination, agreed to without qualification or alteration" (3 *Opinions of the Attorney General* 188-92 [1837]). The opinion cites two unsuccessful attempts by the Senate, one in the J. Q. Adams administration, one in Jackson's, to reshape a nomination to a military grade to the advantage of the nominee.

24. Note 20.

25. U.S. Code, Tit. 4, sec. 6; Marbury v. Madison, 1 Cranch 137 (1803).

26. 1 *Opinions of the Attorney General* 631 (1823); 2 *id.* at 222 (1830); 3 *id.* at 673 (1841); 4 *id.* at 523 (1846); 10 *id.* at 356 (1862); 11 *id.* at 179 (1865); 12 *id.* at 32 (1866) and 455 (1868); 14 *id.* at 563 (1875); 15 *id.* at 207 (1877);

have occurred in the first instance, or for whatever reason, if it still continues after the Senate has ceased to sit and hence cannot be consulted, the President may fill it in the way described. But a Senate "recess" does not include holiday or temporary adjournments,[27] while by an act of Congress, if the vacancy existed when the Senate was in session, the ad interim appointee may receive no salary until he has been confirmed by the Senate.[28] Also there is an informal understanding, although it is not always observed, that the President will not extend a recess appointment to a rejected nominee.[29]

To be distinguished from the power to make recess appointments is the power of the President to make temporary assignments of officials to the duties of other absent or incapacitated officials. Usually a situation of this nature is provided for in advance by a statute which

---

16 *id.* at 523 (1880); 18 *id.* at 28 (1884); 19 *id.* at 261 (1889); 26 *id.* at 234 (1907); 30 *id.* at 314 (1914); 33 *id.* at 20 (1921).

In 4 *id.* at 361, 363 (1845), the general doctrine was held not to apply to a yet unfilled office which was created during the previous session of Congress, but this distinction is rejected in 12 *id.* at 455 (1868); 18 *id.* at 28; and 19 *id.* at 261.

In view of a recent controversy it is interesting to note, on the authority of Mr. Krock, that there have been no fewer than twelve recess appointments to the Supreme Court, and that only one of the appointees, John Rutledge, whom Washington appointed as Chief Justice in 1795, was later rejected by the Senate (*New York Times,* July 29, 1937).

27. 23 *Opinions of the Attorney General* 599 (1901); 22 *id.* at 20 (1898).

28. U.S. Code, Tit. 5, sec. 56.

29. The following extracts from a Washington press dispatch of December 18, 1914, tell how President Wilson once violated the understanding:

"The Bloom case is unprecedented so far as Senators can recall. John H. Bloom was nominated for postmaster. Five hundred citizens of Devils Lake protested. The charges against Bloom were serious and involved his personal character. The Senate Committee rejected it in August.

"The President then sent to the Senate the nomination of Mrs. Marjorie Bloom, wife of the man whose nomination had been rejected. This nomination was in turn rejected. The President then conferred a recess nomination on Mrs. Bloom as soon as Congress adjourned and she took the office under a commission. Today her name was again sent to the Senate.

"It is probable that when the Senate comes to deal with the case at Devils Lake it may go even further than a formal rejection and refer the nomination of Mrs. Bloom back to the President with a direction to the Secretary of the Senate to call his attention to the fact that the nomination was rejected by the Senate in October and citing the Constitution of the United States, which provides that such nominations shall be made 'by and with the advice and consent of the Senate.'"

What the final denouement of this episode was, I have not discovered.

designates the inferior officer who is to act in place of his immediate superior, but in the lack of such provision, theory and practice alike concede the President the power to make a designation.[30]

II

Unlike the British monarch, the President is under no constitutional necessity of acting through agents in order that his official acts may be judicially noticeable. On the contrary, there are many acts which to be done constitutionally must presumably have been done by him personally or in the exercise of his personal judgment. In the words of an opinion rendered by Attorney General Cushing in 1855:

30. 6 *Opinions of the Attorney General* 358 (1854); 12 *id.* at 41 (1866); 25 *id.* at 259 (1904); 28 *id.* at 95 (1909). Probably the most extreme case on record of the assignment of a person — and one apparently without official status at the time — to the duties of an absent official, occurred in Jefferson's second term. Henry Adams tells the story in his *History* as follows:

"When Congress met, Dec. 2, 1805, Breckinridge was attorney-general under a temporary commission, and Robert Smith who had ceased to be Secretary of the Navy on the confirmation of his successor, March 3, was acting as secretary under no apparent authority. Dec. 20, 1805, the President sent a message to the Senate making nominations for vacancies which had occurred during the recess, for which commissions had been granted 'to the persons herein respectively named.' One of these persons was John Breckinridge of Kentucky to be Attorney-General of the United States, and the nomination was duly confirmed. Breckinridge's permanent commission bore {the} date Jan. 17, 1806.

"These dates and facts are curious for the reason that Robert Smith, who had ceased to be Secretary of the Navy, March 3, 1805, ceased necessarily to be attorney-general on the confirmation of Breckinridge, and continued to act as Secretary of the Navy without authority of law. The President did not send his name to the Senate, or issue to him a new commission either permanent or temporary. On the official records of the Department of State, not Robert Smith, but Jacob Crowninshield, was Secretary of the Navy from March 3, 1805, till March 7, 1809, when his successor was appointed, although Jacob Crowninshield died April 15, 1808, and Robert Smith never ceased to act as Secretary of the Navy from his appointment in 1801 to his appointment as Secretary of State in 1809. During the whole period of Jefferson's second administration, his Secretary of the Navy acted by no known authority except the verbal request or permission of the President" (3 *History of the United States* 11-12 [1893]).

For legislation governing this matter today, see U.S. Code, Tit. 5, secs. 4-8.

Washington dispatches bearing the date of December 24, 1938, carry the statement that President Roosevelt has selected Colonel F. C. Harrington to succeed Mr. Harry L. Hopkins as WPA Administrator, but that Harrington's name will not be sent to the Senate, since he will remain on the army payroll and will be designated "acting Administrator." So far I have failed to find any basis in statute or precedent for this assignment of a military officer to a civilian post. The idea obviously has possibilities.

It may be presumed that he, the *man* discharging the Presidential office, *and he alone,* grants reprieves and pardons for offenses against the United States.

And again:

No act of Congress, no act even of the President himself, can, by constitutional possibility authorize or create any military officer not subordinate to the President.[31]

May this type of obligation be enlarged by statute? Dealing with this question in a case before the Civil War, which grew out of a statutory provision expressly prohibiting the advancing of public money to the disbursing officers of the government except under "the special direction of the President," the Court, said:

The President's duty in general requires his superintendence of the administration; yet this duty cannot require of him to become the administrative officer to every department and bureau, or to perform in person the numerous details incident to services which, nevertheless, he is, in a correct sense, by the Constitution and laws required and expected to perform. This cannot be, 1st, Because, if it were practicable, it would be to absorb the duties and responsibilities of the various departments of the government in the personal action of one chief executive officer. It cannot be, for the stronger reason, that it is impracticable — nay, impossible.[32]

31. 7 *Opinions of the Attorney General* 453, 464-65 (1855).
32. Williams v. United States, 1 How. 290, 297 (1843). By the act of August 10, 1846 (9 Stat. 102), as amended, the President, Vice-President, the Chief Justice, and the heads of the executive departments are constituted the Smithsonian Institution, over whose meetings "the President, and in his absence the Vice-President, shall preside." U.S. Code, Tit. 20, secs. 41, 45. This is doubtless a personal duty, but not a very arduous one. Also by 2 Stat. 78, expenditures from the secret service fund had to be vouched for by the President personally, but this provision has dropped out of the statute book.
The *New York Times* of March 12, 1923, contained the following item:
"A little less than two years ago Judson C. Welliver, executive clerk at the White House, stepped across the corridor which separates his office from that of President Harding to place some papers on the President's desk. To his surprise, for it was but a few minutes after 8 o'clock in the morning, he found the President already seated and busily signing papers from a two-foot stack.
"'Good morning, Mr. President,' Mr. Welliver said. 'I didn't know you had come to the office.'
"'Yes, I came in just now,' the President replied. 'I had a lot of papers to sign, and thought I might as well get them out of the way.'
"'Anything important?'

It is true that the Court once held that a certain decree of a court-martial was void because, although it had been confirmed by the Secretary of War, it was not specifically stated to have received the sanction of the President as required by the 65th Article of War;[33] but later decisions call this holding into question.[34] Such legislation is at any rate very exceptional. The general rule as stated by the Court is that when any duty is cast by law upon the President, it may be exercised by him "through the head of the appropriate department," whose acts, if performed within the law, become the President's acts. In fact, as a matter of administrative practice, most orders and instructions emanating from the heads of the departments even when in pursuance of powers conferred by statute on the President do not refer to him.[35]

"'Yes and no,' said the President. 'I am beginning to find out something about being President and the amount of time it demands. You can hardly imagine what I am doing now. This stack of papers is just so much routine. They are the wills of Indians. The President has to countersign the will of every Indian with whom the Government has dealings. If the will is not so countersigned, it is null and void. And so I expect to put in the next hour or so countersigning these wills.'

"'But can't someone else sign them for you?' Mr. Welliver inquired.

"'No; not under the law. There are only two — possibly three — persons in the United States authorized to sign the President's name. They are employees of the General Land Office and they sign the President's name, under certain safeguards and precautions, to the patents granted by that office. But there is no one else who may do so.'

"'I am beginning to find out,' Mr. Harding went on, 'that this job of being President is one that makes almost inordinate demands upon a man's time.'"

I can find no justification in the U.S. Code for the statement that the President is required to sign the wills of Indians; that seems to be the duty of the Secretary of the Interior (Tit. 25, sec. 373). The statement, however, that the President's name is affixed to land patents by authorized clerks of the General Land Office is correct (Tit. 43, secs. 8, 9).

33. Runkle v. United States, 122 U.S. (1887). By the theory of the case the President was in this instance exercising a judicial, and hence non-delegable function; from which it followed that his approval of the decree "must be authenticated in a way to show" that it was "the result of his own judgment."

34. *In re* Chapman, 166 U.S. 661 (1897), and other cases there cited as establishing that "the presumptions in favor of official action . . . preclude collateral attack on the sentences of courts-martial." Confirmation by the President of sentences of courts-martial is still required in several instances (U.S. Code, Tit. 10, sec. 1519). How this may be shown, however, still remains a question, in view of the Chapman case.

35. Wilcox v. Jackson, 13 Pet. 498 (1839); United States v. Eliason, 16 Pet. 291 (1842); Williams v. United States, 1 How. 290 (1843); Confiscation Cases, 20 Wall. 92 (1874); Wolsey v. Chapman, 101 U.S. 755 (1879); etc.; 7 *Opinions of the Attorney General* 479 (1855).

But suppose that the law casts a duty upon a subordinate executive agency *eo nomine,* does the President thereupon become entitled, by virtue of his "executive power" or of his duty to "take care that the laws be faithfully executed," to substitute his own judgment for that of the agency regarding the discharge of such duty? An unqualified answer to this question would invite startling results. An affirmative answer would make all questions of law enforcement questions of discretion, and that the discretion of an independent and legally uncontrollable branch of the government. By the same token, it would render it impossible for Congress, notwithstanding its broad powers under the "necessary and proper" clause, to leave anything to the specially trained judgment of a subordinate executive official with any assurance that his discretion would not be perverted to political ends for the advantage of the administration in power. On the other hand, a flatly negative answer would hold out consequences equally unwelcome. It would, as Attorney General Cushing quaintly phrased it, leave it open to Congress so to divide and transfer "the executive power" by statute as to change the government "into a parliamentary despotism like that of Venezuela or Great Britain, with a *nominal* executive chief or president, who, however, would remain without a shred of actual power."[36] Or, in different words, it would leave it open to Congress to destroy unity of administration in the national government, as it has long since been destroyed in the state governments.

Probably the earliest discussion of this highly important issue is the argument which was made by Madison in the first Congress in behalf of attributing the removal power to the President. It was "the intention of the Constitution," Madison contended, expressed especially in the "faithfully executed" clause, that the first magistrate should be responsible for the executive departments, and this responsibility, he urged, carried with it the power to "inspect and *control*" the conduct of all subordinate executive officers.[37]

Yet, when in the same year it organized the first executive departments, Congress itself adopted a radically different principle. The acts creating the Departments of State and of War specifically recognized the responsibility of the heads of those departments to the President;

36. 7 *Opinions of the Attorney General* 470.
37. 5 *Writings of James Madison* 392; also 398, 401, 402, etc., where he insists upon the *unity* of the Executive Department; although in other passages (*id.* at 362, 364, 399-400), he seems to regard the power of removal as primarily a power to get rid of malfeasant subordinates.

not so with the act organizing the Department of the Treasury. "The Secretary of the Treasury," this act read, and indeed still reads,

shall from time to time . . . make report and give information to either branch of the legislature in person or in writing, as may be required, respecting all matters referred to him by the Senate or House of Representatives, or which shall appertain to his office; and generally shall perform all services relative to finances as he shall be directed to perform[38] —

directed, that is, by Congress. Nor is the reason underlying this difference far to seek. The State and War departments are principally, although not exclusively, organs of the President in the exercise of functions which are assigned him *by the Constitution,* while the Treasury Department is primarily an instrument for carrying into effect Congress' constitutional powers in the field of finance. For like reasons, when in 1794, the Post Office Department was established, it was not placed under the control of the President, nor was the Interior Department when it was formed in 1849; but the Navy Department, established in 1798, was so placed.[39]

And meantime, in Marbury v. Madison, Chief Justice Marshall had suggested a parallel distinction between the duties of the Secretary of State under the original act which had created a "Department of Foreign Affairs," and those which had been added by the later act changing the designation of the department to its present one. The former were, he pointed out, entirely in the "political field," and hence for their discharge the secretary was left responsible absolutely to the President. The latter, on the other hand, were exclusively of statutory origin and sprang from the powers of Congress. For these, therefore, the secretary was "an officer of the law" and "amenable to the law for his conduct."[40]

Nor is the doctrine which was advanced by Attorney General Wirt in 1823 of very different import when it is confined to the field of Congress' delegated powers, which is evidently what Wirt was thinking of. It is that the President's duty under the "faithfully executed" clause requires of him scarcely more than that he should bring a *criminally*

---

38. Act of September 2, 1789, c. 12, sec. 2; U.S. Code, Tit. 5, sec. 242.
39. Cf. U.S. Code, Tit. 5, secs. 156, 190, 361, 412, 481, 485.
40. 1 Cranch 137, 165–66 (1803).

negligent official to book for his derelictions, either by removing him or by setting in motion against him the processes of impeachment or of criminal prosecution,[41] an opinion which voiced the point of view of the "Virginia School" of Presidents, including the later Madison. And the obvious fact is that the President's power to direct his subordinates in the field of Congress' powers can be magnified only at the expense of Congress' own discretion in the exercise of these powers. The doctrine that Congress is unable to vest any subordinate executive agency even within the field of its own specifically delegated powers with any legal discretion which the President is not entitled to appropriate to himself, is, of course, the very hallmark of the Jacksonian conception of the Presidency. The groundwork for it, however, was prepared much earlier, first, by "the decision of 1789," which is treated in the following section, and secondly, by the rise of the President's Cabinet.

Like its British namesake, the American Cabinet is entirely extraconstitutional.[42] The President, the Constitution states, "may require the opinion, in writing, of the principal officer in each of the executive departments, upon any subject relating to the duties of their respective

41. 1 *Opinions of the Attorney General* 624 (1828). Wirt continued: "To interpret this [the "faithfully executed"] clause so as to throw upon the President the duty of personal interference in every specific case of an alleged or defective execution of the laws, and to call upon him to perform such duties himself, would not only be to require him to perform an impossibility himself, but to take upon himself the responsibility of all the subordinate executive officers of the government – a construction too absurd to be seriously contended for." See also 4 *id.* at 515 (1846); 5 *id.* at 287 (1851) and 630 (1852); 11 *id.* at 109 (1864); etc. "The President has, under the Constitution and laws, certain duties to perform, among these being to take care that the laws be faithfully executed; that is, that the other executive and administrative officers of the government faithfully perform their duties; but the statutes regulate and prescribe these duties, and he has no more power to add to, or subtract from, the duties imposed upon subordinate executive and administrative officers by the law, than those officers have to add to or subtract from his duties" (19 *id.* at 686 [1890]).

42. See generally Hinsdale, *A History of the President's Cabinet* (1911); also the same writer's "Again the Cabinet," in 14 *Papers of the Michigan Academy of Science, Arts and Letters* 515-23 (1930). Learned's *The President's Cabinet* (1912) is primarily a legislative history of the executive departments, rather than an account of the development of the Cabinet relationship.

For first-hand Cabinet interiors see the *Memoirs of John Quincy Adams* (1874–1877); *Diary of James K. Polk During His Presidency* (1910); *Diary of Gideon Welles* (1911); and other similar works listed by Binkley in his *Powers of the President* 311-24 (1937).

offices."[43] The consultative relationship thus suggested is an entirely one-sided affair, is to be conducted in writing, with the "principal officers" separately and individually, and is to relate only "to the duties of their respective offices." If an executive council was needed, it was the general idea in 1789 that the Senate would serve the purpose.

"Assembled consultation" of the Cabinet, as Miss Hinsdale points out in her excellent book, first became general practice during the diplomatic crisis of 1793. Two years later, as a result of the fight over the Jay Treaty and the equivocal attitude of Secretary of State Randolph on that occasion, Washington, who had thought at first to maintain recognized spokesmen of the leading political factions of the country in the departmental headships, reconstructed his Cabinet on the avowed basis of loyalty to his own policies, and in so doing created a precedent which, with negligible exceptions, has guided Presidents in their choice of departmental heads ever since. And meantime, by the "decision of 1789," the President had been endowed with an unqualified power of removal over the heads of the executive departments.

So from the first, the heads of these departments occupied, when exercising powers delegated them by statute, a dual role and were subject to a dual responsibility. The inevitable clash between these two roles came in 1833 as an incident of Jackson's "War on the Bank." Convincing himself by a characteristic process of self-hypnosis that the {national} bank was an unsafe depository for the national funds, Jackson ordered secretary of the Treasury Duane to transfer them, which Duane had power under the law to do. As it happened, however, the House of Representatives had recently expressed its confidence in the bank by formal resolution, and Duane's own instructed judgment was to the same effect. He accordingly refused to comply with Jackson's demand, was promptly removed, and his successor Taney at once gave the desired order.[44]

Although in commenting on this episode writers are apt to treat it as the outcome solely of the President's possession of the removal pow-

43. Art. I, sec. 2, par. 1. An "exclusive" construction of this language such as was applied in Marbury v. Madison to the opening clause of Art. III, sec. 2, par. 1, defining the Supreme Court's original jurisdiction, would render the Cabinet "unconstitutional."

44. For a reliable although rather caustic narrative of the episode, see Sumner's *Andrew Jackson* (American Statesman Series, Vol. 17), 339 ff. (1899).

er,[45] this was far from Jackson's own theory of the matter. The latter, as stated in his protest message to Congress, was "that the entire executive power is vested in the President"; that the power to remove "those officers who are to aid him in the execution of the laws" is an incident of that power; that the Secretary of the Treasury is such an officer; that "the custody of the public property and money is an executive function" exercised through the Secretary of the Treasury and his subordinates; that "in the performance of these duties he [the Secretary] is subject to the supervision and control of the President"; and finally that the act establishing the bank "did not and could not change the relation between the President and Secretary — did not release the former from his obligation to see the law faithfully executed nor the latter from the President's supervision and control."[46]

In short, *the Constitution knows only one "executive power," that of the President, whose duty to "take care that the laws be faithfully executed" thus becomes the equivalent of the duty and power to execute them himself.* The removal of Duane was, therefore, the constitutionally ordained result of that officer's attempt to usurp the President's constitutional prerogative; or, in broader terms, the President's removal power, in this case unqualified, was *the sanction provided by the Constitution for his power and duty to control all his subordinates in all their official actions of public consequence.*

Five years later the case of Kendall v. United States[47] arose. The United States owed one Stokes money, and when Postmaster General Kendall, at Jackson's instigation, refused to pay it, Congress passed a special act ordering payment. Kendall, however, still proving non-

45. Wyman, Willoughby, Fairlie, Finley, and Sanderson, all seem to take this general position. Wyman's language is as follows: "This account of this event is worth a hundred cases from the law reports. The President, it appears, has the power in all matters whatsoever to enforce any officer whatsoever to do any act which the officer has the power to do. He can dictate in all matters because of his power of instant dismissal, without giving reasons therefor, and thereupon the right to immediate appointment without limitation therein. . . . Might makes Right. *Whatever the superior commands will be done by the inferior.* Because of this sanction, an administration which is centralized in its organization will always prove to be centralized in action" (Wyman, *Principles of the Administrative Law Governing the Relations of Public Officers* 233 [1903]).

46. 3 Richardson, *Messages of the Presidents* 79-80. The date of the message was April 15, 1834.

47. 12 Pet. 524 (1838).

compliant, Stokes sought and obtained a mandamus in the United States Circuit Court for the District of Columbia, and on appeal this decision was affirmed by the Supreme Court.

While Kendall v. United States, like Marbury v. Madison, involved the question of the responsibility of a head of department for the performance of a *ministerial* duty, the discussion by counsel before the Court and the Court's own opinion covered the entire subject of the relation of the President to his subordinates in the performance by them of statutory duties. The lower court had asserted that the duty of the President under the "faithfully executed" clause gave him "no other control over the officer than to see that he acts honestly, with proper motives," but "no power to construe the law and see that the executive action conforms to it."[48] Counsel for Kendall attacked this position vigorously, relying largely upon statements by Hamilton, Marshall, Wilson, and Story having to do with the President's power in the field of foreign relations.[49]

48. *Id.* at 539-40.

49. The following extract from the argument for the United States is worth quoting:

"The argument of the postmaster general, and of the attorney general, assumes that the post office department is an essential part of the executive department of the government; and from this position infers the want of the jurisdiction claimed. The assumption has been shown to be inaccurate; but even if true, it is not easy to perceive the connection between the premises and the conclusion.

"We are referred to the debates in the convention, to show the anxiety of that body to preserve separate and distinct the three great departments. I will, in return, refer to the 47th and to the succeeding numbers of the Federalist, for a correct exposition of this maxim of political philosophy, and its practical adoption in our constitution.

"Starting from this basis, the constitution is appealed to; and by the aid of some interpolation and some extravagant interpretation, we are told substantially, if not in terms:

"1. That the clause in the constitution which provides that the executive power shall be vested in the President, actually confers upon him all that power which, in any age of the world and under any form of government, has been vested in the chief executive functionary; whether king or czar, emperor or dictator.

"2. That the clause which imposes upon the executive the duty of seeing that the laws are faithfully executed, contains another large grant of power.

"3. That, as a means to the performance of this duty, he is invested with the power of appointment to and removal from office.

"4. That the power of appointment and removal carried with it the power to direct, instruct, and control every officer over whom it may be exercised, as to the manner in which he shall perform the duties of his office.

"My observations upon these points shall be few and brief:

"The first proposition was, perhaps, for the first time distinctly advanced by

The Court rejected the latter argument with emphasis. "There are," it pointed out,

certain political duties imposed upon many officers in the executive departments, the discharge of which is under the direction of the President. But it would be an alarming doctrine that Congress cannot impose upon any executive officer any duty they may think proper, which is not repugnant to any rights secured and protected by the Constitution; and in such cases, the duty and responsibility grow out of and are subject to the control of the law, and not to the direction of the President.[50]

General Hamilton, in his Letters of Pacificus, No. 1, p. 535. A great and revered authority, but subject to occasional error. It was fully answered by Mr. Madison in the Letters of Helvidius, p. 594, etc., and has since remained dormant. The second is now for the first time broadly asserted. Its dangerous tendencies – its hostility to every principle of our institutions, cannot be exaggerated. The true signification of this part of the constitution, I take to be simply this, that the President is authorized to employ those powers which are expressly entrusted to him to execute those laws which he is empowered to administer; or, in the language of the late Chief Justice, he is at liberty to employ any means which the constitution and laws place under his control. 2 Brockenb. 101.

"The third proposition is a palpable and unwarrantable interpolation of the constitution. The fourth, if the power claimed is derived from the power of appointment, would make the judges dependent upon executive dictation; if from that power and that of removal, conjointly, would make it the true theory of the English constitution, that the king might instruct, direct, and control the lord chancellor in the performance of his judicial duties. It would make him the keeper of the chancellor's conscience.

"The right to command, direct and control, involves the correlative duty of obedience. No officer can be criminally or civilly punished for obedience to the lawful command of a superior, which he is bound to obey. This doctrine, then, asserts the entire irresponsibility of all officers, except to this one superior.

"One of the practical inferences from these premises is, that the judiciary department cannot execute its own judgments; a proposition distinctly avowed by the postmaster general in his return, p. 127-8-9, and asserted, in terms equally distinct, by the attorney general, in p. 152" (*Id.* at 571-72).

  50. *Id.* at 610. Further along the Court adds:

"It is urged at the bar, that the postmaster general was alone subject to the direction and control of the President, with respect to the execution of the duty imposed upon him by this law; and this right of the President is claimed, as growing out of the obligation imposed upon him by the constitution, to take care that the laws be faithfully executed. This is a doctrine that cannot receive the sanction of this court. It would be vesting in the President a dispensing power, which has no countenance for its support in any part of the constitution; and is asserting a principle, which, if carried out in its results, to all cases falling within it, would be clothing the President with a power entirely to control the legislation of Congress, and paralyze the administration of justice.

"To contend that the obligation imposed on the President to see the laws faith-

In short, the Court recognized that the underlying question of the case was whether the President's "executive power," coupled with his duty to "take care that the laws be faithfully executed," made it constitutionally impossible for Congress ever to entrust the construction of its statutes to anybody but the President; and it answered this question with an emphatic "no."

How then does this exceedingly important issue stand today? It will aid clarity to distinguish at the outset two types of executive duty. As to the first, or "ministerial" type, the Court has held repeatedly that even a head of department may be compelled by mandamus to perform such a duty.[51] That is to say, not only is a head of department legally entitled to perform such a duty in defiance of the President, but he may be forced by judicial process to do so, and that notwithstanding the fact that he may be immediately removed by the President for compliance with the court's order.

All other executive duties, or powers — for the two terms are interchangeable in this connection — are "discretionary," in that the officer to whom they are entrusted is left a greater or less latitude of judgment respecting the occasion for their exercise, or the manner of it, or both. If such duties, or powers, have their origin in the constitutional prerogatives of the President, then the subordinate to whom they are entrusted is, of course, his mere instrument; and the same is true if they have been delegated by Congress to the President in the first instance.[52] But suppose they have been delegated by Congress, in the exercise of its own constitutional powers, to a subordinate executive officer or agency — then what power may the President constitutionally claim over their discharge? This, in precise terms, is the crucial question.

Again we encounter a dichotomy, inasmuch as discretionary powers may be of a "quasi-judicial" nature or otherwise, depending on whether or not they impinge upon private interests which are entitled to a hearing and other features of "due process of law" before the powers in

---

fully executed, implied a power to forbid their execution, is a novel construction of the constitution, and entirely inadmissible" (*Id.* at 612-13).

Although Stokes got his mandamus, it seems to have netted him little, and his later attempt to recover damages from Kendall was thrown out of Court on the ground that he had already exhausted his right to a remedy (Kendall v. Stokes et al., 3 How. 87 [1845]).

51. Notes 40 and 47; also United States v. Schurz, 102 U.S. 378 (1880); United States v. Black, 128 U.S. 40 (1888); etc.

52. Notes 35 and 40.

question can be exercised. With regard to the former category, Presidents have been more than once informed by their own Attorneys General that they may not substitute themselves for the officer named by the statute, nor entertain appeals from such an officer, nor revise his findings; that in such situations their sole duty is to see that the proper officer acts *with proper diligence.*[53] Indeed it is with just such decisions in mind that Chief Justice Taft remarked in the Myers case that "there may be duties of a quasi-judicial character . . . the discharge of which the President cannot in a particular case properly influence or control."[54] Yet he straightway added that "even in such a case" the President might remove the responsible officer for rendering a decision not to his liking, a paradox of which, as we shall see in a moment, the Court has subsequently tried to disburden itself, although with what degree of success is still a question.

Today, to be sure, the more important discretionary powers of a quasi-judicial character have been entrusted to administrative tribunals like the Interstate Commerce Commission, the Federal Trade Commission, the SEC, and so on, which are not connected with any department. But this is not always the case, for the same kind of duty may be and sometimes is entrusted to officials who are technically the subordinates of a head of a department, or even to heads of departments themselves. Thus the Commissioner of Patents is subordinate of the Secretary of the Interior, while the Secretaries of Agriculture and Commerce and the Attorney General constitute a commission for the enforcement of the Grain Futures Act of 1922, and so on.

Likewise, discretionary powers of a non-judicial type may be delegated to a head of department or subordinate thereof; or to an executive agency outside any department — TVA furnishing, as to most of its powers, an excellent example of the latter category. And it is this category which today furnishes the "no-man's land" between the Jeffersonian and the Jacksonian conception of presidential power and duty in the execution of the law. To state the issue in as concrete terms as possible — is the President entitled, as the law now stands, to con-

---

53. Most of the opinions of Attorneys General cited in Note 41 are to the point. The independence of subordinates in the discharge of quasi-judicial duties cast upon them by statute from a superior's direction is well illustrated in the case of the Commissioner of Patents. See Butterworth v. Hoe, 112 U.S. 50 (1884), and United States v. Duell, 172 U.S. 376 (1899).

54. 272 U.S. 52, 135 (1926).

strue the powers of the TVA for it, or is TVA entitled to construe the law of its creation for itself, subject of course to judicial review? I confess myself to be a Jeffersonian so far as this issue is concerned, and so take the position that the only power which the President can validly claim over TVA is the power — or rather duty — to see that TVA acts honestly and dilligently. Were, however, TVA to be drawn into one of the great executive departments the answer to the above question would have to be framed, so it seems to me, along Jacksonian lines. For when Congress plants an executive agency within the domain of a member of the President's Cabinet, it must be deemed to have done so with its eyes open to the relationship which has developed between the President and his Cabinet — a relationship of unqualified domination on the one hand and of complete subordination on the other.

And it is from this angle that President Roosevelt's plan to reorganize the executive branch of the government should be in part evaluated, although not altogether. Within recent years many "independent agencies" have been set up by Congress outside the precincts of any of the great executive departments, and what the President now proposes is that they shall be brought within one of these departments or that their powers shall be transferred to some bureau or agency which is already there. Thus, if the reasoning of the foregoing paragraphs is correct, the discretionary powers of such agencies, when not of a quasi-judicial nature, would become *properly* subject through the heads of departments to ulimate direction and control by the President; and even those of a quasi-judicial nature would actually become so in time, on account of the inability of judicial power to cope effectively with the President's powers of appointment and removal.

Of course, the advocates of the President's plan strongly urge the claims of administrative *unity* and *efficiency.* But are the two things necessarily synonymous in the case of so vast an organization as the national government? It seems to me clearly not; but rather that efficient administration must in such a case always depend to an important extent upon the expert knowledge and pride in his job of the largely independent bureaucrat. In other words, administration in the sense of the daily task of carrying out the laws and performing the public services for which they provide is a *pluralistic,* not a *monistic* universe; and to imagine the President as a sort of boss of the works under whose all-seeing eye everything takes place, is merely to imagine something that does not exist and never will. To be sure, such considerations do not dispose entirely of the argument for the President's plan; and no one would care to deny that administrative set-up must be constantly tinkered to keep it at all efficient.[55]

We now turn to the President's removal power and the effort of the Court in recent years to equate this power with his supervisory powers; in other words, to stamp upon it the character of a sanctioning power in relation to these, and conversely to confine it to that scope.

III

Save for the provision which it makes for a power of impeachment of "civil officers of the United States,"[56] the Constitution contains no reference to a power to remove from office, a situation in which early resort to the judicial divining rod would seem on first consideration to have been highly likely and necessary. Actually, until its decision in Myers v. United States,[57] October 25, 1926, the Supreme Court had contrived to side-step every occasion for a decisive pronouncement regarding the removal power, its extent and location.

How explain this strange hesitancy on the Court's power to advance the cause of judicial review? Two reasons may be suggested. The first is the strong course taken by the first Congress under the Constitution in undertaking to settle the removal issue by legislation. Throughout the ensuing 140 years the initiative thus asserted, at first in favor of the power of the President and later against it, was respected by the Court.

But in the second place, it may be surmised, the Court has always been uneasily aware of its inability to intervene effectively in this field. So long as Congress chooses to permit it to do so, the Court is free to decree that an official who has been ousted contrary to its view of the constitutional proprieties shall be paid his salary, but it has no power to

---

55. See further Dawson, *The Principle of Official Independence* (1922). It is true that the bureaucrat should not determine policies further than he has been commissioned to do so by the legislature − that is, Congress; but in this respect the President himself, when engaged in seeing to the execution of the laws, is a bureaucrat. Policy comes from the legislative power, and it is in his ability to guide the latter that the President exercises most of his influence upon domestic policy.

56. Art. II, sec. 4.

57. 272 U.S. 52.

reinstate such an official, and ordinarily no power to invalidate his successor's official acts. Curiously enough, in the two principal cases which are reviewed below — the first being the Myers case — the ousted official died while his suit for salary was pending, and so the inadequacy of the Court's remedial powers was conveniently obscured.

The point immediately at issue in the Myers case was the effectiveness of an order of the Postmaster General, acting by direction of the President, to remove from office a first-class postmaster, in view of the following provision of an act of Congress passed in 1876:

> Postmasters of the first, second and third classes shall be appointed and may be removed by the President with the advice and consent of the Senate, and shall hold their offices for four years unless sooner removed or suspended according to law.[58]

A divided Court, speaking through Chief Justice Taft, held the order of removal valid, and the statutory provision just quoted void. Standing by itself this disallowance does not necessarily imply more than that so long as Congress chooses to leave the appointment of an inferior officer with the President, acting with the advice and consent of the Senate, it may not make the officer's removal dependent also on such consent. With this comparatively narrow holding, however, the Court was not content, and in the Chief Justice's elaborate opinion the sweeping doctrine was advanced that the President is endowed by Article II with a power of removal which, so far as "executive officers of the United States appointed by him" are concerned, is not susceptible constitutionally of any restraint or limitation by Congress, and that all such officers are intended by the Constitution to be left removable at the President's will.[59]

The Chief Justice's main reliance was upon "the decision of 1789," previously alluded to. The incident may be described briefly.[60] On June 16 of that year the first House of Representatives under the Constitution went into committee of the whole to consider a bill proposed by Madison for establishing a Department of Foreign Affairs, the opening clause of which provided that the principal officer of the

---

58. 19 Stat. 80, 91. To this day the Postmaster General and the Assistant Postmaster Generals are appointed and removable "by and with the advice and consent of the Senate" (U.S. Code, Tit. 5, secs. 361, 363).

59. Much that I say below is taken from my *President's Removal Power Under the Constitution* (1927).

60. 1 *Annals of Congress* 368 ff., or 383 ff., according to the printing used.

new department was "to be removable from office by the President of the United States." In the debate which ensued three fairly equal parties disclosed themselves: first, those who, headed by Madison, argued that the power of removal was an inherent element both of "executive power" and of the duty to "take care that the laws be faithfully executed"; secondly, those who, headed by Sherman — also a former member of the Philadelphia Convention — contended that the power of removal was conferred as an incident of the power of appointment jointly on the President and Senate; and thirdly, those who held that the Constitution had left it with Congress, by virtue of the "necessary and proper" clause, to locate the power of removal where it thought fit. A fourth party, comprising only three or four members, urged that unless removed for misbehavior in office by the power of impeachment, or by judicial process known to the common law, an officer had a vested right in his office for the term of his appointment as fixed by law.

The mode in which the theoretical issue thus raised was disposed of is somewhat confusing. The objection having been raised to the clause "to be removable by the President" that it represented an attempt by Congress to confer power on the President which was not otherwise provided for in the Constitution, the clause was stricken out, and in its place were inserted the words "whenever the said principal officer shall be removed from office by the President of the United States," which were thought to infer that the President already had the power of removal, in certain cases at least, without grant from Congress. Subsequently the Senate ratified the action of the House by the casting vote of Vice-President Adams, and like action was later taken with regard to the Secretary of the Treasury and the Secretary of War.

Was the "decision of 1789" capable of sustaining the sweeping conclusions of the Chief Justice's opinion? The answer is, no. While the decision undoubtedly avoids the direct implication that the President owed the power of removal to a grant by Congress, yet this result was obtained by the indispensable support of those who throughout the debate had championed the doctrine that Congress could determine the question of the scope and location of the removal power in any way it saw fit. What is more, the question related, as was repeatedly emphasized in the debate by the champions of presidential power, to a high political office, one which was to be the instrument of the President in the principal field of executive prerogative and whose tenure was, for this very reason, being left *indeterminate.* While, therefore, the decision may be fairly considered as ascribing to the President alone the power to remove executive officers appointed with the consent of the Senate whom Congress chooses to leave removable *by not fixing their terms,* it certainly did not establish the proposition of the Myers case that Congress is without power to *fix the terms* of any executive officers whatever as against the President's power of removal.

Nor does the record of opinion respecting the power of removal under the Constitution, prior at least to the Civil War, generally support the results arrived at in the Myers case. In *The Federalist* Hamilton had stated explicitly that the Senate would be associated with the President in the removal of officers, although he seems later to have retracted this opinion.[61] Neither Marshall, Kent, Story, nor Webster regarded the decision of 1789 as reaching offices of determinate tenure; and all but Marshall were quite clearly of opinion that the correct reading of the Constitution located the power of removal in both the President and Senate in the case of officers appointed with the Senate's consent, although they were willing to concede the binding effect of the decision of 1789 as "a practical construction of the Constitution" till Congress should choose to reverse it.[62] And that the Supreme Court of the period shared these views is indicated by its opinion in *Ex parte* Hennen in 1839.[63]

61. *The Federalist* No. 77 at 497 (Earle ed.). "In the Federalist, he [Hamilton] had so explained the removal from office as to deny the power to the President. In an edition of the work at New York, there was a marginal note to the passage that 'Mr. Hamilton had changed his view of the Constitution on that point'" ("Madison to Rives, Jan. 10, 1829," 4 *Letters and Other Writings of James Madison* 5 [1865]).

62. My *Removal Power of the President* 26-31. Webster's position, as set forth in his answer to Jackson's protest message, was as follows:

"The regulation of the tenure of office is a common exercise of legislative authority, and the power of congress in this particular is not at all restrained or limited by anything in the constitution, except in regard to judicial officers. All the rest is left to the ordinary discretion of the legislature. Congress may give to offices which it creates (except those of judges) what duration it pleases. When the office is created and is to be filled, the President is to nominate the candidate to fill it; but when he comes into the office, he comes into it upon the conditions and restrictions which the law may have attached to it."

"If Congress," he continued, "were to declare by law that the Attorney General, or the Secretary of State should hold office during good behavior," its action might be unwise, but it would not be unconstitutional (7 *Writings and Speeches of Daniel Webster* 196-99 [National ed. 1903].

63. 13 Pet. 225, 230 (two cases). The argument of counsel on both sides affords

The literary source of the Chief Justice's opinion is clearly Jackson's famous Message of Protest of April 15, 1834, which was dealt with in the previous section.[64] There all the essential elements of the Chief Justice's doctrine were assembled for the first time, and, it may be added, for the *last* time until the Myers case was decided. Other partial sources are certain opinions of Attorneys General although the real preponderance of opinion from this source by no means supports the sweeping propositions advanced by the Chief Justice. Still another source is the debate stirred by the Tenure of Office Act of 1867, while a fourth source is to be discovered in the arguments developed by President Johnson's counsel at the time of his impeachment trial. Yet even these gentlemen, it is worth noting, generally contented themselves with asserting that Johnson, assuming that he had violated the Tenure of Office Act, had acted in good faith, not that he had beyond peradventure acted constitutionally.[65]

But apart from the verdict of past opinion, the Chief Justice also urged the theory that the power of removal was inherently "executive" on its own merits. His contention was based on the two grounds of

---

an exposition of the common law theory of office. Jones, who appeared against Hennen's application for a mandamus, set forth the theory adopted by the Court, as follows:

"The right to remove is an incident to the power of appointment. It is essential to the exercise of the power to appoint; and the power which is given by the law cannot exist without this incident.

"If the common law has any bearing on this question, it is very remote. The Constitution of the United States, and the laws made in conformity with the provisions of the Constitution, are essentially different from the common law, as to appointments to offices, and as to the tenure by which they are held. 2 Blackstone Commentaries 36, 37. The law of the tenure of office in England is regulated, not by any principles of ethics, or express provision, but by immemorial usage. Office is there an incorporeal hereditament, as a right of way. There is, under the common law, an estate in an office.

But in the United States this is not so. There is in this country no estate in any office. No property in an office. Offices are held for the benefit of the community in which their functions are exercised. As to the tenure and nature of office in England: cited Coke Litt. 378a, 4 Institute 117; Coke Litt. 233b, 2 Institute 388.

"The position in England is, that unless the statute which creates the office limits its tenure, at the time of the creation; it is an office for life, as at the common law. But here no such principles prevail. The common law does not apply to offices, which are all created by the Constitution, or by express statute" (13 Pet. 253-54).

64. Pages above.

65. My *Removal Power of the President* 36-41.

history and of necessity; and in assertion of the former he instanced the power of "the British Crown" in the appointment and removal of officers. The argument proves too much. The power of the British Crown in the appointment and removal of officers, as we saw earlier, is an historical outgrowth of and is still intimately involved with a much wider prerogative in the creation of offices, while the only offices normally known to the Constitution of the United States are those "which shall be established by law."[66]

The ultimate basis, however, of the decision in the Myers case is to be sought far less in constitutional history and legal theory than in certain practical considerations which naturally loomed large in the mind of a Chief Justice who had once been President himself. That this is so is clearly indicated in the following salient passage of the opinion:

> There is nothing in the Constitution which permits a distinction between the removal of the head of a department or a bureau, when he discharges a political duty of the President or exercises his discretion, and the removal of executive officers engaged in the discharge of their other normal duties. The imperative reasons requiring an unrestricted power to remove the most important of his subordinates in their most important duties must, therefore, control the interpretation of the Constitution as to all appointed by him.[67]

That the President ought to be able to remove at will all subordinates whose discretion he is entitled by the Constitution or by the laws of Congress to control, and for whose conduct he is hence responsible, must be granted, as we have seen. But the Chief Justice's conclusion that this fact "must control interpretation of the Constitution as to all appointed by him" was much too drastic and resulted in the paradox that, while the Constitution permitted Congress to vest duties in executive officers in the performance of which they were to exercise their own independent judgment, it at the same time permitted the President to guillotine such officers for exercising the very discretion which Congress had the right to require!

Nor was the menace of this paradox a merely theoretical one. For as was pointed out above, recent decades have witnessed the establishment of a number of "administrative tribunals" outside and independent of any department. The Interstate Commerce Commission was thus established in 1887, the Federal Trade Commission in 1914, the Federal

66. Pages above.
67. 272 U.S. 134.

Tariff Commission in 1916, the Federal Power Commission in 1920, the Federal Communications Commission (succeeding the Federal Radio Commission) in 1934, and the Securities and Exchange Commission, also in 1934. The members of all these bodies are appointed by the President and Senate *for fixed terms,* while the members of the first three are removable by the President for "inefficiency, neglect of duty or malfeasance in office" — a provision which is not repeated as to the last three, possibly because of the influence of the Myers case. Meantime, however, in the act of 1920 creating the Railroad Labor Board, Congress had taken a further step. In an endeavor to confer upon the members of this body a quasi-judicial status, it provided that they should be removable by the President "for neglect of duty or malfeasance in office, but for no other cause"; and a similar tenure was bestowed upon the members of the Board of General Appraisers and the Board of Tax Appeals by the acts of 1922 and 1924 respectively.[68]

Nor should the enactment in 1921 of the Budget and Accounting Act, whereby Congress inaugurated an almost revolutionary reform in methods of national financial legislation, be overlooked in this connection. The act pivots upon the office of Comptroller General of the United States, and the success of the reform unquestionably hinges upon the independence of this or some similar functionary from executive pressure. The act accordingly provides that the Comptroller General shall hold office for fifteen years, and save upon impeachment shall be removable only by joint resolution of Congress and then only after a hearing which shall establish to Congress' satisfaction his incapacity, inefficiency, neglect of duty or malfeasance, or "conduct involving moral turpitude."[69]

There can be little doubt that all these measures, so far as they purported to restrict the President's power of removal, were, by the Chief Justice's opinion in the Myers case constitutionally ineffective, and that the Court would have been compelled sooner or later, had it adhered to that opinion, either to set aside the restrictive provisions or to have interpreted them away. In point of fact, it has since recanted a good deal of the Taft opinion, though just how much may be a question. I refer to its decision in 1935 in Humphrey v. United States.[70]

68. All these provisions can be easily traced through the index to the U.S. Code.
69. U.S. Code, Tit. 31, sec. 43.
70. 295 U.S. 602 (also styled Rathbun v. U.S.).

The material facts of this case were as follows: Humphrey, a member of the Federal Trade Commission, was reappointed to his post by President Hoover, by and with the advice and consent of the Senate, on December 10, 1931, for a term of seven years. On July 25, 1933, and again on August 31, President Roosevelt wrote the commissioner requesting his resignation on the ground that the two entertained divergent views of public policy, but at the same time disclaiming any reflection on Mr. Humphrey personally or on his official conduct. Said the President:

You will, I know, realize that I do not feel that your mind and my mind go along together on either the policies or the administering of the Federal Trade Commission, and, frankly, I think it is best for the people of this country that I should have a full confidence.

Humphrey having declined to resign, the President on October 7 notified him that he was from that date "removed" from office; and in due course Humphrey brought suit for salary.[71]

71. These facts are given at the outset of Justice Sutherland's opinion for the Court. See also *New York Times,* October 8, 1933. The Federal Trade Commission at once recognized "the validity of said Executive order removing Mr. Humphrey"; and declined "to further recognize" him as a member of the Commission (*Id.,* October 10, 1933). Also, in due course, Comptroller General McCarl ruled that Humphrey was no longer entitled to the salary of the post from which he had been ousted (*Id.,* November 12, 1933). Both actions were doubtless based upon the decision in the Myers case.

Subsequently the case gave rise to a discussion in the Senate from which the following colloquy is extracted:

"MR. CLARK. We have referred several times today to the famous Humphrey case. I am one of those who are rather familiar with the record of the late Commissioner Humphrey. I do not think there is any question on earth that if the President of the United States had seen fit to comply with the law in the matter of removing Mr. Humphrey he would have been able to furnish adequate and complete grounds for removing him. Mr. Humphrey had given out interviews which had been published in the public press.

"MR. WHEELER. And I was delighted when the President removed him.

"MR. CLARK. He sent out interviews which would undoubtedly have been held by any court of competent jurisdiction in this country as a ground for his removal. But the President of the United States did not see fit to follow what I would have regarded as the proper course. Instead of giving Mr. Humphrey a hearing, as required by law, and removing him for cause, he saw fit simply to remove him on the basis of a letter in which he stated that Mr. Humphrey's mind did not run along with his.

"This instance shows the danger which generally exists, although it did not exist in this particular case, because it so happened that the law was not complied with; but it is a danger that we might encounter were another President to come into office, no matter how upright he might be, or how fixed his mind as to his right to remove or not to remove individuals. As far as I am concerned,

The principal basis of the Court's unamimous decision sustaining Humphrey's claim that he was wrongfully removed from office is indicated in the following paragraphs of Justice Sutherland's opinion. Distinguishing the Myers case, the Justice says:

A postmaster is an executive officer restricted to the performance of executive functions. He is charged with no duty at all related to either the legislative or judicial power. The actual decision in the Myers Case finds support in the theory that such an office is merely one of the units in the executive department and hence inherently subject to the exclusive and illimitable power of removal by the chief executive, whose subordinate and aid he is. . . .

The Federal Trade Commission is an administrative body created by Congress to carry into effect legislative policies embodied in the statute. . . . Its duties are performed without executive leave and in the contemplation of the statute must be free from executive control. . . .
We think it plain under the Constitution that illimitable power of removal is not possessed by the President in respect of officers of the character of those just named [the Interstate Commerce Commission, the Federal Trade Commission, the Court of Claims]. The authority of Congress, in creating quasi-legislative or quasi-judicial agencies, to require them to act in discharge of their duties independently of executive control, cannot well be doubted; and that authority includes, as an appropriate incident, power to fix the period during which they shall continue, and to forbid their removal except for cause in the meantime. For it is quite evident that one who holds his office only during the pleasure of another cannot be depended upon to maintain an attitude of independence against the latter's will.[72]

Elsewhere in his opinion Justice Sutherland takes pains to point out

along with the Senator from Montana I was glad to see Mr. Humphrey removed, but I thought it should have been accomplished in line with the law rather than in the manner in which it was brought about."
What makes the above data interesting is the possibility which is foreshadowed in the concluding paragraph of Justice Sutherland's opinion:
"To the extent that, between the decision in the Myers case, which sustains the unrestrictable power of the President to remove purely executive officers, and our present decision that such power does not extend to an office such as that here involved, there shall remain a field of doubt, we leave such cases as may fall within it for future consideration and determination as they may arise."
Suppose such a doubtful case to arise, what attitude would the Trade Commission, or other similar body, and the Comptroller General be apt to take? Or suppose the Senate to have joined in a removal contrary to statute, would the Court itself interpose? Theoretically it ought to; but it would unquestionably be very astute to obviate such a situation. Cf. Blake v. U.S., 103 U.S. 227 (1880), and Wallace v. U.S., 257 U.S. 541 (1922).
72. 295 U.S. 627-29.

that "the decision of 1789" concerned an office which "was not only purely executive" but an officer "who was responsible to the President and to him alone, in a very definite sense."[73]

That this holding, considered in the light of this opinion, goes a long way toward scrapping the Myers case seems to me fairly clear. Not only does the opinion entirely ignore Chief Justice Taft's invocation of the opening clause of Article II, but it employs the "executive power" throughout in the narrow sense of non-discretionary powers. All other powers which grow out of and succeed to legislation by Congress within the field of its delegated powers are comprised, when they do not fall to the regular courts, under the captions of "quasi-legislative" and "quasi-judicial." It seems to follow that the President's unrestricted power of removal can reach only two classes of officials: (1) those whose statutory powers are ministerial merely; (2) those who exercise the President's own powers, whether of statutory or constitutional origin.[74]

At the same time, it should not be too hastily inferred that the President is entirely without a certain minimum power of removal of broader range, in which connection President Roosevelt's recent removal of Dr. A. E. Morgan from the chairmanship of TVA is of considerable interest. Dr. Morgan had made certain statements about his fellow

73. *Id.* at 631.

74. But this interpretation of the decision still leaves doubtful the constitutionality of the act of August 24, 1912, c. 389, 36, 37 Stat. 555, which provides that "no person in the classified civil service of the United States shall be removed therefrom except for such cause as will promote the efficiency of said service and for reason given in writing, and the person whose removal is sought shall have notice of the same and of any charges preferred against him, and be furnished with a copy of the same, and also be allowed a reasonable time for personally answering the same in writing; and affidavits in support thereof; but no examination of witnesses nor any trial or hearing shall be required except in the discretion of the officer making the removal. . ." (U.S. Code, Tit. 5, sec. 652).

Even if this be considered as restrictive of the President's removal power, it seems to me to be entirely constitutional so far as it protects officers with merely ministerial duties vested in them by statute. The distinction in the Humphrey case between such an officer and those protected by that decision is not altogether logical. For there is no reason why Congress should not have power to protect against *arbitrary* removal even the humblest agents of its delegated powers, a conclusion to which Shurtleff v. United States, 189 U.S. 311, lends aid and comfort. On the other hand, once Congress designates any officer or agency of the government as an instrument of the President's constitutional or statutory powers, it thereby automatically renders such officer or agency, whatever may be its other powers or duties, removable by the President at will.

directors which amounted to charges of gross malfeasance on their part, but when the President demanded that he produce evidence in support of these statements, Dr. Morgan refused to do so, and his dismissal thereupon followed.

The act of Congress creating the TVA contains two provisions regarding removal.[75] The first says that "any member of said board may be removed from office at any time by a concurrent resolution of the Senate and House of Representatives"; the other reads that "any member of said board who is found by the President of the United States to be guilty of a violation of this section [forbidding the application of political tests in the selection or promotion of the corporation's employees and officials] shall be removed from office by the President of the United States." The question raised by Dr. Morgan's dismissal is whether the latter provision should be given an exclusive construction. The answer is both yes and no. Inasmuch as it was the obvious intention of Congress that the board of directors of the TVA should be an independent body, the President has no right to construe their legal duties for them, and hence no right to remove them for a refusal on their part to permit him to do so. But the President was not attempting to construe Dr. Morgan's legal duties for him. He was merely requiring his cooperation in attempting to clear up a charge which had called into question the honesty of the other directors and which had virtually brought the activities of the board to a standstill. To deny the President the power of removal in such a case would be to make it impossible for him to discharge his duty to "take care that the laws be faithfully executed" under the most modest interpretation of that duty.[76]

The provision of the TVA Act which purports to make the directors removable by a concurrent majority of the houses raises a rather different question. Nothing but a vote which the President has approved, or which has been passed over his veto, is recognized by the Constitution as capable of effecting a legal change. How then can a concurrent resolution remove from office one who has been appointed

75. U.S. Code, Tit. 16, secs. 831^c, c and e.
76. Or put the matter this way: if Dr. Morgan's charges were *untrue* he deserved to be removed for false and libellous statements damaging to *esprit de corps;* while if they were *true,* his associates deserved removal, and he with them for hampering inquiry into their misconduct (83 Cong. Rec. 3896 [March 23, 1938]).

thereto by constitutional authority? Plainly, only on the theory that liability to removal in that way is one of the characteristics of the office as it was created by Congress. The question, despite its novelty, is not an entirely one-sided one. To deny Congress the power thus to qualify the tenure of an agent would be to force it to choose between relying solely on presidential control or leaving the agent uncontrolled. When private rights are not at stake the more flexible conception of constitutional arrangements is usually the more desirable one.[77]

And this brings us back to the case of the Comptroller General, which seems to be a somewhat special one. Whether Congress may constitutionally restrict the President's removal power in his case depends on

77. President Wilson, on June 4, 1920, vetoed the first Budget Bill, on account of the provision in it which made the Comptroller General and Assistant Comptroller General removable by a concurrent resolution of the houses. He said:

"I am convinced that the Congress is without Constitutional powers to limit the appointing power and its incident power of removal derived from the Constitution.

"The section referred to not only forbids the Executive to remove these officers, but undertakes to empower the Congress by a concurrent resolution to remove an officer appointed by the President with the advice and consent of the Senate.

"I can find in the Constitution no warrant for the exercise of this power by the Congress. There is certainly no expressed authority conferred and I am unable to see that authority for the exercise of this power is implied in any expressed grant of power. On the contrary, I think its exercise is clearly negatived by Section 2 of Article II.

"That section, after providing that certain enumerated officers and all officers whose appointment are not otherwise provided for shall be appointed by the President with the advice and consent of the Senate provides that Congress may, by law, vest the appointment of such inferior officers as they think proper in the President alone, in the course of law, or in the heads of departments. It would have been within the constitutional power of the Congress, in creating these offices, to have vested the power of appointment in the President without the advice and consent of the Senate, or even in the head of a department. Regarding as I do the power of removal from office as an incident to the appointment power, I cannot escape the conclusion that the vesting of this power of removal in the Congress is unconstitutional and therefore I am unable to approve the bill."

So far as this argument depends upon the theory of an illimitable power of removal, it is of course invalidated by the Humphrey decision. For another illustration, besides that afforded by the TVA act of legislation endowing the houses with power to act by concurrent resolution, see the act of June 16, 1933, c. 101, sec. 1 (48 Stat. 291), whereby it is stipulated that "after June 16, 1933, no new investigations shall be initiated by the [Federal Trade] Commission as the result of a legislative resolution, except the same be by a concurrent resolution of the two Houses of Congress" (U.S. Code, Tit. 15, sec. 46[a]). Prior to this, investigations were initiated on the request of either house.

whether his power is to be deemed an extension of the legislative power over appropriations or of the executive power over expenditure. That the Constitution recognizes expenditure to be an executive function seems evident; and this too is the verdict of history (early appropriation acts were in the most general terms). But of course expenditure is conditional upon appropriation, and so the Comptroller's office may be regarded — and on historical grounds also — as a descendant of the British Comptroller and Auditor, "who holds his office during good behavior, with a salary paid by statute out of the Consolidated Fund and who considers himself in no sense a servant of the Treasury but an officer responsible to the House of Commons."[78] That Congress could protect the tenure of an Auditor General who would be vested merely with the function of post-audit, as is proposed in President Roosevelt's Reorganization Plan, seems even clearer, inasmuch as his powers would not commence until expenditure was past.[79]

78. 1 Lowell, *The Government of England* 289 (1908). For an excellent discussion of certain aspects of the Comptroller General's powers under present legislation, see Mansfield, "Administrative Finality and Federal Expenditures," 47 *Yale Law Journal* 603–21 (1938).

79. President Coolidge attempted at least once, although unsuccessfully, to evade statutory restraints upon his removal power by demanding a blank resignation beforehand from the person whom he contemplated appointing. The story is told in the following memorandum of a conversation between the President and Hon. Wm. F. Culbertson, Vice Chairman of the Tariff Commission at the time, and a letter from Culbertson to the late Senator Costigan of Colorado:

"Contemporary memorandum of the interview with the President, Sept. 8, 1924:

"Shortly after I reached my office this morning, about 9:30, I received a request over the telephone to come to the White House to see the President. I went over immediately. The President was reasonably cordial. He began by saying that the subject of the interview was Mr. David J. Lewis's reappointment. Mr. Lewis's term as a member of the Tariff Commission expired yesterday. The President stated that he intended to reappoint Mr. Lewis, but that he desired that Mr. Lewis prepare and give to him a letter of resignation as a member of the Tariff Commission. At first I did not fully comprehend the nature of this request.

"I spoke of Mr. Lewis's term having already expired. Then the President explained that he wanted Mr. Lewis to submit his resignation under the new commission, to be effective in case he (the President) desired at any time in the future to accept it.

"The President at this point called in Mr. Forster, one of his secretaries, and instructed him to make out Mr. Lewis's commission of reappointment as a member of the Tariff Commission, effective today.

"The President then handed me a sheet of White House paper so that I could take down the tenor of the letter which he wished Mr. Lewis to write. I wrote

To sum up: the Constitution refers specifically to only one kind of removal from office, that by the impeachment process. It early became accepted doctrine, however, that in the absence of constitutional or

---

down the following words: 'I hereby resign as a member of the Tariff Commission, to take effect upon your acceptance.'

"I raised the objection at this point that an unqualified resignation of this kind would imply on the record that Mr. Lewis did not desire to continue as a member of the Tariff Commission.

"The President replied that this was a matter for Mr. Lewis to decide. In explanation of his request, the President said he desired to be free after the election concerning the position filled by Mr. Lewis. He said that if he were not {re-} elected, the Democrats might undertake to hold up other appointments which he made during the next session of the Senate, and he implied that he desired to use the appointment of Mr. Lewis for trading purposes in case of necessity.

"I thereupon asked the President whether I could have his assurance that if he were re-elected Mr. Lewis could be continued as a member of the Tariff Commission. He said that he could not at this time make any commitments.

"We then talked of other matters, and at the end the President asked me to have Mr. Lewis see him during the afternoon, when he said he would give him his commission."

The letter, which bore the date of September 9, 1924, read as follows:

"My Dear Costigan: You will perhaps have seen today in the press that Mr. Lewis was reappointed yesterday. I reached Washington Sunday evening and had not been in office very long Sunday morning before I was sent for by the President. The result of my interview is covered by a memorandum, a copy of which I enclose.

"When I returned to the office I took the President's suggestions up with Lewis, and later he reached the decision that he would not write the letter of resignation requested by the President. He, however, went to see the President during the afternoon and I presume he will write you the details of what took place. In general this is what happened.

"He (Lewis) went into the President's office and the President had before him the commission. He took up his pen and signed it in Lewis's presence. He then turned to Lewis and asked him whether he had 'that letter.' Lewis then explained that he did not feel free to furnish the President with the letter which he requested. Lewis said that the President was visibly disturbed and said with a little heat that it did not make any difference any way, that the position would be held only at the pleasure of the President.

"Lewis then said to the President that only the two of them knew that the commission was signed, and he suggested that the President was at liberty to destroy the commission. The President, however, did not respond to this suggestion, and Lewis left the President's office with his commission. A little later he was sworn in.

"Thus ends another curious chapter in the Tariff Commission's history. It indicates clearly, I think, that there is a line beyond which the President will not go in opposing the principle for which the three of us have stood in the development of the Tariff Commission.

"We miss your counsels very much, but I suggest that you stay in the Colorado

statutory provision to the contrary, all appointive officials are subject to removal by the appropriate authority, that there is "no estate in office." Previous to the Myers case the weight of opinion treated the removal power as an element of the power of appointment and on that ground attributed to the Senate a participation in the removal of officers appointed with its consent. At the same time, by the "decision of 1789" the first Congress planted "a practical construction" upon the Constitution which ascribed the power to the President alone so far as "executive" officers were concerned; and by the decision in the Myers case this "practical construction" was converted temporarily into a rule of constitutional law which severely restricted Congress' power in the creation of offices to determine their tenure. But the pronouncement in the Myers case was from any point of view much too sweeping, and it has since been largely replaced by the doctrine of the Humphrey case, that Congress is entitled in creating an administrative agency which it intends to vest with discretionary powers to qualify or restrict the removability of such agency. Conversely, the general principle which governs the President's power of removal is fairly clear too. *It is a function of his supervisory powers,* and where these are unlimited it also is unlimited. But in addition the President enjoys as do all non-judicial officers a minimum supervisory power and hence a minimum removal power which arises from his duty to "take care that the laws be faithfully executed," which is to say, that their legally designated enforcers act *diligently and honestly;* yet even in this case Congress is probably entitled to prescribe a fair procedure for the determination of such questions.

In short, to a very great extent, the President's removal power is constitutionally subject to control by Congress. Actually it is very, very broad, partly because Congress has not chosen to fetter it; partly because, on the other hand, it has chosen so frequently to delegate the discretionary powers which its legislation has called into existence to

---

climate until you are certain that your return here will not bring with it a return of your hay fever.

"Very cordially yours, Culbertson.

"Hon. Edward P. Costigan,

"Palmer Lake, Col."

New York Times, January 17, 1926. See also 68 Cong. Rec. 1952, 2187-89 (January 13 and 16, 1926). Of course, a really successful enterprise of this sort, in evasion of the laws, would not be apt to leak out.

the President himself. Furthermore, most of the heads of the great executive departments have at least some powers which have been delegated to them by the President. They, therefore, continue subject to the President's uncontrolled removal power, even though no account be taken of that course of history which, in Chief Justice Taft's words in the Myers case, renders them the President's "alter ego's."[80]

80. Myers v. United States, 272 U.S. 52.

8. The War and the Constitution: President and Congress

The chief lesson of the war to date for constitutional interpretation is that the Constitution is an easily dispensable factor of our war effort — perhaps one might say an "expendable" factor. That the Constitution is not needed as a source of national power for war purposes has been stated by the Court itself. Speaking in 1936 for himself and brethren in United States v. Curtiss-Wright Export Corporation, Justice Sutherland said: "The investment of the Federal government with the powers of external sovereignty did not depend upon the affirmative grants of the Constitution. The powers to declare and *wage war* [my italics], to conclude peace, to make treaties, to maintain diplomatic relations with other sovereignties, if they had never been mentioned in the Constitution, would have been vested in the Federal government as necessary concomitants of nationality" (299 U.S. 304, 318).

From this it follows that silence of the Constitution is not a denial but an affirmance of power in the national government to adopt any measures that seem best calculated to bring a foreign war to a successful conclusion. Even so, it may be contended that the Constitution is still of some importance in distributing the power which the above doctrine attributes to "the Federal government" as a whole. The suggestion is certainly a tenable one logically, but is hardly borne out by certain recent developments, of which the President's Labor Day address to

From 37 *American Political Science Review* 18–25 (February, 1943). Reprinted by permission.

Congress is an outstanding instance. Demanding on that occasion that Congress should repeal a provision of the Emergency Price Control Act of February 2, 1942, which prohibited ceilings on food products until farm prices had gone, on the average, sixteen percent beyond "parity prices," Mr. Roosevelt said:

> I ask the Congress to take this action by the first of October. Inaction on your part by that date will leave me with an inescapable responsibility to the people of this country to see to it that the war effort is no longer imperiled by threat of economic chaos.
> In the event that the Congress should fail to act, and act adequately, I shall accept the responsibility, and I will act.
> At the same time that farm prices are stabilized, wages can and will be stabilized also. This I will do.
> The President has the power, under the Constitution and under Congressional acts, to take measures necessary to avert a disaster which would interfere with the winning of the war.
> I have given the most thoughtful consideration to meeting this issue without further reference to the Congress. I have determined, however, on this vital matter to consult with the Congress. . . .
> The American people can be sure that I will use my powers with a full sense of my responsibility to the Constitution and to my country. The American people can also be sure that I shall not hesitate to use every power vested in me to accomplish the defeat of our enemies in any part of the world where our own safety demands such defeat.
> When the war is won, the powers under which I act automatically revert to the people — to whom they belong.

I interpret these words as saying to Congress, in effect, "unless you repeal a certain statutory provision forthwith, I shall nevertheless treat it as repealed." On what grounds does Mr. Roosevelt rest his case for power in these premises? He makes a vague gesture toward "Congressional acts," and it is true that he and certain of his advisers have from time to time achieved some rather striking results in the name of statutory "interpretation" — the $25,000 limit on salaries, which purports to be based on the Anti-Inflation Act of October 2, being a notable example. Nevertheless, I opine, Mr. Roosevelt's principal reliance is on his "powers under . . . the Constitution." Now it is a fact that Presidents have before this on a few occasions announced that they did not consider themselves to be constitutionally obligated by something which Congress had enacted but which, they asserted, trenched on presidential prerogatives. But the position advanced by Mr. Roosevelt in the above quoted passage goes beyond this, for therein he claims the right and power to disregard a statutory provision which he does not deny, and indeed could not possibly deny, that Congress had full constitutional authority to enact, and which, therefore, he was under obligation by the Constitution to "take care" should be "faithfully executed." And yet to anyone who followed with care the controversy over the "fifty destroyer" deal, the course projected by the President in his Labor Day address can hardly appear surprising, inasmuch as he thrust aside on that occasion legislation which was undeniably enacted by Congress in the exercise of its constitutional powers.

Currently, moreover, the President has not hesitated either to add to or subtract from statutory provisions the enactment of which lay within the national legislative province beyond any possibility of challenge. One instance is afforded by his now famous order to Montgomery Ward and Company to accord CIO a maintenance of membership contract; and another is furnished by section 5 of his recent order on manpower, which declares that "no employer shall retain in his employ any worker whose services are more urgently needed in any establishment, plant, facility, occupation, or area designated as more esential by the chairman" of the War Manpower Commission. So far as I can discover, there is nothing in either of the War Powers acts, the Selective Service Act, or any other act, that remotely supports such a decree. And the vast proliferation of "defense agencies" embracing some forty "administrations," "agencies," "boards," "offices," "commissions," "committees," "authorities" — what have you? — have almost all (OPA is one exception) been summoned into existence by the magic wand of the President without reference to statutory authorization.

The President's main reliance, in fact, is upon his powers as "Commander-in-Chief of the Army and Navy" — or at times as "Commander-in-Chief in time of war." To the latter term it has been pertinently objected that the Constitution knows no such office. But whichever term is employed, the intention is generally the same, namely, to claim for the President the constitutional power and duty to take any steps which he may deem helpful in prosecuting the war, any act of Congress to the contrary notwithstanding. Indeed, in the final sentence of his Labor Day address, the President seems to invoke for his measures an even higher sanction than the Constitution. He there says: "When the war is won, the powers under which I act automatically revert to the people — to whom they belong." This seems to suggest that the President derives his war powers *directly* from the people, and not *via* the Constitution, a doctrine closely akin to the Leadership principle which our armed forces are combating today in the four quarters of the globe. The sentence was unfortunate.

So much for what may be called the *civil* aspect of the President's power as Commander-in-Chief as that power is interpreted by Mr. Roosevelt. Let us now turn to its *martial* aspect. In this connection, two presidential acts are of outstanding importance to date: the order of February 19 last, directed primarily to the danger of Japanese sabotage on the West Coast, and the order of July 2 creating a military commission for the trial of the eight saboteurs. The essential paragraphs of the former document read as follows:

> Whereas the successful prosecution of the war requires every possible protection against espionage and against sabotage to national-defense material, national-defense premises, and national-defense utilities. . . .
>
> Now, therefore, by virtue of the authority vested in me as President of the United States, and Commander-in-Chief of the Army and Navy, I hereby authorize and direct the Secretary of War, and the military commanders whom he may from time to time designate, whenever he or any designated commander deems such action necessary or desirable, to prescribe military areas in such places and of such extent as he or the appropriate military commander may determine, from which any or all persons may be excluded, and with respect to which, the right of any person to enter, remain in, or leave shall be subject to whatever restrictions the Secretary of War or the appropriate military commander may impose in his discretion.
>
> The Secretary of War is hereby authorized to provide for residents of any such area who are excluded therefrom, such transportation, food, shelter, and other accommodations as may be necessary, in the judgment of the Secretary of War or the said military commander, and until other arrangements are made, to accomplish the purpose of this order. . . .
>
> I hereby further authorize and direct all executive departments, independent establishments and other Federal agencies, to assist the Secretary of War or the said military commanders in carrying out this Executive order, including the furnishing of medical aid, hospitalization, food, clothing, transportation, use of land, shelter, and other supplies, equipment, utilities, facilities and services.

In pursuance of this order, about one hundred thousand Japanese residents of western states, the great majority of them native-born citizens of the United States, were in due course removed from their farms and homes and put in concentration camps, where many of them still are. In the entire history of the country, no comparable interference with the private security and private rights of citizens has been witnessed. How is it to be justified in terms of constitutional law?

By the tests imposed by the decisive opinion in the Milligan case, the President's order was totally unconstitutional, and even by the Chief Justice's concurring opinion for himself and three associates, it would have had to be authorized by Congress. Since the Milligan case, however, a new kind of martial law has been identified by the Court — "preventive" as against "punitive" — and in the leading case of Moyer v. Peabody {212 U.S. 78 (1909)} a situation roughly analogous to that which confronted the President was solved on the basis of this distinction. The facts, briefly, were these: Moyer, a labor leader, brought suit against Peabody, a former governor of Colorado, for ordering his imprisonment in the course of a strike which occurred during Peabody's incumbency. Speaking for the Court, Justice Holmes conceded that the state courts were open at the time; also, "as it must be, that the governor's declaration that a state of insurrection existed is conclusive on the Courts"; and, finally, "that the governor, *without sufficient reason but in good faith* [my italics], in the course of putting the insurrection down, held the plaintiff until he thought he could safely release him." In the face of these admissions, the Court held that Moyer had no action. Conforming, therefore, the President's order of February 19 to the pattern furnished by the Moyer case, that order may be regarded as representing the President's judgment that the war situation on the West Coast threatened imminent violence that would be disastrous to our war effort. And the good faith of such a judgment being conceded, as it undoubtedly must be, the question of its reasonableness becomes, on the basis of the Moyer precedent, irrelevant. In short, the order of February 19 represents a qualified and limited declaration of martial law.*

*Editor's Note: Corwin concludes here that the Japanese incarceration was "justified in terms of constitutional law." But in 1951, again discussing the Japanese incarceration, he noted that under the act of March 21, 1942, "a military commander operating under the protection of the act would not be answerable to the civil courts once the war was over for his orders during its continuance. Could there be more conclusive proof of the triumph in wartime of personal rule, in which as Aristotle says there is always 'an element of the bestial,' over the rule of law?" ("The Impact of War on the Constitution," lecture at Emory University, 1951, Corwin Papers, Princeton University Library).

The material facts in the case of the saboteurs {*Ex parte* Quirin, 317 U.S. 1 (1942)} are given sufficiently in the appended note.[1] The trial instituted under the President's order of July 2 began on July 8. While it was still going on, but after all the evidence was in, counsel for seven of the saboteurs petitioned both the Supreme Court and the United States District Court for the District of Columbia for leave to bring habeas corpus proceedings. Early in his opinion for the unanimous Court — Justice Murphy being absent — the Chief Justice makes it plain that the Court is not going to attempt to draw any line between the powers of Congress and those of the President in the premises of the case. "We are concerned only," he says, "with the question whether it is within the constitutional power of the national government to place petitioners upon trial before a military commission for the offenses with which they are charged." In arriving at an affirmative answer to this question, the opinion rebuts three principal contentions of the petitioners, the first of which was that "violation of the laws of war" — the first offense charged against the petitioners, and apparently the one which the Court regarded as best supported by the evidence — was not an offense known to the laws of the United States. The Chief Justice admits that Congress has never attempted to codify violations of the laws of war, but holds that the reference in the 15th Article of War to "offenses that . . . by the laws of war are triable by a military

1. Only seven saboteurs were parties to the case, Dasch being the exception. All except Haupt, an American citizen, were citizens of the Third Reich and hence enemy aliens. All of them following the outbreak of war between Germany and this country, being then in Germany, took a course of training in sabotage in a school near Berlin, their tutor being a member of the German High Command. Thereafter three of them, together with Dasch, boarded a German submarine at a French port and proceeded to Long Island; while the remaining four found their way in like fashion to the Florida coast. The courses pursued by the two groups on their arrival in this country were substantially identical. Coming ashore during hours of darkness on June 13 and June 17, respectively, they divested themselves of the German uniforms or parts of uniforms which they had been wearing and buried them, along with a quantity of explosives, fuses, and timing devices in the sand. One party then went to New York City, the other to Jacksonville, Florida, all members being in civilian dress. In the course of the ensuing fortnight, all were picked up, either in New York or Chicago, by the FBI; and on July 2 the President appointed a military commission to try them for offenses against the laws of war and the 81st and 82nd Articles of War, which trial began on July 8. I ought to add that I prepared this article before I was aware of Professor Cushman's excellent review of the same case in the December issue of this *Review*.

commission" is sufficient to meet the objection, particularly when it is read in connection with the Rules of Land Warfare promulgated by the War Department and with the Hague Convention of 1907 (ratified by the Senate in 1909) by which is recognized a class of "unlawful belligerents" not entitled to be treated as prisoners of war, among them being combatants not wearing fixed emblems. In short, petitioners' conduct fell within well-established legal categories which are addressed particularly to military tribunals.

Secondly, however, the petitioners urged that they were entitled by the Fifth and Sixth amendments to a civil trial, inasmuch as theirs was not a case "arising in the land or naval forces." The premise of this argument the Chief Justice concedes in effect. "We may assume, without deciding," he says, "that a trial prosecuted before a miliary commission created by military authority is not one 'arising in the land . . . forces,' when the accused is not a member of or associated with these forces." But that concession, he immediately proceeded to add, did not affect petitioners' position, since "no exception is necessary to exclude from the operation of these provisions [of the Fifth and Sixth amendments] cases never deemed to be within their terms"; and petitioners' cases were of that kind. Nor was Haupt, although a citizen of the United States, in any different situation in this respect from the other petitioners, for all alike were enemy belligerents who by entering the country with hostile intent and in civilian garb had violated the usages of war. Nor did Milligan's case aid Haupt's cause, inasmuch as Milligan was found by the Court to be a non-belligerent, "not being a part of or associated with the armed forces of the enemy."

Lastly, the petitioners pointed out that the presidential order under which the trial was conducted departed sharply in certain respects from the requirements of the Articles of War. Thus, whereas the 43rd Article of War provides that "no person shall, by general court martial [no mention here of military commission] be convicted of an offense for which the death penalty is made mandatory by law, nor sentenced to death, except by the concurrence of all members of said court martial present at the time the vote is taken," the President's order expressly declared that the concurrence of only two-thirds of the members of the Commission should be necessary for conviction or sentence; and other material departures by the order from Articles 38, 46, 50½, and 70 were noted by counsel. Dealing with this argument, the Chief Justice says:

We need not inquire whether Congress may restrict the power of the Commander-in-Chief to deal with enemy belligerents. For the Court is unanimous in its conclusion that the Articles in question could not at any stage of the proceedings afford any basis for issuing the writ. But a majority of the full Court are not agreed on the appropriate grounds for decision. Some members of the Court are of opinion that Congress did not intend the Articles of War to govern a Presidential military commission convened for the determination of questions relating to admitted enemy invaders and that the context of the Articles makes clear that they should not be construed to apply to that class of cases. Others are of the view that — even though this trial is subject to whatever provisions of the Articles of War Congress has in terms made applicable to "commissions" — the particular Articles in question, rightly construed, do not foreclose the procedure prescribed by the President or that shown to have been employed by the Commission, in a trial of offenses against the law of war and the 81st and 82nd Articles of War, by a military commission appointed by the President.

The main question which arises on the opinion as a whole is that of its necessity. In other words, was not the Court here performing a work of supererogation? The Chief Justice himself appears to have some such thought in mind when, in close proximity to the passage just quoted, he remarks: "Petitioners do not argue and we do not consider the question whether the President is compelled by the Articles of War to afford unlawful enemy belligerents a trial before subjecting them to disciplinary measures." And petitioners' reticence in this regard was, it seems to me, the better part of valor, although I do not think it should have precluded the Court from speaking on the point. These saboteurs were invaders, their penetration of the boundary of the country, projected from units of a hostile fleet, was essentially a military operation, their capture, followed by their surrender to the military arm of the government, was but a continuation of that operation. Punishment of the saboteurs was therefore within the President's power as Commander-in-Chief in the most elementary, the purely martial, sense of that power. Moreover, six of the petitioners were enemy aliens, and so, strictly speaking, without constitutional status. As to Haupt, the American citizen, the better course would possibly have been to try him in the civil courts as a traitor. It is certainly curious to compare the apparent hesitation of the President on this occasion to assert his indubitable authority as Commander-in-Chief with his lack of hesitation to appropriate the powers of Congress in his putative role of "Commander-in-Chief in wartime."

Also, in view of a certain recent development, a glance should be paid the theory, so often voiced by writers (including the present one) that in its control of the purse-strings Congress posseses its most effective check on presidential power. At best, the promise of this rule is seriously impaired by war, inasmuch as legislative prying into presidential budgets at such a time always involves the danger of revealing military secrets. But when the President lays before Congress a budget which calls for appropriations amounting in the total to the national income, Congress' difficulties are multiplied indefinitely; and that is the situation which confronts Congress at this moment.

In an address which he gave early in World War I, the Honorable Charles Evans Hughes said: "While we are at war we are not in revolution. We are making war as a Nation organized under the Constitution, from which the established national authorities derive all their powers either in war or in peace. The Constitution is as effective today [i.e., in the midst of war] as it ever was and the oath to support it is just as binding. . . ."

I doubt if as circumspect a gentleman as Mr. Hughes would venture such a statement on the basis of the events of this war to date. The crucial matter is, of course, the question of the right of the President to invade the field of Congress and to set aside congressional legislation on his own finding that our war effort will be aided by his doing so. That this question should have been raised is, however, by no means the fault of the President alone — Congress, too, is to blame. Moreover, until recently it is the President rather than Congress that has enjoyed the support of dominant public opinion in this matter, a warning which Congress needs to take to heart. Unless Congress can, by improving its organization and reforming some of its procedures, render itself a more consistently useful public agency, it seems likely to be gradually reduced to the level of a badly tarnished pageant, and little more. And in this connection it should not escape attention that the operative Constitution of World War I has become since then, under the New Deal, the everyday Constitution of the country. There is always a tendency, even in democracies, for the emergency device to become the normal.

IV. Truman and Presidential Prerogative

9. The Steel Seizure Case: A Judicial Brick Without Straw

President Truman's seizure of the steel industry without specific statutory warrant[1] brings to a new pitch a developing reliance on the "executive power" which began almost at the inception of the federal government. True, this development has not always proceeded at the same pace; while at times it has seemed to be arrested, during the last fifty years its maturation has been virtually uninterrupted. Moreover, the forces, interests, and events which have energized the development are today more potent than ever.

The opening clause of Article II of the Constitution reads: "The executive Power shall be vested in a President of the United States of America." The records of the Constitutional Convention make it clear that the purposes of this clause were simply to settle the question whether the executive branch should be plural or single and to give the executive a title.[2] Yet, in the very first Congress to assemble under the Constitution, the opening clause of Article II was invoked by James Madison and others in order to endow the President with power to remove officers whose appointments had been made with the advice and consent of the Senate. Madison's view prevailed,[3] and was finally ratified by the Supreme Court in 1926.[4] The same theory was invoked by Hamilton in support of President Washington's Proclamation of

From 53 *Columbia Law Review* 53–66 (June, 1953). Reprinted by permission.
1. Youngstown Sheet & Tube Co. v. Sawyer, 343 U.S. 579 (1952).
2. 2 Farrand, *The Records of the Federal Convention* 171, 185 (rev. ed. 1937).
3. Corwin, *The President: Office and Powers* 102–114, 428 (3d ed. 1948).
4. Myers v. United States, 272 U.S. 52 (1926).

Neutrality upon the outbreak of war between France and Great Britain.[5] This time the Court's acquiescence was not long delayed. Even in the act of asserting the power of the Court to pass upon the constitutionality of acts of Congress, Chief Justice Marshall said: "By the Constitution of the United States the President is invested with certain important political powers, in the exercise of which he is to use his own discretion, and is accountable only to his country in his political character, and to his own conscience."[6] Even Thomas Jefferson, cousin and congenital enemy of Marshall, had said of the executive power in an official opinion as Secretary of State in 1790: "The Executive [branch of the government], possessing the rights of self-government from nature, cannot be controlled in the exercise of them but by a law, passed in the forms of the Constitution."[7]

Throughout the last half century the theory of presidential power has recruited strength from a succession of "strong" Presidents, from an economic crisis, from our participation in two world wars and a "cold" war, and finally from organization of the labor movement. Moreover, the constitutional basis of the doctrine has shifted somewhat since the early nineteenth century. It no longer relies exclusively, or even chiefly, on the opening clause of Article II. To the terminology of political disputation in the Jacksonian period it is indebted for such concepts as "residual," "resultant," and "inherent" powers. Thanks to Lincoln, it is able to invoke the President's duty to "take care that the laws," i.e., all the laws, "be faithfully executed," and his power as Commander-in-Chief of the armed forces. Of more recent origin is the quite baffling formula of an "aggregate of powers vested in the President by the Constitution and the laws."[8]

The chief constitutional value which overextension of presidential power threatens is, of course, the concept of a "government of laws and not of men" — the "rule of law" principle. In 1882 Justice Samuel Miller gave classical expression to this principle in the following words: "No man . . . is so high that he is above the law. . . . All officers of the government . . . are creatures of the law, and are bound to obey it."[9]

5. Corwin, *President: Office and Powers* 217 *et seq.,* 465, 474-75.
6. Marbury v. Madison, 1 Cranch 137, 166 (1803).
7. 5 *Writings of Jefferson* 209 (Ford ed. 1895).
8. 40 *Opinions of the Attorney General* 312, 319 (1944).
9. United States v. Lee, 106 U.S. 196, 220 (1882).

Yet eight years later this same great judge queried whether the President's duty to "take care that the laws be faithfully executed is limited to the enforcement of the acts of Congress or treaties . . . [in] their *express terms,*" or whether it embraces also "the rights, duties and obligations growing out of the Constitution itself . . . and all the protection implied by the nature of the government under the Constitution?"[10] The answer assumed is evident.

In 1895 the Debs case,[11] a landmark in the judicial history of Article II, was decided. Here the Court held that the United States has at all times the right to enter its courts to ask for an injunction to protect "matters which by the Constitution are entrusted to the care of the nation." The "United States" here meant the President. The significance of the Court's choice of terminology is that it was not basing its holding on the duty of the President "to take care that the laws be faithfully executed," but on a broader principle – national interest.

The procession of "strong" Presidents was headed by Theodore Roosevelt, who asserts in his *Autobiography* that the principle which governed him in his exercise of the presidential office was that he had not only a right but a duty "to do anything that the needs of the Nation demanded unless such action was forbidden by the Constitution or by the laws."[12] Although in his book, *Our Chief Magistrate and His Powers,* ex-President Taft warmly protested against the notion that the President has any constitutional warrant to attempt the role of a "Universal Providence,"[13] yet, as Chief Justice, he later relied on the opening clause of Article II as a grant of power.[14] He also interpreted the Debs case as signifying that the national executive may seek an injunction in any case involving a widespread public interest.[15]

As for the influence of the labor movement and the resultant consolidation of labor's political strength in a few great organizations subject to a highly autocratic leadership, it is sufficient to mention that, between the anthracite strike of 1902 and the bituminous coal strike of 1946, Presidents intervened in a purely personal or political capacity

10. *In re* Neagle, 135 U.S. 1, 64 (1889).
11. *In re* Debs, 158 U.S. 564 (1895).
12. Roosevelt, *An Autobiography* 389 (1913).
13. Taft, *Our Chief Magistrate and His Powers* 144 (1916).
14. See Myers v. United States, 272 U.S. 52, 118 (1926).
15. See Taft, *The Presidency* 90 *et seq.* (1916).

in no fewer than twenty-six strikes.[16] Indeed, President Truman's course of action in dealing with the bituminous coal situation in 1946 may be regarded as having both foreshadowed his conduct in the steel strike of 1952[17] and influenced judicial attitudes in some measure in the Youngstown (Steel Seizure) case.[18]

The Facts of the Youngstown Case

To avert a nationwide strike of steel workers which he believed would jeopardize the national defense, President Truman, on April 8, 1952, issued Executive Order 10340[19] directing the Secretary of Commerce to seize and operate most of the country's steel mills. The order cited no specific statutory authorization, but invoked generally the powers vested in the President by the Constitution and laws of the United States. Secretary Sawyer forthwith issued an order seizing the mills and directing their presidents to operate them as managers for the United States in accordance with his regulations and directions. The President promptly reported these events to Congress,[20] conceding Congress' power to supersede his order; but Congress failed to take action either then or a fortnight later, when the President again raised the problem in a special letter.[21] Of course, in the Defense Production Act of 1950,[22] the Labor Management Relations (Taft-Hartley) Act of 1947,[23] and the Selective Service Act of 1948,[24] Congress had in fact provided other procedures for dealing with such situations; and in the elaboration of these statutory schemes it had repeatedly declined to authorize governmental seizures of property to settle labor disputes. The steel companies sued the Secretary in a federal district court, praying for a declaratory judgment and injunctive relief. The district judge issued a preliminary injunction, which the court of appeals stayed. On certiorari to the court of appeals, the Supreme Court affirmed the

16. Corwin, *President: Office and Powers* 453-54 (figures compiled by Professor Dishman of Dartmouth College).

17. Corwin, *A Constitution of Powers in a Secular State* 76 n.20 (1951). See also *id.* at 62 n.8a.

18. Youngstown Sheet & Tube Co. v. Sawyer, 343 U.S. 579 (1952).

19. 17 Fed. Reg. 3139 (1952).

20. 98 Cong. Rec. 3962 (April 9, 1952).

21. 98 Cong. Rec. 4192 (April 21, 1952).

22. 64 Stat. 798 (1950), as amended, 50 U.S.C. App. sec. 2071 (Supp. 1952).

23. 61 Stat. 136 (1947), as amended, 29 U.S.C. secs. 141–97 (Supp. 1952).

24. 62 Stat. 604 (1948), 50 U.S.C. App. secs. 451–62 (Supp. 1952).

district court's order by a vote of six to three. Justice Black delivered the opinion of the Court in which Justices Frankfurter, Douglas, Jackson, and Burton concurred; Justice Clark expressly limited his concurrence to the judgment of the Court. All these Justices presented what are termed "concurring" opinions. The Chief Justice, speaking for himself and Justices Reed and Minton, dissented.

The Doctrine of the Opinion of the Court

The chief point urged in Justice Black's opinion is that there was no statute which expressly or impliedly authorized the President to take possession of the steel mills. On the contrary, in its consideration of the Taft-Hartley Act in 1947, Congress refused to authorize governmental seizures of property as a method of preventing work stoppages and settling labor disputes. Authority to issue such an order in the circumstances of the case was not deducible from the aggregate of the executive powers under Article II of the Constitution; nor was the order maintainable as an exercise of the President's powers as Commander-in-Chief of the armed forces. The power sought to be exercised was the lawmaking power. Even if it were true that other Presidents have taken possession of private business enterprises without congressional authority in order to settle labor disputes, Congress was not thereby divested of its exclusive constitutional authority to make the laws necessary and proper to carry out all powers vested by the Constitution "in the Government of the United States, or in any Department or Officer thereof."[25]

The pivotal proposition of the opinion is, in brief, that inasmuch as Congress could have ordered the seizure of the steel mills, there was a total absence of power in the President to do so without prior congressional authorization. To support this thesis no proof in the way of past opinion, practice, or adjudication is offered. Justice Black's attitude toward this matter of authority is, in fact, decidedly cavalier. The closing paragraph of his opinion reads:

The Founders of this Nation entrusted the lawmaking power to the Congress alone in both good and bad times. It would do no good to recall the historical events, the fears of power and the hopes for free-

---

25. U.S. Constitution, Art. I, sec. 8. See Youngstown Sheet & Tube Co. v. Sawyer, 343 U.S. 579, 660–61 (1952).

dom that lay behind their choice. Such a review would but confirm our holding that this seizure order cannot stand.[26]

The somewhat different truth of the matter is that the framers of the Constitution were compelled to defend their handiwork against the charge that it violated "the political maxim that the legislative, executive, and judicial departments ought to be separate and distinct."[27] To meet this charge Madison sought to show in *The Federalist* that the three departments ought not to be so far separated as to have no control over each other.[28] In his opinion for the Court in *Ex parte Grossman*,[29] decided 137 years later, Chief Justice Taft adopted the same point of view: the fact that when two departments both operate upon the same subject matter the action of one may cancel that of the other *affords no criterion of the constitutional powers of either.* Rather the question is what does *the pertinent historical record* show with regard to presidential action in the field of congressional power?

The Historical Record

Our history contains numerous instances in which, contrary to the pattern of departmental relationship assumed in the Black opinion, presidential action has occurred within a recognized field of congressional power and has, furthermore, fully maintained its tenancy until Congress adopted superseding legislation. And Congress' right to supersede was not contested. In brief, the mere existence in Congress of power to do something has not, of itself, excluded the President from the same field of power until Congress finally acted. But once this happened, its legislation was forthwith recognized as governing the subject and as controlling presidential action in the area.

An early example of this pattern of departmental relationship is

26. *Id.* at 589.
27. *The Federalist* No. 47 at 245 (Everyman's ed. 1929).
28. *The Federalist* No. 48 (Madison).
29. 267 U.S. 87 (1925). "The Federal Constitution nowhere expressly declares that the three branches of the Government shall be kept separate and independent. All legislative powers are vested in a Congress. The executive power is vested in a President. The judicial power is vested in one Supreme Court and in such inferior courts as Congress may from time to time establish. The Judges are given life tenure and a compensation that may not be diminished during their continuance in office, with the evident purpose of securing them and their courts an independence of Congress and the Executive. Complete independence and separation between the three branches, however, are not attained, or intended, as other provisions of the Constitution and the normal operation of government under it easily demonstrate" (*id.* at 119–20).

afforded by the case of the *Flying Fish*,[30] in which Chief Justice Marshall denied that the President had power to order the seizure of a vessel bound from a French port, *because* Congress had acted in the same field of power:

It is by no means clear that the president of the United States whose high duty it is to "take care that the laws be faithfully executed," and who is commander in chief of the armies and navies of the United States, might not, without any special authority for that purpose, in the then existing state of things, have empowered the officers commanding the armed vessels of the United States, to seize and send into port for adjudication, American vessels which were forfeited by being engaged in this illicit commerce. But when it is observed that [an act of Congress] gives a special authority to seize on the high seas, and limits that authority to the seizure of vessels bound, or sailing to, a French port, the legislature seem to have prescribed that the manner in which this law shall be carried into execution, was to exclude a seizure of any vessel not bound to a French port.[31]

Another field which the President and Congress have occupied successively is extradition. In 1799 President Adams, in order to execute the extradition provisions of the Jay Treaty, issued a warrant for the arrest of one Jonathan Robbins. As Chief Justice Vinson recites in his opinion:

This action was challenged in Congress on the ground that no specific statute prescribed the method to be used in executing the treaty. John Marshall, then a member of the House of Representatives, in the course of his successful defense of the President's action, said: "Congress, unquestionably, may prescribe the mode, and Congress may devolve on others the whole execution of the contract; but, till this be done, it seems the duty of the Executive department to execute the contract by any means it possesses."[32]

Not until 1848 did Congress enact a statute governing extradition cases and conferring on the courts, both state and federal, the duty of handling them.[33]

The power of the President to act until Congress acts in the same field

---

30. Little v. Barreme, 2 Cranch 170 (1804).

31. *Id.* at 177–78, quoted in Youngstown Sheet & Tube Co. v. Sawyer, 343 U.S. 579, 660–61 (1952), Clark, J., concurring. Justice Clark added: "I know of no subsequent holding of this Court to the contrary" (*ibid.*).

32. Youngstown Sheet & Tube Co. v. Sawyer, 343 U.S. 579, 684 (1952), citing 10 *Annals of Congress* 619 (1948).

33. Rev. Stat. secs. 5270-79 (1878), as amended, 18 U.S.C. secs. 651–76 (1946).

is also shown in these instances. The first Neutrality Proclamation, issued by President Washington in 1793, was also without congressional authorization.[34] The following year Congress enacted the first neutrality statute,[35] and subsequent proclamations of neutrality have been based on an act of Congress governing the matter. The President may, in the absence of legislation by Congress, control the landing of foreign cables in the United States and the passage of foreign troops through American territory, and has done so repeatedly.[36] Likewise, until Congress acts, he may govern conquered territory[37] and, "in the absence of attempts by Congress to limit his power," may set up military commissions in territory occupied by the armed forces of the United States.[38] He may determine in a manner binding on the courts whether a treaty is still in force as law of the land, although again the final power in the field rests with Congress.[39] One of the President's most ordinary powers and duties is that of ordering the prosecution of supposed offenders against the laws of the United States. Yet Congress may do the same thing under the "necessary and proper" clause.[40] On September 22, 1862, President Lincoln issued a proclamation suspending the privilege of the writ of habeas corpus throughout the Union in certain classes of cases. By an act passed March 3, 1863, Congress ratified his action and at the same time brought the whole subject of military arrests in the United States under statutory control.[41] Conversely, when President Wilson failed in March, 1917, to obtain Congress' consent to his arming American merchant vessels

34. For the controversy thereby precipitated between Hamilton (Pacificus) and Madison (Helvidius), see Corwin, *The President's Control of Foreign Relations* c. 1 (1917).

35. 1 Stat. 381 (1794). The act was the direct outcome of suggestions made by Washington in his message of December 3, 1793. See 1 Richardson, *Messages and Papers of the Presidents* 139 (1896).

36. 22 *Opinions of the Attorney General* 13 (1898); see Tucker v. Alexandroff, 183 U.S. 424, 434-35 (1902). An act was passed May 27, 1921, 42 Stat. 8 (1921), 47 U.S.C. sec. 34 (1946) which requires presidential license for the landing and operation of cables connecting the United States with foreign countries. See Wright, *The Control of American Foreign Relations* 302 n.75 (1922).

37. Santiago v. Nagueras, 214 U.S. 260 (1909).

38. Madsen v. Kinsella, 343 U.S. 341 (1952).

39. Charlton v. Kelly, 229 U.S. 447 (1913). See also Botiller v. Dominguez, 130 U.S. 238 (1889).

40. See Sinclair v. United States, 279 U.S. 263, 289, 297 (1929).

41. 12 Stat. 755 (1863).

with defensive arms, he went ahead and did it anyway, "fortified not only by the known sentiments of the majority in Congress but also by the advice of his Secretary of State and Attorney General."[42]

To turn to the specific matter of property seizures, Justice Frankfurter's concurring opinion in the Youngstown case is accompanied by appendices containing a synoptic analysis of legislation authorizing seizures of industrial property and also a summary of seizures of industrial plants and facilities by Presidents without definite statutory warrant. Eighteen such statutes are listed, all but the first of which were enacted between 1916 and 1951. Of presidential seizures unsupported by reference to specific statutory authorization he lists eight as occurring during World War I. One he fails to mention is the seizure of the Marconi Wireless Station at Siasconset in the late summer of 1914, as a result of the company's refusal to give assurance that it would comply with naval censorship regulation.[43] To justify these seizures it was deemed sufficient to refer to "the Constitution and laws" generally. For the World War II period he lists eleven seizures in justification of which no statutory authority was cited. The first of these was the seizure of North American Aviation, Inc., of Englewood, California. In support of this action Attorney General Jackson, as Chief Justice Vinson points out in his dissenting opinion, "vigorously proclaimed that the President had the moral duty to keep this Nation's defense effort a 'going concern.'"[44] Said the then Attorney General:

For the faithful execution of . . . [the] laws the President has back of him not only each general law-enforcement power conferred by the various acts of Congress but the aggregate of all such laws plus that wide discretion as to method vested in him by the Constitution for the purpose of executing the laws.[45]

In the War Labor Disputes Act of June 25, 1943,[46] all such seizures were put on a statutory basis. Congress having at last acted on the subject, its expressed will thereafter governed.

42. Berdahl, *War Powers of the Executive in the United States* 69 (1921).
43. Attorney General Gregory's justification of this action, 30 *Opinions of the Attorney General* 291 (1914), more or less set the style for similar future opinions.
44. Youngstown Sheet & Tube Co. v. Sawyer, 343 U.S. 579, 695 (1952).
45. 89 Cong. Rec. 3992 (1943).
46. 57 Stat. 163 (1943).

In United States v. Pewee Coal Co.,[47] the Court had before it the claim of a coal mine operator whose property was seized by the President without statutory authorization, "to avert a nation-wide strike of miners." The company brought an action in the Court of Claims to recover under the Fifth Amendment for the total operating losses sustained during the period in which this property was operated by the United States. The court awarded judgment for $2,241.46 and the Supreme Court sustained this judgment, a result which, by implying the validity of the seizure,[48] supported the government's position in the Youngstown case.[49]

The doctrine dictated by the above considerations as regards the exercise of executive power in the field of legislative power was well stated by Mr. John W. Davis, principal counsel on the present occasion for the steel companies, in a brief which he filed nearly forty years ago as Solicitor General. The brief defended the action of the President in withdrawing certain lands from public entry, although his doing so was at the time contrary to express statute. "Ours," the brief reads,

is a self-sufficient Government within its sphere. (*Ex parte Siebold,* 100 U.S. 371, 395; *in re Debs,* 158 U.S. 56, 564, 578.) "Its means are adequate to its ends" (*McCulloch v. Maryland,* 4 Wheat. 316, 424), and it is rational to assume that its active forces will be found equal in most things to the emergencies that confront it. While perfect flexibility is not to be expected in a Government of divided powers, and while divi-

47. 341 U.S. 114 (1951).
48. Such suits are based on the Tucker Act, 24 Stat. 505 (1887), as amended, 28 U.S.C. secs. 41 (20), 250 (1)(2), 287 (1946), and are founded upon the Constitution of the United States. "The constitutional prohibition against taking private property for public use without just compensation is directed against the Government, and not against individual or public officers proceeding without the authority of legislative enactment" (Hooe v. United States, 218 U.S. 322, 335-36 [1910]). See United States v. North American Co., 253 U.S. 330, 333 (1920). While the above quoted language is doubtless correct as an interpretation of the Tucker Act, it ignores the constitutional obligation of the United States to compensate for acts of "taking" which stem from the President's power, especially his power as Commander-in-Chief. See United States v. Causby, 328 U.S. 256, 267 (1946), and notes 58-61.
49. "The relatively new technique of temporary taking by eminent domain is a most useful administrative device: many properties, such as laundries, or coal mines, or railroads, may be subjected to public operation for a short time to meet war or emergency needs, and can then be returned to their owners" (United States v. Pewee Coal Co., 341 U.S. 114, 119 [1951], Reed, J., concurring).

sion of power is one of the principal features of the Constitution, it is the plain duty of those who are called upon to draw the dividing lines to ascertain the essential, recognize the practical, and avoid a slavish formalism which can only serve to ossify the Government and reduce its efficiency without any compensating good. The function of making laws is peculiar to Congress, and the Executive can not exercise that function to any degree. But this is not to say that all of the *subjects* concerning which laws might be made are perforce removed from the possibility of Executive influence. The Executive may act upon things and upon men in many relations which have not, though they might have, been actually regulated by Congress. In other words, just as there are fields which are peculiar to Congress and fields which are peculiar to the Executive, so there are fields which are common to both, in the sense that the Executive may move within them until they shall have been occupied by legislative action. These are not the fields of legislative prerogative, but fields within which the law-making power may enter and dominate whenever it chooses. This situation results from the fact that the President is the active agent, not of Congress, but of the Nation. As such he performs the duties which the Constitution lays upon him immediately, and as such, also, he executes the laws and regulations adopted by Congress. He is the agent of the people of the United States, deriving all his powers from them and responsible directly to them. In no sense is he the agent of Congress. He obeys and executes the laws of Congress, not because Congress is enthroned in authority over him, but because the Constitution directs him to do so.

Therefore it follows that in ways short of making laws or disobeying them, the Executive may be under a grave constitutional duty to act for the national protection in situations not covered by the acts of Congress, and in which, even, it may not be said that his action is the direct expression of any particular one of the independent powers which are granted to him specifically by the Constitution. Instances wherein the President has felt and fulfilled such a duty have not been rare in our history, though, being for the public benefit and approved by all, his acts have seldom been challenged in the courts.[50]

Some Logical Considerations

If the legislative power and executive power are not always mutually exclusive, neither, on the other hand, are the legislative and judicial powers. Replying to the contention in Wayman v. Southard that it was unconstitutional for Congress to delegate to the courts its power

50. Brief for Appellant, pp. 75–77, United States v. Midwest Oil Co., 236 U.S. 459 (1915). Assistant Attorney General Knaebel's name was also on the brief.

to regulate their practice,[51] Chief Justice Marshall answered that while Congress cannot delegate powers which are "strictly and exclusively legislative," the courts do have certain rule-making powers with respect, for example, to the returning of writs and processes and the filing of pleadings which Congress might have retained but which it had the right to confer on the judicial department.[52] Indeed, if the President was forbidden to seize the steel mills by virtue of the fact that Congress could have done so, the right of the Court to "invalidate" the seizure becomes highly questionable; and, as all admitted, Congress could have invalidated the seizure.

Actually the President was exercising the same *kind* of power that he would have exercised had the Taft-Hartley Act, for example, made provision for such a seizure "when necessary to avert a serious strike." The Court's opinion says, however:

> The President's order does not direct that a congressional policy be executed in a manner prescribed by Congress — it directs that a presidential policy be executed in a manner prescribed by the President. The preamble of the order itself, like that of many statutes, sets out reasons why the President believes certain policies should be adopted, proclaims these policies as rules of conduct to be followed, and again, like a statute, authorizes a government official to promulgate additional rules and regulations consistent with the policy proclaimed and needed to carry that policy into execution.[53]

So what? The same thing can be said of orders of the Interstate Commerce Commission setting "reasonable rates," something which Congress can do directly any time it chooses to bypass or override the commission. Besides, the chief factors of the "national emergency" described in Executive Order 10340 put into operation "cognate powers" of President and Congress which may be merged indefinitely in the former at the option of Congress.[54]

The Concurring Opinions

Justice Frankfurter begins the material part of his opinion with the statement:

51. 10 Wheat. 1 (1825).
52. See *id.* at 42-43.
53. Youngstown Sheet & Tube Co. v. Sawyer, 343 U.S. 579, 588 (1952).
54. United States v. Curtiss-Wright Corp., 299 U.S. 304, 319-29 (1936).

We must . . . put to one side consideration of what powers the President would have had if there had been no legislation whatever bearing on the authority asserted by the seizure, or if the seizure had been only for a short, explicitly temporary period, to be terminated automatically unless Congressional approval were given.[55]

He then enters upon a review of the proceedings of Congress which attended the enactment of the Taft-Hartley Act, and concludes that Congress expressed its intention to withhold the seizure power "as though it had said so in so many words."[56]

Justice Douglas' contribution consists in the argument that a necessary result of the condemnation provision of the Fifth Amendment is that the branch of government with "the power to pay compensation for a seizure is the only one able to authorize a seizure or make lawful one that the President has effected."[57] This contention overlooks such cases as Mitchell v. Harmony,[58] United States v. Russell,[59] Portsmouth Harbor Land & Hotel Co. v. United States[60] and United States v. Pewee Coal Co.,[61] in all of which a right of compensation was recognized to exist in consequence of a taking of property or damage to property which resulted from acts stemming ultimately from constitutional powers of the President. In United States v. Pink,[62] Justice Douglas quoted with approval the following words from *The Federalist:* "All constitutional acts of power, whether in the executive or in the judicial department, have as much . . . validity and obligation as if they proceeded from the legislature."[63] If this is so as to treaty obligations, then all the more must it be true of obligations which are based directly on the Constitution.[64]

Justice Jackson's rather desultory opinion contains little that is of direct pertinence to the constitutional issue. Important, however, is his contention, which seems to align him with Justice Frankfurter, that Congress has "not left seizure of private property an open field but has

55. Youngstown Sheet & Tube Co. v. Sawyer, 343 U.S. 579, 597 (1952).
56. *Id.* at 602.
57. *Id.* at 631–32.
58. 13 How. 115 (1852).
59. 13 Wall. 623 (1871).
60. 260 U.S. 327 (1922).
61. 341 U.S. 114 (1951).
62. 315 U.S. 203, 230 (1942).
63. *The Federalist* No. 64 at 330 (Everyman's ed. 1929).
64. See 40 *Opinions of the Attorney General* 250, 253 (1942).

covered it by three statutory policies inconsistent with this seizure."
From this he reasons that "we can sustain the President only by holding
that seizure of such strike-bound industries is within his domain and
beyond control by Congress."[65] The opinion concludes:

> In view of the ease, expedition and safety with which Congress can
> grant and has granted large emergency powers, certainly ample to
> embrace this crisis, I am quite unimpressed with the argument that we
> should affirm possession of them without statute.... But I have no
> illusion that any decision by this Court can keep power in the hands of
> Congress if it is not wise and timely in meeting its problems. A crisis
> that challenges the President equally, or perhaps primarily, challenges
> Congress. If not good law, there was wordly wisdom in the maxim
> attributed to Napoleon that "The tools belong to the man who can
> use them." We may say that power to legislate for emergencies belongs
> in the hands of Congress, but only Congress itself can prevent power
> from slipping through its fingers.[66]

Justice Burton says that the Taft-Hartley Act, read in the light of its
legislative history,[67] significantly fails to provide authority for seizures.
He also agrees that "Congress authorized a procedure which the President declined to follow."[68] Justice Clark bases his position directly on
Little v. Barreme.[69] The President must, he says, follow the procedures
laid down in the Taft-Hartley, Selective Service and Defense Production
acts.[70] At the same time he endorses the view, "taught me not only by
the decision of Chief Justice Marshall in Little v. Barreme, but also by
a score of other pronouncements of distinguished members of this
bench," that "the Constitution does grant to the President extensive
authority in times of grave and imperative national emergency."[71]

Dissenting Opinion

Chief Justice Vinson launched his dissent, for himself and Justices
Reed and Minton, with a survey of the elements of the emergency
which confronted the President: the Korean War, the obligations of
the United States under the United Nations Charter and the Atlantic

65. Youngstown Sheet & Tube Co. v. Sawyer, 343 U.S. 579, 639-40 (1952).
66. *Id.* at 653-54.
67. 93 Cong. Rec. 3835-36 (1947).
68. Youngstown Sheet & Tube Co. v. Sawyer, 343 U.S. 579, 659 (1952).
69. 2 Cranch 170 (1804).
70. Youngstown Sheet & Tube Co. v. Sawyer, 343 U.S. 579, 663-65 (1952).
71. *Id.* at 662.

Pact, the appropriations acts by which Congress voted vast sums to be expended in our defense and that of our European allies, the fact that steel is a basic constituent of war matériel. He reproaches the Court for failing to give consideration to the President's finding of an emergency. According to the Court, he said, "the immediacy of the threatened disaster" is "irrelevant"; and the President, unable to use the executive power to avert the disaster, "must confine himself to sending a message to Congress." The opinion of the Chief Justice musters impressive evidence to show that the steel seizure, considering the emergency involved, fits into the picture of past presidential emergency action. And "plaintiffs admit that the emergency procedures of Taft-Hartley are not mandatory."[72]

Résumé and Evaluation

Youngstown will probably go down in history as an outstanding example of the *sic volo, sic jubeo* frame of mind into which the Court is occasionally maneuvered by the public context of the case before it. The doctrine of the case, as stated in Justice Black's opinion of the Court, while purporting to stem from the principle of the separation of powers, is a purely arbitrary construct created out of hand for the purpose of disposing of this particular case, and is altogether devoid of historical verification. Nor do the concurring opinions contribute anything to the decision's claim to be regarded seriously as a doctrine of constitutional law. Their importance consists in the suggestion, cogently urged by Justice Frankfurter and endorsed by Justices Jackson, Burton, and Clark, that the President should have heeded the intention of the Taft-Hartley Act. Only Justice Clark, however, guided by Marshall's opinion in the early case of Little v. Barreme, had the courage to draw the appropriate conclusion: Congress having entered the field, its ascertainable intention supplied the law of the case. Justice Clark accordingly refused to concur in the opinion of the Court, while voting for its decision.

The Chief Justice's dissenting opinion is impressive for its delineation of the emergency and convincing in its summation of evidence regarding presidential emergency power. In view of the attitude of the concurring justices, however, his assertion as to the bearing of Taft-Hartley on the problem before the Court is deceptive. The statement that Taft-

72. *Id.* at 705.

Hartley was "not mandatory" is equivocal. Granting that the act was not intended to require the President to resort to it in preference to permitting the situation to take an uncontrolled course, yet resort to it may very well have been intended as an indispensable preliminary to a seizure. This conclusion is borne out by the fact that when the procedures provided by the act fail, the President is required to submit a report and recommendations to Congress for action. In the opinion of the writer the case was rightly decided, but for wrong reasons. The line of reasoning suggested by Justices Frankfurter, Jackson, Burton, and Clark should have been pursued to its logical end, as by Justice Clark it was.[73]

The question remains whether the record of the case is of value for constitutional law and practice. It is. (1) That the President does possess "residual" or "resultant" powers over and above, or in consequence of, his specifically granted powers to take temporary alleviative action in the presence of serious emergency is a proposition to which all but Justices Black and Douglas would probably have assented in the absence of the complicating issue that was created by the President's refusal to follow the procedures laid down in the Taft-Hartley Act. (2) Such residual powers being conceded, it would follow logically that a seizure of property made by exercise of them would give rise to a constitutional obligation on the part of the United States to render "just compensation" in accordance with the requirements of the Fifth Amendment. (3) It is also fairly evident that the Court would never venture to traverse a presidential finding of "serious" emergency which was prima facie supported by judicially cognizable facts, but would wave aside a challenge to such a finding as raising a "political question." (4) The Court would unquestionably have assented to the proposition that in all emergency situations the last word lies with Congress when it chooses to speak such last word. And the moral from all this is plain:

73. The case for the President is not improved by Congress' adoption of the following provision as a part of the Defense Production Act amendments of 1952, Pub. L. No. 429, 82nd Cong., 2d sess., sec. 115 (June 30, 1952): "Section 503 of the Defense Production Act of 1950, as amended, is hereby amended by adding at the end thereof the following: 'It is the sense of the Congress that, by reason of the work stoppage now existing in the steel industry, the national safety is imperiled, and the Congress therefore requests the President to invoke immediately the national emergency provisions (sections 206 to 210, inclusive) of the Labor-Management Relations Act, 1947, for the purpose of terminating such work stoppage.'"

namely, that escape must be sought from "presidential autocracy" by resort not to the judicial power, but to the legislative power — in other words, by resort to timely action by Congress and to procedures for the meeting of emergency situations so far as these can be intelligently anticipated.

And — not to give the thing too fine a point — what seems to be required at the present juncture is a new Labor Disputes Act which ordains procedures for the handling of industry-wide strikes in terms so comprehensive and explicit that the most headstrong President cannot sidestep them without manifest attaint to the law, the Constitution, and his own oath of office. "Presidential autocracy," when it is justified, is an inrush of power to fill a power vacuum. Nature abhors a vacuum; so does an age of emergency. Let Congress see to it that no such vacuum occurs.

10. The President's Power

When in 1800 President Adams signed a deed conveying property to his "great and good friend" the Queen of Portugal for a legation in the Federal City, he was informed by his Attorney General that only Congress had the constitutional power to dispose of public property. When, 140 years later, President Franklin Roosevelt handed over fifty naval units to Great Britain in return for leases of some West Atlantic naval bases, he was told by his Attorney General, now a member of the Supreme Court, that he was entirely within his rights, that his power to *dispose* the forces of the United States included the power to dispose *of* them. These two episodes stand at either end of a course of constitutional development, practical and polemical, which ascribes to the President a truly royal prerogative in the field of foreign relations, and does so without indicating any correlative legal or constitutional control to which he is answerable.

Indeed, our high-flying prerogative men appear to resent the very idea that the only possible source of such control, Congress to wit, has any

Reprinted by permission of *The New Republic*, © 1951, The New Republic, Inc., January 29, 1951, pp. 15–16.

effective power in the premises at all. Thus when Mr. Taft in his speech of January 5 asserted that President Truman "had no authority to commit American troops to Korea without consulting Congress and without Congressional approval," and that he "has no power to agree to send American troops to fight in Europe in a war between members of the Atlantic Pact and Soviet Russia," one of the aforesaid high prerogative spokesmen declared that "his [Taft's] statements are demonstrably irresponsible." The public "is entitled to know what provisions of the law or of the Constitution have been violated by President Truman in sending troops overseas. From the day that President Jefferson ordered Commodore Dale and two-thirds of the American Navy into the Mediterranean to repel the Barbary pirates, American Presidents have repeatedly committed American armed forces abroad without prior Congressional consultation or approval."[1]

The proffered demonstration is inconclusive at best. Jefferson, in reporting his action to Congress, explained that he had been careful to authorize only self-defensive measures on the part of our forces, and that when they had captured one of the pirate vessels they had, after disabling it for committing further hostilities, liberated it with its crew. He wished, he said, to have Congress, who "exclusively" had the power, to consider whether it would not be well to authorize measures of offense. Hamilton expressed great contempt for Jefferson's scruples, but that does not alter the record to which appeal has been made.

As to the cases in which "American Presidents have repeatedly committed armed forces abroad" without "Congressional consultation or approval," the vast majority involved fights with pirates, landings of small naval contingents on barbarous or semi-barbarous coasts, the dispatch of small bodies of troops to chase bandits or cattle rustlers across the Mexican border, and the like. Except for Polk's deliberate precipitation of war with Mexico in 1846 and a few cases occurring in the Caribbean area since 1902, they exhibit a uniform pattern of measures undertaken for the protection of American lives and property against impending or actual violence or for punishment of such violence. Such episodes are small compared with Truman's claim of power to put an indefinite number of troops in Europe for an indefinite time in anticipation of war, without consulting Congress.[2]

1. Arthur Schlesinger, Jr., in the *New York Times*, January 9, 1951.
2. On this paragraph see Rogers, *World Policing and the Constitution* (1945).

The power of Congress over the employment of the armed forces was repeatedly recognized in early legislation. The President's power to call forth the militia stems immediately from the act of February 28, 1795; and I should like to inform Professor Commager[3] that it was this act and not the Constitution which "the magisterial Story" was construing in the case of Martin v. Mott (12 Wheat. 19 [1827]); also, the President's power to employ the armed forces to suppress insurrections and enforce the law rests on the act of March 8, 1807. Formal declarations of war by Congress have always included a clause "authorizing" and "directing" the employment of the forces to support the declaration, and it may be remembered that the Conscription Act of September, 1940, specifically provided that the forces to be conscripted would not be sent abroad without the consent of Congress. When we were precipitated into the war by the Japanese attack on Pearl Harbor, this consent was given. It is also pertinent to recall that when President Wilson landed troops at Vera Cruz on April 21, 1914, he consulted Congress, which approved his action the following day; and President Franklin Roosevelt's "utmost sympathy" message to France, June 14, 1940, contained the caveat that "these statements carry no implication of military commitments. Only Congress can make such commitments."

Besides, the Constitution does not consist primarily of precedents but of principles with which precedents, to be valid, must be squared. The Administration's interpretation of the precedents which illustrate routine activities of the executive departments upsets the most fundamental principle of the Constitution, the balance between the departments. It distorts the Constitution.

The fact that a certain power is ascribable to the President does not prove that Congress possesses no power whereby Presidential employment of it may be brought under control and direction. This precise question was involved in the case of Little v. Barreme (2 Cranch 170, 177 [1804]). There Chief Justice Marshall, speaking with reference to the seizure of a vessel under the act of February 9, 1809, suspending intercourse with France, said:

> It is by no means clear that the President of the United States whose high duty it is to "take care that the laws be faithfully executed," and who is Commander-in-Chief of the armies and navies of the United States, might not, without any special authority for that purpose, in

3. See his article in the *New York Times Magazine*, January 14, 1951.

the then existing state of things, have empowered the officers commanding the armed vessels of the United States, to seize and send into port for adjudication, American vessels which were forfeited by being engaged in this illicit commerce.

The court held, nevertheless, that since Congress had acted in the matter the President was bound to follow its directions and that the seizure had been illegal.

While the shadowy line that separates congressional power when raising an army and creating a navy or air force to specify the purposes for which they may be employed and the President's right to dispose the forces thus brought into existence has come to be drawn in the course of the years inside what was once deemed to be legislative domain, yet there are conceded to be other powers of Congress which are constitutionally unlimited and Congress' use of which is capable of upsetting the presidential applecart at any time. Congress can refuse to raise armies and navies at all, to borrow money, to levy taxes, to make appropriations. It can abrogate "so far as the people and authorities of the United States are concerned" any treaty to which the United States is a party, and has repealed a considerable number in whole or in part. (La Abro Silver Mining Co. v. United States, 175 U.S. 423, 460 [1899], citing cases.)

What then is the answer? Futile and embittered debate between the holders of powers that must be exercised in close cooperation if at all, or a decent consultation and accommodation of views between the two departments of government concerned? And surely, it is paradoxical in the extreme to reduce the legislative organ of government to the level of a mere rubber stamp of policies the professed purpose of which is the preservation of free institutions. Either the Brussels Agreement should be formally submitted to the Senate for approval by a constitutional two-thirds majority, or something akin to Coudert's resolution should be adopted. Our foreign policy has been elaborated in a political, and at times an intellectual, vacuum long enough.

V. After the Constitutional Revolution

11. The Dissolving Structure of Our Constitutional Law

There is a story that once upon a time a doctor, an engineer, and a politician were debating which of these callings was the most ancient. The doctor rested his case on the contention that the removal of the rib from Adam's side was obviously a surgical operation; to which the engineer rejoined that before Adam had even appeared on the scene the world itself had to be created out of chaos, and that this was clearly an engineering operation. "Very true," chimed in the politician, "but who do you think created chaos?"

Accepting the Clausewitz thesis that "war is only an extension of policy," we are free to say that the politicians have created chaos in these latter days in a rather wholesale way. But that is another story. The world revolution is not my topic, but the comparatively limited revolution which we have been witnessing in our own country the last few years in consequence of the New Deal and more recently of the war. How has this revolution affected conceptions of governmental power in the United States; how is it to be evaluated in terms of American constitutional law? For constitutional law has always been the most distinctive feature of the American system of government, the result of a unique infusion of politics with jurisprudence, of current opinion with established principles. Today this remarkable product of American political genius appears to be undergoing a fundamental revision — even to be in process of dissolution.[1]

From 20 *Washington Law Review* 185–98 (November, 1945). Reprinted by permission.
1. The writer is indebted to the Claremont Colleges, publishers of his *Constitutional Revolution, Ltd.* (1941), for the privilege of using some of the matter in that volume in the preparation of this paper.

What is constitutional law? As the term is employed in this country, it denotes a body of rules resulting from judicial interpretation of a written constitution, and particularly the interpretation of the Constitution of the United States by the Supreme Court at Washington. Its parental elements are, therefore, the constitutional document and the power of the Supreme Court to pass upon the validity of legislation both state and national in relation to that document — more briefly, judicial review. The latter is the active, generative element; the former is, *in theory*, the matrix, the receptive element.

Actually, when the subject is considered statistically, the theory that the constitutional document contained in embryo from the outset the entirety of constitutional law puts credulity to a quite impossible test. First and last the Supreme Court has handed down some fifteen or sixteen thousand opinions, occupying in the published *Reports* probably two hundred thousand pages, large octavo; and of this total, probably one-third comprises cases involving points of constitutional interpretation. But even more striking is the fact that by far the greater number of these have arisen out of four or five brief phrases of the constitutional document, "power to regulate commerce," "obligation of contracts," deprivation of "life, liberty or property without due process of law" (which phrase occurs both as a limitation on the national government and — since 1868 — on the states), and out of three or four theories or doctrines which the Constitution is supposed to embody.

The latter are, in fact, the essence of the matter. That is to say, the effectiveness of constitutional law as a system of restraints on governmental power depends for the most part on the effectiveness of these doctrines as they are applied by the Court for that purpose. The doctrines to which I refer are (1) the doctrine or concept of dual federalism; (2) the doctrine of the separation of powers; (3) the doctrine and *practice* of judicial review; and finally, the substantive concept of due process of law, by which judicial review has been put beyond statable limits both as to subject matter and also as to the considerations determining its exercise. What I propose to do is to take up each of these four doctrines in turn, briefly sketch its origins, and then project against that background a short account of what has been happening to it in recent years.

Federalism in the United States embraces the following elements: (1) as in all federations, the union of several autonomous political entities, or states, for common purposes; (2) the division of legislative powers between a national government, on the one hand, and constituent states, on the other; (3) the direct operation for the most part of each of these centers of government, within its assigned sphere, upon all persons and property within its territorial limits; (4) the provision of each center with the complete apparatus of law enforcement, both executive and judicial; (5) the supremacy of the national government within its assigned sphere over any conflicting assertion of state power; (6) dual citizenship.

The third and fourth of the above-listed salient features of the American federal system are the ones which at the outset marked it off most sharply from all preceding systems, in which the member states generally agreed to obey the mandates of a common government for certain stipulated purposes, but retained to themselves the right of ordaining and enforcing the laws of the union. This, indeed, was the system provided in the Articles of Confederation. The Convention of 1787 was well aware, of course, that if the inanities and futilities of the confederation were to be avoided in the new system the latter must incorporate "a coercive principle"; and as Ellsworth of Connecticut expressed it, the only question was whether it should be "a coercion of law, or a coercion of arms," that "coercion which acts only upon delinquent individuals" or that which is applicable to "sovereign bodies, states, in their political capacity." In judicial review the former principle was established, albeit without entirely discarding the latter, as the Civil War was to demonstrate.

The sheer fact of federalism comes within the purview of constitutional law, that is, becomes a judicial *concept*, in consequence of the conflicts which have at times arisen between the idea of state autonomy (state sovereignty) and the principle of national supremacy. Exaltation of the latter principle, as it is recognized in the supremacy clause (Article VI, paragraph 2) of the Constitution, was the very keystone of Chief Justice Marshall's constitutional jurisprudence. It was his position that the supremacy clause should be applied literally, with the result that if an unforced reading of the terms in which legislative power was granted to Congress confirmed its right to enact a particular statute, the circumstance that the statute projected national power into an accustomed field of state power became a matter of complete indifference. State power, in short, was no ingredient of national power, and hence no independent limitation thereof.

Quite different was the outlook of the Court over which Marshall's successor, Chief Justice Taney, presided. That Court took as its point of departure the Tenth Amendment, which reads, "The powers not delegated to the United States by the Constitution, nor prohibited by it to the States, are reserved to the States respectively, or to the people." In construing this provision the States Rights Court sometimes talked as if it regarded *all* the reserved powers of the states as limiting national power. At other times it talked as if it regarded certain "subjects" as reserved exclusively to the states, slavery being the outstanding instance.

But whether following the one line of reasoning or the other, the Court subtly transformed its function, and so that of judicial review, in relation to the federal system. Marshall viewed the Court as primarily an organ of the national government and of its supremacy. The Court under Taney regarded itself as standing outside of and above both the national government and the states, and as vested with a quasi-arbitral function between two centers of diverse but essentially equal, because "sovereign," powers. Thus in Ableman v. Booth,[2] which was decided on the eve of the Civil War, we find Taney himself using this arresting language:

> This judicial power was justly regarded as indispensable, not merely to maintain the supremacy of the laws of the United States, but also to guard the States from any encroachments upon their reserved powers by the general government. . . . So long . . . as this Constitution shall endure, this tribunal must exist with it, deciding in the peaceful form of judicial proceeding, the angry and irritating controversies between sovereignties, which in other countries have been determined by the arbitrament of force.

Other justices of the period committed themselves even more unqualifiedly to the state sovereignty thesis.

It is the Taney Court, therefore, rather than the Marshall Court, which elaborated the concept of *dual federalism*. Marshall's federalism is more aptly termed *national* federalism; and turning to modern issues, we may say without exaggeration that the broad general constitutional issue between the Court and the New Deal in such cases as Schechter Corp. v. U.S. and Carter v. Carter Coal Co.[3] was, whether dual federalism or national federalism should prevail. More narrowly, the issue in these cases was whether Congress' power to regulate commerce must

2. 21 How. 406 (1859).
3. 295 U.S. 495 (1935); 298 U.S. 238 (1936).

stop short of regulating the employer-employee relationship in industrial production, that having been hitherto regulated by the states. We all know how this issue was finally determined. In the Fair Labor Standards Act of 1938 Congress not only prohibits interstate commerce in goods produced by substandard labor, but it directly forbids, with penalties, the employment of labor in industrial production for interstate commerce on other than prescribed terms.[4] And in United States v. Darby[5] this act was sustained by the Court in all its sweeping provisions, on the basis of an opinion by Chief Justice Stone which purports to be based — and logically is based — on Chief Justice Marshall's famous opinions in McCulloch v. Maryland[6] and Gibbons v. Ogden[7] of 120 years ago. In short, as a principle capable of limiting the national legislative power, the concept of dual federalism is today at an end, with consequent aggrandizement of national power.

This, however, is only a part of the story — perhaps even less than half of it. For in another respect even the great Marshall has been in effect overruled in support of enlarged views of national authority. Without essaying a vain task of "tithing mint, anise and cummin," it is fairly accurate to say that throughout the 100 years which lie between Marshall's death and the first New Deal cases, the conception of the federal relationship which on the whole prevailed with the Court was a *competitive conception*, one which pitted the national government and the states against each other. It is true that we occasionally get some striking statements of contrary tendency, as in Justice Bradley's opinion in 1880 for a divided Court in the Siebold case,[8] where is reflected recognition of certain results of the Civil War; or much later in a frequently quoted dictum by Justice McKenna, in Hoke v. United States,[9] in which the Mann White Slave Act was sustained in 1913:

Our dual form of government has its perplexities, State and Nation having different spheres of jurisdiction . . . but it must be kept in mind that we are one people; and the powers reserved to the states and those conferred on the nation are adapted to be exercised, whether indepen-

4. 52 Stat. 1060, 29 U.S.C. sec. 201 (1938).
5. 312 U.S. 100 (1941).
6. 4 Wheat. 316 (1819).
7. 9 Wheat. 1 (1824).
8. *Ex parte* Siebold, 100 U.S. 371 (1880).
9. 227 U.S. 328 (1913).

dently or concurrently, to promote the general welfare, material and moral.

The contrary outlook is nevertheless the one much more generally evident in the outstanding results for American constitutional law throughout three-quarters of its history. Consider, for example, the doctrine of tax exemption which converted federalism into a principle of private immunity from taxation, so that, for example, neither government could tax as income the official salaries paid by the other government. Consider, too, the paradox which is illustrated in the case of Hammer v. Dagenhart,[10] overruled in the Darby case, in which it was held that an attempt by Congress to exclude child-made goods from the channels of interstate commerce was not a regulation of commerce, but an invasion of the police powers of the states, although by other decisions then in good standing a similar attempt by a state would have been an invasion of Congress' power to regulate commerce. Thus was a realm of no-power created — a veritable laissez-faire Utopia! And all such results sprang from a conception of the federal relationship which regards the national government and the states as rival governments bent on mutual frustration, and on a conception of the judicial role which made it the supreme duty of the Court to maintain the two centers of government in theoretical possession of their accustomed powers, however incapable either might be in fact of exercising them. Indeed, maintenance of the federal equilibrium became — the due process clause aside — the be-all and end-all of judicial review.

By the *cooperative* conception of the federal relationship, on the other hand, the states and the national government are regarded as mutually complementary parts of a *single* governmental mechanism all of whose powers are intended to realize the current purposes of government according to their applicability to the problem in hand. *This is the conception on which the New Deal rests.* It is, for example, the conception which the Court invokes throughout its decisions in sustaining the Social Security Act of 1935[11] and supplementary state legislation. It is also the conception which underlies congressional legislation of recent years making certain crimes against the states, like theft, racketeering, kidnaping, crimes also against the national government whenever the of-

10. 247 U.S. 251 (1918).
11. 49 Stat. 620, 42 U.S.C. 7 (1935).

fender extends his activities beyond state boundary lines. The usually cited constitutional justification for such legislation is that which was established more than a quarter of a century ago in the Hoke case, from which I quoted just previously.

It has been argued, however, that the cooperative conception of the federal relationship, especially as it is realized in the policy of federal subventions to the states, tends to break down state initiative and to devitalize state policies. Actually, its effect has, to date, usually been just the contrary, and for the reason pointed out by Justice Cardozo in Helvering v. Davis,[12] also decided in 1937, namely that the states, competing as they do with one another to attract investors, have not been able to embark separately upon expensive programs of relief and social insurance. The other great objection to cooperative federalism is, however, much more difficult to meet. This is, that cooperative federalism spells further aggrandizement of national power. Unquestionably it does, for when two cooperate it is the stronger member of the combination who calls the tunes. Resting as it does primarily on the superior fiscal resources of the national government, cooperative federalism has been, to date, a short expression for a constantly increasing concentration of power at Washington in the instigation and supervision of local policies.

The second great structural principle of American constitutional law is supplied by the doctrine of the separation of powers. How has this principle fared at the hands of recent tendencies, and more particularly, at the hands of the New Deal?

The notion of three distinct functions of government approximating what we today term the legislative, the executive, and the judicial, is set forth in Aristotle's *Politics*, but it was "the celebrated Montesquieu" who by joining the idea to the notion of a "mixed constitution" of "checks and balances," in Book XI of his *Spirit of the Laws*, brought Aristotle's discovery to the service of the rising libertarianism of the eighteenth century. It was Montesquieu's fundamental contention that "men entrusted with power tend to abuse it." Hence it was desirable to divide the powers of government, first, in order to keep to a minimum the powers lodged in any single organ of government; secondly, in order to be able to oppose organ to organ. So vague a principle, nevertheless,

12. 301 U.S. 619 (1937).

was bound to take color from the institutional landscape against which it chanced to be projected. In England, where the principle formerly had currency in the "literary theory" of the British constitution, it early became subordinated to the doctrine of parliamentary sovereignty and to the cabinet system. On the other hand, while the principle was formerly thought to support the accountability of administrative officials to the ordinary courts — the so-called "rule of law" — in France it was invoked from the outset in behalf of the contrasted system of "droit administratif." Nor is the explanation of the difference far to seek. Whereas England was made a nation by her law courts and her Parliament, France was the creation primarily of the Capetian administrative system.

In the United States libertarian application of the principle was originally less embarrassed by inherited institutions. In its most dogmatic form the American conception of the separation of powers may be summed up in the following propositions: (1) there are three intrinsically distinct functions of government, the legislative, the executive, and the judicial; (2) these distinct functions ought to be exercised respectively by three separately manned departments of government; which, (3) should be constitutionally equal and mutually independent; and which, (4) taken together, cover the entire field of governmental power.

Even prior to the New Deal this entire colligation of ideas had been seriously impaired by three developments in national governmental practice: first, the growth of presidential initiative in legislation; secondly, the delegation by Congress of legislative powers to the President; thirdly, the delegation in many instances of like powers to so-called "independent agencies" or commissions, in which are merged "the three powers of government" of Montesquieu's postulate. The first two of these developments have been brought under the New Deal to a pitch not formerly approximated except temporarily during the war with Germany; the third development the Roosevelt Administration resisted and even attempted to nullify in the interest of further concentration of power in the hands of the President, and during the war succeeded more or less in doing so through the creation of such agencies as WPB, WMC, OWI, etc. I cannot, of course, go into detail; I can only indicate certain achieved results.

When people talk about "presidential autocracy" they are apt, especially under war conditions, to be thinking chiefly of those powers which the President gets directly from the Constitution. Actually, a vast proportion of the great powers which the President exercises even in wartime are the immediate donation of Congress. The reassurance afforded by this fact turns out on examination, nevertheless, to be rather meager. For the truth is that the practice of delegated legislation is inevitably and inextricably involved with the whole idea of governmental intervention in the economic field, where the conditions to be regulated are of infinite complexity and are constantly undergoing change. In this situation it is simply out of the question to demand that Congress should attempt to impose upon the shifting and complex scene the relatively permanent molds of statutory provision, unqualified by a large degree of administrative discretion.

Nor again, can the presidential role in the formulation of legislation for congressional consideration be reasonably expected ever to become less than it is today. One of the major reasons urged for governmental intervention is furnished by the need for gearing the different parts of the industrial process with one another for a planned result. In wartime this need is freely conceded by all; but its need in peacetime is conceivably even greater, the results sought being so immeasurably more complex.

So, both in the interest of unity of design and of flexibility of detail, presidential power today takes increasing toll from both ends of the legislative process — both from the formulation of legislation and from its administration. In other words, the principle of the separation of powers as a barrier preventing the fusion of presidential and congressional power is today pretty shaky if it is not altogether defunct.

To sum up the argument to this point: the New Deal, and the doctrines of constitutional law on which it rests, and the conception of governmental function which it incorporates, have all tremendously strengthened forces which even earlier were making, slowly, to be sure, but with "the inevitability of gradualness," for the *concentration of governmental power in the United States, first in the hands of the national government; and, secondly, in the hands of the national executive.* In the constitutional law which the validation of the New Deal has brought into full being the two main structural elements of government in the United States in the past, the principle of dual federalism and the doctrine of the separation of powers, have undergone a radical and enfeebling transformation which the war has, naturally, carried still further.

We come now to judicial review. The matter of primary interest to us in connection with this unique institution is that it is not referable — as is, for example, the President's veto power — to a specific constitutional clause, but depends on a justifying *doctrine*. In brief, this doctrine claims for the courts the power to interpret with finality the standing law, of which the Constitution is a part — indeed, the supreme part. This is on the theory that when performed by a court in connection with the decision of a case, interpretation of the standing law is an act not of *will* or *power*, but of *knowledge*; and is hence preservative of the law, and so of the Constitution when that happens to be a part of the standing law which is applicable to the case under decision. As Chief Justice Marshall phrased the matter, "Judicial power, as contradistinguished from the power of the law, has no existence. Courts are the mere instruments of the law, and can will nothing."[13]

Now whether judicial interpretation of the Constitution does preserve — or on the contrary, does *not* preserve it — is frequently a question which lies outside the realm of verifiable phenomena, it being obviously impossible in this year of grace to know what *was* intended "by the Constitution," or by the framers or the ratifiers thereof, with regard to matters which did not exist in 1787. One is reminded of an old conundrum. Query: "Does your brother like cheese?" Answer: "I have no brother." Query: "But if you had a brother, would he like cheese?"

But the critics of judicial review have never been content with this agnostic position. The earliest of them, indeed, asserted that judicial review was itself a standing refutation of the proposition that it preserved the Constitution inasmuch as it was never intended by the framers of the Constitution — was, in other words, founded on usurpation. Although this thesis has produced a whole library either in reaffirmation or refutation thereof, it can be disposed of for our purposes fairly briefly.

The words of the Constitution itself make it amply clear that the framers intended that both state and national courts, and ultimately the Supreme Court, should be entrusted with the duty of maintaining the supremacy of the Constitution and of acts of Congress "made in pursu-

13. Osborn v. The Bank, 9 Wheat. 738, at 866 (1824).

ance thereof" against all conflicting State constitutional and legal provisions. Furthermore, there is evidence to show that many of the framers anticipated that the Supreme Court would be entitled, and hence obligated, to interpret and apply against acts of Congress direct prohibitions upon the national legislative power, as, for example, the provision against *ex post facto* laws.[14] But at this point anything approaching certainty ends, inasmuch as the experience of the framers in 1787 with judicial review was much too fragmentary to enable them to foresee the problems to which the institution would give rise, much less, to provide adequate and binding solutions for such problems.

Even so, to characterize judicial review, or to characterize Chief Justice Marshall's opinion in the leading case of Marbury v. Madison,[15] as "usurpation," is an altogether extravagant use of that term. Besides, a usurpation which still stands after 142 years must long since have outgrown its original taint.

Today's critics of judicial review delve much deeper, and bring to the surface more fundamental issues. They assert that interpretation — and hence the judicial function — is not separable from the legislative, but is a continuation of it; that preservation of the law is a superstition, and a malignant one, in that the law must constantly change to meet social needs; and finally, that since it is the tendency of judicial review to hamper this process of change it is undesirable; while some add that it is incompatible with the underlying principle of democracy — that when the majority want change they are entitled to get it, and in short order.

The thesis of the total disinterestedness of the judicial process was first brought into question by a critic whose own disinterestedness could not be challenged, in Oliver Wendell Holmes' *Common Law*, published in 1881. On the opening page of this famous work one reads: "The law draws all its juices of life from considerations which judges rarely mention, and always with apology, I mean considerations of what is expedient for the community concerned." A generation later, a friend of Justice Holmes, Professor John Chipman Gray of Harvard, enlarged upon the former's thesis in his *Law, Its Nature and Sources*. Gray, in fact, went to the extent of asserting that interpretation is *the* law-

14. Art. I, sec. 9, par. 3.
15. 1 Cranch 137 (1803).

making function par excellence, and he quoted repeatedly and with gusto
the assertion of a certain Bishop Hoadly of the seventeenth century that
"Whoever hath an absolute authority to interpret any written or spoken
law, it is he who is truly the law-giver . . . and not the person who first
wrote or spoke them."

Then a few years ago Mr. — now Judge — Jerome Frank brought out
his *Law and the Modern Mind.* Here the notion of the stability of the
law is attacked as an old wives' tale, belief in which has been kept up by
"the father complex," the inclination, that is, of most people — or so
Judge Frank alleges — when they leave the paternal roof to seek security
from some other source. In the last analysis, Judge Frank, enlarging
on Gray, as the latter had enlarged before on Holmes, denies that even
the interpreters of the law give us *law* — they give us only decisions, he
says. The Supreme Court of the United States is, therefore, one must
conclude, only an enlarged version of the wise man of primitive communities who, to keep the communal peace, dispensed a ready-made
justice by the wayside to settle neighborhood quarrels.

Frank's avowed anarchism fluttered the dove-cotes even of many self-
proclaimed "legal pragmatists," but it must be admitted that he has
been vindicated by subsequent events in two respects at least. The demand for *social* security has today reached a volume which is utterly
dismaying both because of the expectation which it voices and because
of the decline in what Frank himself calls "the spirit of adventure."
The second way in which Frank has been vindicated is more immediately relevant to our theme; I mean, by the extent to which the Supreme
Court has overruled earlier decisions in upholding the New Deal legislation. Many of these earlier decisions were, to my mind, erroneous and
needed to be overturned. Nevertheless, the confession by the Court of
having committed error on such a scale and involving constitutional
interpretations of such magnitude, has presented the thesis of the
Court's preservative function with the sharpest challenge it has ever
met.

More than that, however, when this confession of error and the consequent acts of restitution by the Court are set against the background
of the ideological motivation of the New Deal legislation, they force
the conclusion that judicial review has today become, like dual federalism and like the principle of the separation of powers, a secondary and

subordinate factor of national power, whether wielded by President or by Congress.

And this brings us to the fourth structural element of our Constitutional Law which has latterly undergone enfeeblement. I mean the doctrine of substantive due process of law.

The due process of law clause of the Fifth Amendment reads: "nor shall any person . . . be deprived [that is, by the national government] of life, liberty, or property, without due process of law." The clause derives, via a statute of Edward III's time, from the thirty-ninth chapter of Magna Carta (chapter 29 of the issue of 1225). There the King promises that "no free man" shall be imprisoned or deprived of his estate, or otherwise despoiled except "in accordance with the judgment of his peers or the law of the land (*legem terrae*)." By the phrase *legem terrae* here was meant that mode of trial which eventually ripened into the grand jury — petit jury process of the common law; and there can be little doubt that it was the main concern of the men who were responsible for the Fifth Amendment to consecrate this process.

But the circumstances which render the due process clause a fundamental element of American constitutional law was the role it has played in articulating transcendental theories of private immunity with the constitutional document. Particularly did the framers subscribe to the notion that the property right, which they regarded as anterior to government, set a moral limit to the latter's powers. Yet could judicial review pretend to operate on a merely moral basis? Both the notion that the Constitution was an emanation from the *sovereignty* of the people, and the idea that judicial review was but a special aspect of normal judicial function, forbade the suggestion. It necessarily followed that unless judicial protection of the property right against legislative power was to be waived, it must be rested on some clause of the constitutional document; and, inasmuch as the due process clause, and the equivalent "law of the land" clause of certain of the early state constitutions, were the only constitutional provisions which specifically mentioned property, they were the ones selected for the purpose.

The absorptive power of the due process clause and the equivalent law of the land clause was foreshadowed as early as 1819 in a dictum by Justice William Johnson of the United States Supreme Court: "As to the words from *Magna Charta* . . . after volumes spoken and written with a view to their exposition, the good sense of mankind has at length settled down to this: that they were intended to secure the individual from the arbitrary exercise of the powers of government, unrestrained by the established principles of private rights and distributive justice."[16] Thirty-eight years later the prophecy of these words was realized in the famous Dred Scott case in which section 8 of the Missouri Compromise, whereby slavery was excluded from the territories, was held void under the Fifth Amendment, not on the ground that the procedure for enforcing it was not due process of law, but because the Court regarded it as unjust to forbid people to take their slaves, or other property, into the territories, the common property of all the states.[17] Due process of law came, in short, to mean the Court's idea of what was just.

Then with the adoption of the Fourteenth Amendment in 1868 the Court found itself presented with a vast new jurisdiction by the clause which forbids any *state* to "deprive any person of life, liberty, or property, without due process of law." Although at first the Court manifested the greatest reluctance to enter upon its tempting heritage, when it finally did so, about 1895, it discovered that the clause had meantime acquired a new dimension in the conception of liberty as *freedom of contract*. The Court now became for more than a generation the ultimate guardian, in the name of the constitutional document, of the laissez-faire conception of the proper relation of government and private enterprise — a rather inconstant guardian, however, for its fluctuating membership tipped the scales now in favor of business, now in favor of government, that is, of "the power of numbers," as Justice Matthews once put it. And in the New Deal cases, the latter tendency appears to have won out definitely. Due process of law in those cases means Congress' view of what is just, without ordinarily any correction by the Court.

In short, the same dissolving tendency is seen to be operating today upon the due process clause as upon the separation of powers principle and the dual federalism principle, in favor of legislative power and in limitation of judicial review.

The fundamental elements of American constitutional law reduce, therefore, to a single element, judicial review, and this has gradually

16. The Bank of Columbia v. Okely, 4 Wheat. 235 (1819).
17. Scott v. Sanford, 19 How. 393 (1857).

emancipated itself from all documentary and doctrinal restraints, and even from the restraint which was originally implicit in common law jurisdictions in the judicial function as such — the principle of *stare decisis*. But now the result of this self-achieved emancipation has been to extend and at the same time to obliterate the frontier between constitutional law and policy; and without a definite boundary to defend, judicial review itself becomes an instrument of policy, and thereby exposes itself more and more to political criticism.

The consequence is that today American constitutional law appears to be in a highly deliquescent state. The old hard-and-fast distinctions are no more. As the final oracle of due process of law the Court is still able to defend certain values like fair trial and freedom of utterance against local prejudices and unfairness; but national legislative power itself tends to become a due process of law which is coextensive with an already nationalized social and industrial life.

The question naturally arises whether these changes in the structure of our constitutional law are likely to persist. Considering their reach and scope, the answer would seem, on the face of things, to be yes; but there is an even more compelling reason for holding that they will endure and even be enlarged in the future. This is that they spring from a common underlying cause, one moreover which transcends juridical concepts and permeates popular outlook itself. I mean, of course, that altered conception of governmental function to which I have previously referred. American constitutional law came to maturity under, and received those characteristic features which I have been sketching, from the notion that government exists simply for the purpose of supplementing and reinforcing the non-political controls of society, and especially those which rest on social superiority and economic power. The theory to which our present-day constitutional law testifies increasingly is that government should correct these non-political controls from the point of view of the theory of the equality of man. Fusion of governmental functions translates to an increasing extent into a policy of social levelling.

Although the statement is subject to important correction at points — the case of the tariff furnishing the outstanding instance — yet it can be fairly said that from the fall of the Federalist Party in 1801 to the capture of the government at Washington by the New Deal 132 years later, the Jeffersonian, libertarian conception of governmental function generally prevailed in this country, the demand for equality meantime finding satisfying expression in purely political terms, more especially in the establishment of white manhood suffrage. Nor is the reason for this far to seek; it was stated indeed by the younger Pinckney in the Federal Convention in these words: "There is more equality of rank and fortune in America than in any other country under the sun, and this is likely to continue as long as the unappropriated western lands remain unsettled. . . . I lay it therefore down as a settled principle that equality of condition is a leading axiom of our government."

So when the great panic of 1837 stimulated demands for governmental intervention, these demands met a confident rebuke from the shrewdest politician of the period. I quote from President Van Buren's message of September 4, 1837, dealing with the then burning issue of banks and currency:

All communities are apt to look to government for too much. Even in our own country, where its powers and duties are so strictly limited, we are prone to do so, especially at periods of sudden embarrassment and distress. But this ought not to be. The framers of our excellent Constitution and the people who approved it with calm and sagacious deliberation acted at the time on a sounder principle. They wisely judged that the less government interferes with private pursuits the better for the general prosperity. It is not its legitimate object to make men rich or to repair by direct grants of money or legislation in favor of particular pursuits losses not incurred in the public service.

What, therefore, the government ought to do, Van Buren urged, was not to revive the defunct Bank of the United States, but get out of the banking business altogether — and this in due course is just what it did do.

What a contrast is this picture to what happened ninety-six years later! That the contrast is due to an important extent to difference in political leadership is no doubt true, but political leadership does not function in a vacuum. The fact is that the *New Deal came to power because it appeared to an altered outlook on the part of a large section of the American people toward the nature and purpose of government,* to an altered expectation on their part of what government can do if it only tries hard enough. Nor did this change in outlook come in a day — it was in its inception a gradual development. Yet there can be no doubt that the collapse of 1929 and the succeeding depression strengthened and confirmed this change in outlook immensely. By the same token, the new outlook is likely to persist, as is shown for example in the confident talk about sixty million jobs and the commitments which many of our public men have assumed in this connection.

So again we must conclude that the changes in the structure of our constitutional law which this article traces will be on the whole permanent ones. In Thomas Wolfe's poignant words, "We can't go home again" — if indeed we should wish to.

12. Our Constitutional Revolution and How to Round It Out

The Constitution of the United States contains provisions of the following three types, among others: first, those which delineate the structure of the national government; second, those which define its powers; third, those which affirm certain rights of the individual as against the powers of the national government. In the course of the last thirty-one years the Constitution has been subjected to the impact of American participation in two world wars and to that of an economic crisis which was described by the late President as "a crisis greater than war." The effect of these impacts upon the formal structure of the national government has been slight, but its effect on the other two types of constitutional provision has been such as to convert what was originally deemed to be a *Constitution of Rights* into a *Constitution of Powers*. And it is this revolutionary reversal of constitutional values which furnishes the occasion for this discourse. I have in mind *two* purposes: first, to exhibit in detail just how this reversal has been brought about — the *modus operandi* of it; and secondly, to suggest that unless we are prepared to forego altogether the values of constitutionalism, we need to give some deliberate attention to that element of the Constitution which has remained comparatively unresponsive to crisis; I mean the structural element. The point is, that a structural arrangement which once served very well may have ceased to

From 19 *Pennsylvania Bar Association Quarterly* 261-84 (April, 1948). Reprinted by permission.

do so, just because it has not changed along with the rest of the Constitution with which it is integrated. Let me add that most of my examples of constitutional change are based on World War II, that being by far the greatest of the three crises as well as the one in which the effects of the other two were cumulative, so to speak.

What, then, do I mean by saying that the Constitution has been transformed from a *Constitution of Rights* into a *Constitution of Powers*? I certainly do not mean to suggest that the provisions of the Constitution which deal with either rights or powers have undergone visible, verbal change, for they have not. Rather, what I have in mind is the altered actual force of these provisions nowadays as compared with what it was forty years ago. But just how has this change come about — what has been the method of it? The change has been caused by the impact of certain crises, to be sure; but in just what terms precisely has this impact been translated into constitutional terms? The answer to this question is not recondite. It is discovered as soon as we turn to consider the effect of these crises, and particularly of World War II, upon certain principles or doctrines of constitutional interpretation which have always been held to apply to the *powers* of the national government. There are five of these, and I will now proceed to describe them briefly.

The first one is the doctrine that the national government, in contrast to the state governments, is one of *enumerated* powers only. Thus, as Cooley points out in his *Constitutional Limitations*, whereas the primary purpose of a state constitution is to impose limitations on otherwise plenary power, the primary purpose of the national constitution is to grant powers that would be otherwise non-existent. And especially does this contrast hold, Cooley adds, as to the provisions of the two types of Constitution which have to do with the legislative power.

The second principle of constitutional interpretation to which I refer is a corollary of the principle of the separation of powers. It is the doctrine that the legislature, i.e., Congress, may not delegate its powers. The source of this doctrine is John Locke's *Treatise on Civil Government*, where Locke is at great pains to emphasize the distinction between the prerogative of the King and the "legislative power" of Parliament. Of course what Locke was thinking of was that if Parliament ever did delegate its powers to the King, the King could by virtue of his absolute veto always prevent the delegated power from being recovered.

The third doctrine above referred to is the doctrine that *this is a government of laws and not of men.* What is meant, more distinctly, is that everything that is done by an agent of government must be traced to some legal warrant; that is, the executive may not, for the most part, act except on the basis of a very definite delegation from the Constitution or on the basis of an act of Congress.

The fourth principle or doctrine is that *the powers of government are limited by certain outstanding rights of the individual.* Our forefathers were brought up in the belief that certain rights of the individual are anterior to government and that government was not endowed with power to transgress such rights. On the contrary, it was a trustee of them. Indeed, one of the main, if not the *principal*, reason for government was the protection it could afford such rights.

Fifth, and finally, we have what is not so much a doctrine as an *institution* or *practice*, the recognized right of the courts, and ultimately of the Supreme Court, to set their interpretation of the Constitution above even that of the legislature when they are asked to enforce its laws. And the consequence of the judiciary's acting after the legislature is that it is in a position to make its view of the Constitution prevail in particular cases, while that view will also be very influential in determining future readings of the Constitution by the other branches of the government as well as by the Court itself.

Let us now see what has happened to these different doctrines within late years and especially as the result of World War II. To begin with, war has itself undergone great development in recent times. The war power, as it was known to the framers of the Constitution, embraced, if we are to follow Hamilton's language in *The Federalist,* three relatively simple elements. In the first place, there was recruiting, which was on a voluntary basis for the most part. Secondly, there was the problem of supply, and in the main it would seem from Hamilton's language that this problem was expected to be met by purchases in the open market. Of course once war started, on the battlefield and in the war theater, there might be "requisitions," a subject which was discussed at great length in those days by writers on the law of nations. In the third place, there was the power to command the forces; that is, to dispose them. That, of course, belonged to the President of the United States, as Commander-in-Chief.

War today is a very different affair. In World War II the whole of our American society was regimented. Labor was regimented, industry and agriculture were regimented, even talent was regimented for use in propaganda work; and so on and so forth. War today is, in the functional sense, *total war*, in that it brings into operation all of the forces of the society that is involved. This functional totality is, in turn, the result of two things: conscription and technical progress. The first great conscript army was the *levée en masse*, which was proclaimed by the first French Republic in the fall of 1792 when the European powers began invading French territory. Prior to that time, forces were largely volunteer and mercenary. As to technical progress, I don't need to go into that subject further than to point to the culmination of it in the atomic bomb. But technical progress and the necessity of maintaining at the front the vast forces which are the product of conscription, those two facts simply mean that war while it is waging absorbs all the energies of society, which means in turn that a tremendous strain is placed on governmental powers and so on the Constitution itself.

What, then, has been the effect of war on the idea that this is a government of enumerated powers. In a word, the effect has been to water this idea down very decidedly. It is an interesting fact that while the Constitution says Congress has the power "to declare war," it doesn't say that anybody has the power to *wage* war. That no doubt was the result of the rather simple idea that people had of war in those days. As early, nevertheless, as 1795 a Philadelphia lawyer got up in the Supreme Court, which then sat in Philadelphia, and argued that the power to wage war did not come from the Constitution but stemmed from the fact that the United States is a nation. The power, he contended, was inherent in the American people as a community which possessed all the rights of any nation at international law, one of which was the right to wage war. One of the Justices accepted the argument, another one repudiated it, while the rest of the Court thought it unnecessary to pass on the question.

One hundred and forty-one years later, in 1936, the doctrine that the Court snubbed in 1795 was accepted by it *in toto*, and indeed with certain extensions and improvements. I quote Justice Sutherland's words for the Court on the occasion referred to:

A political society [reads the passage referred to] cannot endure without a supreme will somewhere. Sovereignty is never held in suspense. When, therefore, the external sovereignty of Great Britain in respect of the colonies ceased, it immediately passed to the Union.

It results that the investment of the Federal government with the powers of external sovereignty did not depend upon the affirmative grants of the Constitution. The powers to declare and wage war, to conclude peace, to make treaties, to maintain diplomatic relations with other sovereignties, if they had never been mentioned in the Constitution, would have vested in the Federal government as necessary concomitants of nationality [299 U.S. 304, 317–18].

But, you may ask, what difference does it make whether ours is a government of *enumerated* power or a government of *plenary* powers in the waging of war? It makes just this difference, that under the doctrine of enumerated powers you must go to the Constitution to find a special warrant for the things that are necessary to be done, but that under the doctrine of a plenary *inherent* war power, you resort to the Constitution only to find out if there is definite language which *forbids* the things necessary to be done. The doctrine of inherent powers, in other words, *makes constitutionally available all of the resident forces of the United States as a national community in the waging of war.* It makes all of the resources of the nation constitutionally available.

We now turn to the proposition that the legislature cannot delegate its powers. That was cast overboard for purposes of war as early as World War I. The Congress of the United States was suddenly confronted with the problem of adapting legislative power to the exigencies of war, a vast new range of subject matter that had never before been brought within the national government's orbit, and at the same time to give its legislation affecting this enlarged subject matter a form which would render it easily responsive to the ever-changing requirements of a naturally fluid war situation. How could that be done? There was only one way and that was to say to the President, you may do this, you may do that and the other thing, and to lay down only a minimum of restraints upon the exercise of these broad powers. Take, for example, the Lend-Lease Act that preceded World War II. In this Act the Congress of the United States told the President that he could beg, borrow, steal, manufacture, or "otherwise procure" anything that he thought would be conducive to the waging of war and that he could lend, loan, grant, give away, or "otherwise dispose of" these things to anybody on the face of the earth whose possession and use of them might be deemed "to contribute to the defense of the United States."

But now, the precedents for the Lend-Lease Act and other legislation of the same kind in World War II were created in World War I. For example, there was the Food and Fuel Control Act which delegated to President Wilson the power to deal in foods and fuels, power which he turned over to Mr. Garfield and Mr. Hoover, and there was very little language indeed used in the act which was of a restrictive character. Also there was the Trading with the Enemy Act, the Espionage Act, the Selective Service Act. All of these committed vast powers to the President of the United States. It is interesting, I think, to note the fact that World War I was to a very great extent a rehearsal for World War II from the point of view of the solution of certain important problems of constitutional law.

We come now to our third doctrine; that this is a government of laws and not of men. It was the Civil War which brought about the demise of that doctrine so far as war is concerned. Under the Constitution the President is Commander-in-Chief of the army and navy and of the militia of the several states when in the service of the United States. This clause is expounded by Alexander Hamilton in *The Federalist* No. 69. I shall not bother to read the passage; what it boils down to is this: Hamilton points out there how very different the President's power as Commander-in-Chief is from the power of the King of Great Britain, that the President's power is merely that of top general and top admiral. Thus no officer can be created who can give orders to the President; no officers of the armed services can be created to whom the President may not give orders, but the integration of the power of Commander-in-Chief with that of President is not apparently regarded by Hamilton as being significant at all. There was, in other words, no particular reason from Hamilton's point of view why somebody other than the President might not be made top admiral and top general. For it was a purely military power that Hamilton found in the clause.

And as late as 1850 you find the United States Supreme Court, speaking by Chief Justice Taney, also contrasting the power of the President as Commander-in-Chief with the power of the King of England, in the following words:

> His [the President's] duty and his power are purely military. As commander-in-chief, he is authorized to direct the movements of the naval and military forces placed by law at his command, and to employ them in the manner he may deem most effectual to harass and conquer and subdue the enemy.
>
> In the distribution of political power between the great departments of government, there is such a wide difference between the power con-

ferred on the President of the United States, and the authority and sovereignty which belong to the English crown, that it would be altogether unsafe to reason from any supposed resemblance between them, either as regards conquest in war, or any other subject where the rights and powers of the executive arm of the government are brought into question [9 How. 603].

And the Commander-in-Chief clause remained "the forgotten clause" of the Constitution until April 14, 1861, when Fort Sumter surrendered, whereupon President Lincoln proceeded to take a series of measures of the most remarkable character. There was a period of more than ten weeks between the surrender of Fort Sumter and the convening of Congress by the President's summons. During that period the President elected to handle the war situation entirely on his own without any assistance from Congress. As to why he did this there has always been a great deal of speculation. For one thing, he was by no means persuaded that Congress would agree with him as to the necessity of meeting the situation with force. And there were other reasons. But whatever they were, let me show you into what extraordinary courses Mr. Lincoln was driven in sustaining his policy.

During this period of ten weeks he enrolled the state militias in a huge volunteer army to serve for ninety days; created a volunteer army of forty thousand men to serve for three years; added twenty-three thousand men to the regular army; eighteen thousand men to the navy; paid out two million dollars from unappropriated funds in the Treasury; closed the Post Office to "treasonable correspondence"; subjected passengers to and from foreign countries to new passport regulations; suspended the writ of habeas corpus in certain localities; caused the arrest and military detention of persons who were "represented to him as being engaged in treasonable practices" — and all this, except for the call to the state militias, without any statutory authorization.

In his message of July 4, Lincoln informed Congress of most of the things he had done. He didn't tell them quite all, He didn't tell them about the two million dollars until after the thing was smoked out in May of the following year, when he had to admit he had done that too. But at any rate Congress promptly ratified everything the President had done with respect to the army and navy. The habeas corpus suspension, however, was not ratified, and the year following Lincoln effected a general suspension of the writ throughout the country. By the act of

March 3, 1863, this more sweeping measure was ratified in language which seemed to indicate that Congress conceded the President's right to take it. In the meantime, in August, 1862, Lincoln had established a limited draft by presidential order, although the great Draft Act was not passed by Congress until July, 1863.

But to get to the point. Some of these things were ratified by Congress, some were not. Some of them, indeed, had had their intended effect before Congress met. What conclusion is forced upon us? It is obvious that many of these acts assert for the President for the first time in our history *an initiative of indefinite scope in meeting the domestic aspects of a war emergency;* and in meeting them, by what was virtually an exercise of *legislative* power.

And, in World War I, Mr. Wilson imitated Lincoln to some, although not to a great extent. That war was far removed from the country and there was time for Congress to act. Even so, in some cases Mr. Wilson fell back upon his powers as Commander-in-Chief. Thus Mr. Creel's Committee on Public Information was a creation of the President, and the War Industries Board was another such creation. From early 1918, this latter agency, under Mr. Baruch's chairmanship, constituted a highly important segment of the government of the United States internally, and for as long as the war lasted.

In World War II you get a great expansion of this quasi-legislative power of the President, one that is simply amazing when you come to study it in detail. The precedents were there, to be sure, but these precedents were certainly blessed with a prolific progeny. What is more, Mr. Roosevelt took his first step of this nature some fifteen months *before* the outbreak of "shooting war." I mean his action in handing over fifty destroyers in September, 1940, to Great Britain in return for some leases of naval bases in British possessions in the West Atlantic. That measure gave rise to considerable controversy at the time and Mr. Jackson, then Attorney General, felt called upon to render an opinion in support of it. The Attorney General being the Administration's family lawyer, it is not his business to criticize what the family wants, but to show how well justified the family is in wanting it. So Mr. Jackson rendered an opinion on the "destroyer deal," and his argument boiled down to a neat little pun. First proving that the President had long been recognized as having the power to *dispose* the forces, he next inserted after the word "dispose," the word "of"!

But the most remarkable development of presidential legislative power is to be found in the creation of the so-called "war agencies." In April, 1942, I wrote the Executive Office of the President and asked them to give me a list of all these war agencies and to specify to me the warrant by which they had been brought into existence. I got back a very polite answer which listed forty-three executive agencies, of which thirty-five were admitted to be of purely executive provenience. Six of these raised no question because what they amounted to was an assignment by the President of additional duties to already existing officers, and of officers whose appointment had been, in most cases, ratified by the Senate. For example, our participation in the Combined Chiefs of Staff was an additional duty, of course, of certain military and naval commanders, and the Combined Raw Materials Board was a like creation. Nobody was assigned to such duties who was not already in an office to which they were logically relevant. But take the Board of Economic Warfare, the National Housing Agency, the National War Labor Board, the Office of Censorship, the Office of Civilian Defense, the Office of Defense Transportation, the Office of Facts and Figures, the Office of War Information, the War Production Board, which superseded the earlier Office of Production Management, the War Manpower Commission, and later on the Economic Stabilization Board, all these and many others I could recite were created by the President simply by virtue of power which he claimed as Commander-in-Chief.

One result of the creation of these agencies was this: the President conferred upon them certain powers, some of which he had from statute, some of which he claimed as "Commander-in-Chief in wartime." But in either case the agencies themselves rested on no statutory foundation. And the result of this defect was curious enough. The question came up finally in the Court of Appeals of the District of Columbia whether an order issued by the War Labor Board was enjoinable and the court said, "No, it is not enjoinable because the law knows nothing about it. What we are asked to enjoin is only 'advice' to the President, the War Labor Board being only an 'advisory body.'" That is, the court did not have before it a situation in which anybody was *doing* anything of which the court could take any notice. In short, the strictly legal status of these agencies was that of *advisory bodies merely*, although actually the President almost invariably followed their advice, that is, converted their advice into governing policy.

Oftentimes, moreover, even the powers concerning the exercise of which an agency "advised" the President were not to be traced to any statute, in which case violation of the orders of the President based on such "advice" was not an offense against the United States. What penalty was there, then? It is here that you encounter a very interesting phenomenon called *indirect sanctions*. When the President, for example, ordered Montgomery Ward to put a "maintenance clause" in their labor contracts, he had no statutory authority to do so, nor did the War Labor Board. Nevertheless, when Montgomery Ward refused to do as they were bid they speedily found that the seventy Post Office employees who had been handling their parcel post orders for years hadn't put in an appearance. But ordinarily the indirect sanctions took this form: if the employers didn't follow the presidential line, they were informed they couldn't have priorities; and if the employees failed to comply with the orders, the director of the Selective Service was ordered to make a re-check of these gentlemen and the recalcitrants were confronted with the prospect of being put on the firing line.

An interesting illustration that occurred in World War I of indirect sanctions was furnished by the following episode involving the Remington Arms Company of Bridgeport, Connecticut, in the fall of 1918. The narrative is by a member of President Wilson's War Labor Board: "After a prolonged strike and the War Labor Board had rendered a decision, the strikers still refused to return to work. The President of the United States wrote the strikers upholding the board, pointing out that an appeal from it should be made through the regular channels and not by strike; and that if the strikers did not return to work, they would be barred from any work in Bridgeport for a year; that the United States Employment Service would not obtain positions for them elsewhere, and that the government would no longer consider their exemptions based on the theory that they were useful in war production. This ended the strike." Indirect sanctions *can* be very effective.

Nor did Mr. Roosevelt hesitate to state very early the theory on which he was operating. I refer to his famous address to Congress of September 7, 1942, when, in asking Congress to repeal certain provisions of the Emergency Price Control Act, he said:

I ask the Congress to take this action by the first of October. Inaction on your part by that date will leave me with an inescapable responsibility to the people of this country to see to it that the war effort is no longer imperiled by threat of economic chaos.

In the event that the Congress should fail to act, and act adequately, I shall accept the responsibility, and I will act.

At the same time that fair prices are stabilized, wages can and will be stabilized also. This I will do.

The President has the powers, under the Constitution and under Congressional acts, to take measures necessary to avert a disaster which would interfere with the winning of the war.

I have given the most thoughtful consideration to meeting this issue without further reference to the Congress. I have determined, however, on this vital matter to consult with the Congress. . . .

The American people can be sure that I will use my powers with a full sense of my responsibility to the Constitution and to my country. The American people can also be sure that I shall not hesitate to use every power vested in me to accomplish the defeat of our enemies in any part of the world where our own safety demands such defeat.

When the war is won, the powers under which I act automatically revert to the people — to whom they belong.

Here certainly is a very remarkable proposition. The President of the United States is claiming the right to repeal an act of Congress although he does not deny that Congress had the power to pass the act. To be sure, other Presidents have occasionally refused to enforce acts of Congress, though very rarely, and always on the ground that the acts in question were unconstitutional, and particularly that they constituted an invasion of the President's powers. That is what Andrew Johnson did in 1867, but nobody on the face of the earth can deny that Congress had the right to pass the Emergency Price Control Act, or that it was the only organ of government that did have that right; and yet the President is claiming the right to repeal the law. Undoubtedly that is a claim of power to suspend the Constitution and as to a very important feature of it, namely the division of power between the President and Congress. Any candid man must admit that a situation may arise in war in which it would be necessary to suspend the Constitution. Thus Abraham Lincoln admitted that he didn't know whether or not he had suspended the Constitution when he suspended the writ of habeas corpus; but said he, "Are all the laws to go unenforced in order that one law may be preserved?" But on the occasion when Mr. Roosevelt spoke, Congress was in session and it seems to me that if the situation is so desperate as to require suspension of the Constitution, the safe view to take is that

Congress ought to be considered to be aware of the fact as well as the President, and so be joined in the enterprise.

I turn now to *the effect of war on private rights.* I think perhaps the best illustration of the effect of war on private rights is the growth of the use of military conscription. To begin with, when the Constitution was framed Congress was authorized to provide for the calling of the militia into the service of the United States to enforce the laws, to suppress insurrection and repel invasion. The clause of the Constitution bestowing this power reflects the old common law, and indeed legislation from the time of Edward III, when the King of England was conceded to have the power to call the militia out from the counties for the purpose of repelling invasion. Otherwise the militia could be required to serve only within the county's borders.

The first suggestion of conscription in this country for the raising of a national army was made by James Monroe when he was President Madison's Secretary of State during the War of 1812. Daniel Webster, then a member of the House of Representatives, made a most savage attack on the measure, calling it a "dance of blood" and a "gamble with death" and the House of Representatives failed to act till the end of the war made it unnecessary to do so. During the Civil War you get a draft to suppress "insurrection," that at least was the theory of the federal government. So you see the draft was still kept within the categories of repelling invasion, suppressing insurrection, and enforcement of the laws.

During World War I, of course, we had the Selective Service Act under which an army was raised to serve abroad. That circumstance gave rise to a very interesting case, in which Mr. Hannis Taylor made an attack on the constitutionality of the act with an interesting argument which was well buttressed with history. Chief Justice White, speaking for the Court, brushed the argument aside and sustained the draft. No doubt he necessarily must have done so, but he might have exhibited better manners.

Next we have in the act of September, 1940, the first *peacetime* draft, and there was assurance given that these men would not serve abroad, but when war came fifteen months later that clause of the act was quickly repealed. But the final step was President Roosevelt's surprise message of February 5, 1944, in which he asked for a conscription of labor, a suggestion which did not get to first base in Congress.

This growth I have traced of the idea of conscription is an instructive illustration of the way in which previous privileges and immunities are eroded by the impact of war, or even by its imminence.

Finally, I wish to devote a moment or two to the subject of judicial review — the power of the Court to pass on the constitutionality of laws and other acts of public authority. The War Emergency Price Control Act of 1942 contained a clause to the effect that only the Emergency Court which the act created could enjoin an order of the OPA and that only in that court could the question of the validity of the act be raised. In the Yakus case, decided in 1944, the Supreme Court, after having avoided the issue as long as it could, finally found it necessary to consider the constitutional question thus provoked. Yakus was convicted in a United States District Court of violating an OPA order and sentenced to fine and imprisonment. He appealed to the United States Supreme Court on the ground that the District Court had not permitted him to plead the unconstitutionality of the act and of the order which he was charged with violating. The Supreme Court, however, sustained the sentence. In other words, Yakus was convicted without being permitted to plead his constitutional rights.

That is a pretty serious business. Our lawyers and judges have always maintained that there is a fundamental distinction between *jurisdiction* and *judicial power*. A court has no jurisdiction except such as Congress has specifically given it. That is perfectly clear from the Constitution. On the other hand, once a court has jurisdiction of a case it is thereby put in possession of the power — the *judicial power* — to decide it in accordance with the law. Now, however, the Congress of the United States comes along and says, "Yes, you can decide cases under the Price Control Act in accordance with the law, except that you may not consider the Constitution, the Supreme Law, in this connection." Three of the Justices — one being former Justice Roberts — dissented along the line I have suggested, but unavailingly. For the country was engaged in *total war*, and the judicial power was regimented, like everything else.

But this, you will say, is simply the law of war. A great deal of it is *rather* the law of "emergency," a term which has come to have, nowadays, a very indefinite connotation. The first case ever decided by the United States Supreme Court in which an emergency was recognized that was not plainly war was the case of Wilson v. New, back in 1916. In the New Deal period, however, the justification of "emergency" was repeatedly invoked by the Court in support of legislation which by the older tests of constitutional law were at least of doubtful validity. I have in mind the Minnesota Moratorium case, the Gold Clause cases, and some of the Social Security Act cases. Furthermore, it is a lesson of our constitutional history that a power claimed successfully on the justification of war emergency may come later to be assimilated to the normal peacetime powers of government. This happened in respect to the power of the national government to give its paper notes the legal tender quality; and I am not at all certain that some, if not most, of the measures put into operation over industry and labor by the government during World War II may not be justified under certain New Deal cases as regulations of commerce. It is, in short, impossible to say yet to what extent World War II has remade the Constitution not only for war, but for peace as well.

But I have dwelt too long on these details, I am afraid. I come now to my second main point. What you have here, in consequence of all these developments, is a tremendous increase in the powers of the national government. These additional powers of the *national government* are, moreover, all brought to focus and application upon the situations for which they were devised *by the President* — in other words, *the aggrandizement of the national government has meant the aggrandizement of the presidential office.*

Is there any change in the structural constitution indicated or demanded by this tremendous flow of power into the national government and through it into the hands of the President? That is the question to which I wish now to address myself briefly.

Of course, we want two things: an efficient government, a government that is capable of acting on serious matters before it is too late; we also, however, wish to preserve some of our constitutional liberties. What, then, can we do in the present situation?

In answering this question we need to look around and see what materials we have for constitutional reconstruction — for structural improvement, if such improvement is demanded. What materials have we got? I do not think that judicial review need be taken into account. We can not rely upon judicial power in time of war or in time of great emergency; and, very naturally, since the Supreme Court is not going to take the risk of forbidding that things be done the failure to do which might turn out eventually to have been fatal to the country. No judiciary can assume such a risk. We still have, however, Congress, and Congress has one great power which, although it has sometimes been defied, sometimes circumvented, is yet a very great power, and that is *the power of the purse.*

Can we establish, then, a relationship between the President and Congress that will, on the one hand, *support* the President, and on the other hand *control* him? In 1940 I published a book called *The President: Office and Powers,* and in that book I made a suggestion which some writers have taken up since, and which I myself still think is a good suggestion, and that was *that a new type of Cabinet be created.* The existing cabinet is not a success at all from the point of view of controlling the President, and not very much of a success from the point of view, even, of informing him. I have read Miss Perkins' book and I am now reading Mr. Hull's *Memoirs;* and each of them has said things which are not designed to strengthen one's admiration for the Cabinet as a body. The history of the Cabinet is to no small extent the history of a board the meetings of which are more or less ceremonial and casual. Meanwhile, the President gets his real counsel and advice from other quarters entirely. Andrew Jackson had his "kitchen cabinet," President Roosevelt had his "brain trust," and other Presidents have had the equivalent of these. And in a recent article in the *American Political Science Review,* an authoritative writer, Mr. Don K. Price, expressed the opinion that the Cabinet was not a success, even from an administrative point of view, i.e., from the point of view of coordinating administration. The individual members of the Cabinet are doubtless very useful persons, often very well qualified persons, but the joint wisdom of the Cabinet is frequently very much less than the sum total of the wisdom of its individual members.

How, then, should this new Cabinet be made up? As I have said, we want a body which will support the President, and which, on the other hand, will be able to control him. We want a body which will facilitate action and which, on the other hand, will keep it within bounds. I think that a Cabinet made up in part of leading members of Congress would answer our prescription. Thus let us suppose the creation of a joint legislative council by the Senate and the House of Representatives, and let us suppose further a custom by which the President of the United States was required to consult that body regularly. He would then have to consult people who were not eating his salt, and who were under no obligation to him whatsoever, and yet who, on the other hand, by putting the stamp of their approval upon his proposals, would be able to facilitate their enactment into law. You would have a body, in other words, that would be both capable of controlling and, on the other hand, of supporting the President, of securing that the things needing to be done would be done on time; but, on the other hand, that the judgment that they needed to be done represented a wide consensus, a vastly wider consensus than the President can by himself supply.

The question may arise in your minds whether such an arrangement would be constitutional, inasmuch as office-holders cannot hold seats in Congress. But notice that I am not saying that there shouldn't be a Secretary of State, I am not saying that there shouldn't be a Secretary of the Treasury or an Attorney General. They are the chiefs of certain administrative departments. And then, of course, the Chairman of the Interstate Commerce Commission and the Chairman of the Federal Trade Commission, and so on and so forth, also are administrators, and are disqualified by the Constitution for election to Congress. But the answer is that membership in the Cabinet has no necessary connection with an administrative job. *Membership in the Cabinet is not an office*, it is simply a function which the Presidents of the United States have come automatically to fasten upon the chiefs of the great executive departments. But there is no reason in the world why the President of the United States should not make up a Cabinet consisting of the leaders of Congress — or, for that matter, of participants in this gathering.

Imagine the President of the United States desiring a Cabinet of the sort I have indicated. He would say to Mr. John Doe, "Now, I am making you Secretary of the Treasury, but So-and-So, the Chairman of the House Ways and Means Committee, is the man with whom I shall devise my fiscal policies, and you are expected to follow those out." And the same as to the Secretary of State, "Now, I am going to make you Secretary of State, Mr. Roe, but I am going to settle my policy on foreign affairs in conference with Mr. So-and-So, the Chairman of the Foreign Relations Committee of the United States Senate, and you will take orders from him, or from me — take the orders that he and I agree are the ones that are desirable in the present situation."

I see no constitutional objection to this. Another objection, perhaps, is a little more difficult to meet, and that is that oftentimes, as is the case at present, the Congress of the United States represents one party and the President represents another party. What about that? I think that that is really an argument *for* the proposal I am making. I think that the President of the United States has accumulated into his hands such vast powers — or, let us put it more justly — he has had such vast powers thrust into his hands, that it is high time that *the political significance* of the office be watered down a bit.

In time of emergency, the President and Congress cooperate, whether the President be of one party and Congress of another or otherwise. In time of war that happens; and in addition we have a maxim that partisanism should stop at the water's edge. In short, it is recognized that in very serious situations there ought not to be all this tugging and hauling between the President and Congress, this political competition between them. *But why should we reserve best methods for crises?* Why shouldn't we use best methods in times when there isn't a crisis, and when the use of best methods would perhaps prevent a crisis from arising? So I think that the argument which is urged on that ground, that the President might belong to one party and the Congress to another, really constitutes, in the last analysis, a good argument for the proposal.

Frankly, I think there is a great deal of nonsense to what I might describe as "the political racket." The attitude that should be taken toward government, to my mind, on the part of those who exercise its powers is that they are confronted with a job of housekeeping, and more and more is that the case as the government extends its guidance more and more to the normal activities of the people. To repeat, it seems to me that the attitude has to be taken toward *government*, that it *has become today a species of communal housekeeping*, and from that point of view the relationship between the President and Congress should not be one of political competition and bicker; it should be one of trying to arrive by compromise at those solutions which are, as the result of conference and consultation, agreed upon as being the best.

The President of the United States today occupies a very paradoxical position. Mr. Wilson says in his *Constitutional Government of the United States* that the President is "the leader of his party," and that he is "the leader of the nation." But the fact of the matter is that the two roles don't harmonize always. The President of the United States, as the leader of the party, will be tempted to do things that as leader of the nation he would not think of doing, and sometimes he will do them.

Take the situation in which Mr. Truman found himself in relation to the Taft-Hartley Act. I am not saying that the Taft-Hartley Act is a perfect law by any means; but it could have been made a better one if Mr. Truman and the people who were promoting the measure had gotten together and discussed matters with the purpose in mind of arriving at the best solution, that is to say, the solution that came nearest to meeting popular expectation. You would then have had a better act. Mr. Truman, however, sat back and saw the bill going through Congress with what he considered its objectionable features, and then when it was finally laid on his desk he proceeded to write a venomous veto message of it. Presently, however, the bill was passed over his veto; and the day following he came out with the statement, "I am still opposed to the law, but as the President of the United States I recognize that it is my duty to enforce it, and shall do so" — or words to that effect. Well, I think that that represents an ambivalent attitude toward the presidential office that is not wholesome, one for which, however, the present stereotyped relationship between President and Congress rather than Mr. Truman is to blame.

As a matter of fact, if I had my way I would go a considerable step farther. Thus I think those people in Congress who tinkered up the pending amendment to limit presidential tenure to ten years at the outside, simply missed a splendid opportunity, owing to the fact that they were so intent on showing how strongly they reprobated the late President Roosevelt's action in running for a fourth term. As somebody has said, having been unable to beat F.D.R. when he was alive, they decided that they could at least smear him in the grave. At any rate, the controlling motive was obviously political, and so the authors of the proposal did not give themselves the opportunity of discussing an amendment that would have been worth discussing. I mean an amendment which would disqualify the President of the United States from succeeding himself. The point is that *the President of the United States ought not have to think about his political future, because when he has to think about his political future his party demands that he do so* inasmuch as his political future is the party's. Relieved from that necessity, the President could be the kind of a President that George Washington was, or as close an approximation thereto as his character and abilities enabled him to be.

And in this connection the following passage from the famous Farewell Address is worthy of thoughtful consideration. The spirit of party, it reads, "serves always to distract the public councils and enfeeble the public administration. It agitates the community with ill-founded jealousies and false alarms, kindles the animosity of one party against the other, foments confusion, riot and insurrection. It opens the door to foreign influence and corruption, which find a facilitated access to the government itself through the channels of party passion. Thus the policy and the will of one country is subjected to the policy and will of another. There is an opinion that parties in free countries are useful checks upon the government and serve to keep alive the spirit of liberty. This, within certain limits, is probably true, and in governments of monarchical character patriotism may look with indulgence, if not with favor, upon the spirit of party. But in those of a popular character, in governments purely elective, it is a spirit not to be encouraged. From their natural tendency it is certain there will always be enough of that spirit for every salutary purpose, and there being constant danger of excess, the effort ought to be by force of public opinion to mitigate and assuage it. A fire not to be quenched, it demands vigilance to prevent its bursting into a flame lest instead of warming it should consume."

I think there is a stupendous amount of good sense to that, good even, or indeed especially, for the present hour.

Well, now, ladies and gentlemen, I have laid my case before you. In a word, what I have said is that the Presidency of the United States needs reintegration, and the legislative power comprising the President and Congress needs reintegration. This end could be greatly furthered by a new type of Cabinet, but the achievement could be greatly reinforced by neutralizing the Presidency politically.

"I see no need to amend our Constitution," said Louis Brandeis in 1915. "It has not lost its capacity for expansion to meet new conditions unless interpreted by rigid minds which have no such capacity. Instead of amending the Constitution, I would amend men's economic and social ideas. Law has always been a narrowing, conservatizing profession. What we must do in America is not to attack our judges, but to educate them."

When those words were spoken, they had a timely wisdom, a prophetic wisdom. Indeed, they might be fittingly termed the prologue of the New Deal revolution. But that revolution, plus two great wars, has raised new constitutional problems and especially the problem of *the sufficiency of the structural Constitution*, for its dual task of adequate action in crisis and the preservation of democratic values. I am not saying, mind you, that the Presidency has become a matrix of dictatorship. What could be more trite? But I am saying that the Presidency has reached a position of unhealthy dominance in the system, one which instead of expediting the formation of national policy stands often in the way of it.

How is this problem to be met? We certainly can not rely on the judges to do it, we must needs rely on the political branches, so first of all upon popular understanding and demand. If given the opportunity to lay my case before this distinguished company I have made no contribution to that end, the fault is my own; the pleasure of the occasion is also mine.[1]

1. In 1879, his senior year at Princeton, Woodrow Wilson published an article in the *International Review* entitled "Cabinet Government in the United States." In his Introductory Note to a reissue of this piece last year under the auspices of The Woodrow Wilson Foundation, Judge Finletter says, "The key suggestion . . . was to set up a Cabinet from among members of the House and Senate." But Wilson himself, putting the question, "What is the change proposed?" answers thus: "Simply to give to the heads of the Executive departments — the members of the Cabinet — seats in Congress, with the privilege of the initiative in legislation and some part of the unbounded privilege now commanded by the Standing Committees," and he invokes the authority of "Chief-Justice [*sic*] Story" in support of a similar suggestion (see pp. 8-9). Despite some rather confusing language at one point, it seems clear that Wilson did not contemplate putting members of Congress at the head of the executive departments, or on the other hand, making the latter members of Congress, otherwise he would have been obliged to discuss — certainly to indicate his awareness of — the constitutional ban on office-holders being members of Congress. His proposal was apparently only an elaboration of the one which George H. Pendleton of Ohio had been agitating ever since the close of the Civil War and which in 1881 received the endorsement of a distinguished Senate committee. Congressman Kefauver of Tennessee has revived it within recent years.

Additions to the Mason-Garvey Bibliography*

"The Pelatiah Webster Myth," 10 *Michigan Law Review* 619-26 (May, 1912).

"Tenure of Office and the Removal Power Under the Constitution," 27 *Columbia Law Review* 353-99 (April, 1927).

"Moratorium Over Minnesota," 82 *University of Pennsylvania Law Review* 311-16 (1934).

"The Schechter Case — Landmark, or What?" 13 *New York University Law Quarterly Review* 151-90 (January, 1936).

"The Constitution as Instrument and as Symbol," 30 *American Political Science Review* 1071-85 (December, 1936).

"Liberty and Juridical Restraint," in Anshen, ed., *Freedom: Its Meaning* 84-103 (1940).

"Some Aspects of the Presidency," 218 *Annals of the American Academy of Political and Social Science* 122-31 (November, 1941).

"The Presidency in Perspective," 11 *Journal of Politics* 7-13 (1949).

"The Impact of the Idea of Evolution on the American Political and Constitutional Tradition," in Persons, ed., *Evolutionary Thought in America* 182-99 (1950).

"Of Presidential Prerogative," 47 *Whittier College Bulletin* 3-29 (September, 1954, first edition; revised July 1, 1955).

"Presidential 'Inability,'" *National Review* 9-10 (November 26, 1955).

"Franklin and the Constitution," 100 *Proceedings of the American Philosophical Society* 283-88 (August, 1956).

*Alpheus Mason and Gerald Garvey, eds., *American Constitutional History: Essays by Edward S. Corwin* 216-29 (1964).

Table of Cases

Index

*Presidential Power and
the Constitution*

Designed by R. E. Rosenbaum.
Composed by Jay's Publishers Services, Inc.,
in 10 point Selectric Press Roman, 2 points leaded,
with display lines in Friz Quadrata.
Printed offset by LithoCrafters, Inc.,
on Warren's Number 66 text, 50 pound basis.
Bound by LithoCrafters, Inc.,
in Joanna book cloth
and stamped in All Purpose foil.

Library of Congress Cataloging in Publication Data

Corwin, Edward Samuel, 1878-1963.
  Presidential power and the Constitution.

  Bibliography: p.
  Includes index.
  1. Executive power--United States. I. Title.
KF5053.C6   342'.73'062   75-38000
ISBN 0-8014-0982-9